The Quality of Democracy

RECENT TITLES FROM THE HELEN KELLOGG INSTITUTE
FOR INTERNATIONAL STUDIES

Scott Mainwaring, *general editor*

The University of Notre Dame Press gratefully thanks the Helen Kellogg Institute for International Studies for its support in the publication of titles in this series.

Kevin Healy
Llamas, Weavings, and Organic Chocolate: Multicultural Grassroots Development in the Andes and Amazon of Bolivia (2000)

Ernest J. Bartell, C.S.C., and Alejandro O'Donnell
The Child in Latin America: Health, Development, and Rights (2000)

Vikram K. Chand
Mexico's Political Awakening (2001)

Ruth Berins Collier and David Collier
Shaping the Political Arena (2002)

Glen Biglaiser
Guardians of the Nation? (2002)

Sylvia Borzutzky
Vital Connections (2002)

Alberto Spektorowski
The Origins of Argentina's Revolution of the Right (2003)

Caroline C. Beer
Electoral Competition and Institutional Change in Mexico (2003)

Yemile Mizrahi
From Martyrdom to Power (2003)

Charles D. Kenney
Fujimori's Coup and the Breakdown of Democracy in Latin America (2003)

Alfred P. Montero and David J. Samuels
Decentralization and Democracy in Latin America (2004)

Katherine Hite and Paola Cesarini
Authoritarian Legacies and Democracy in Latin America and Southern Europe (2004)

Robert S. Pelton, C.S.C.
Monsignor Romero: A Bishop for the Third Millennium (2004)

For a complete list of titles from the Helen Kellogg Institute for International Studies, see http://www.undpress.nd.edu

The Quality of Democracy

Theory and Applications

Edited by

Guillermo O'Donnell,
Jorge Vargas Cullell, *and*
Osvaldo M. Iazzetta

University of Notre Dame Press

Notre Dame, Indiana

Manufactured in the United States of America

Library of Congress Cataloging-in-Publication Data
The quality of democracy : theory and applications / edited by Guillermo O'Donnell,
Jorge Vargas Cullell, and Osvaldo M. Iazzetta.
p.   cm.
"From the Helen Kellogg Institute for International Studies."
Based on a workshop on the quality of democracy and human development in Latin
America, held in Heredia, Costa Rica, Feb. 1–2, 2002.
Includes bibliographical references and index.
ISBN 0-268-03719-1 (cloth : alk. paper) — ISBN 0-268-03720-5 (pbk. : alk. paper)
1. Democracy—Latin America—Congresses.   2. Human rights—Latin America—
Congresses.   3. Political participation—Latin America—Congresses.   4. Latin
America—Economic conditions—1982– —Congresses.   I. O'Donnell, Guillermo A.
II. Vargas Cullel, Jorge.   III. Iazzetta, Osvaldo Miguel.   IV. Helen Kellogg Institute
for International Studies.   V. Title.

JL966.Q83   2004
321.8—dc22

2004016399

∞ *This book is printed on acid-free paper.*

We dedicate this book to the memory of Norbert Lechner,
a great intellectual, an inspiring colleague, a loyal friend
and, above all, a wonderful human being.

contents

PART I THEORETICAL AND EMPIRICAL FOUNDATIONS

PART II COMMENTS BY WORKSHOP PARTICIPANTS

acknowledgments

The authors want to express their gratitude to the United Nations Development Program's Regional Bureau for Latin America and the Caribbean (UNDP-RBLAC) for its support for the workshop on the "Quality of Democracy and Human Development in Latin America," which took place in Heredia, Costa Rica, and which generated the writings published in this volume. We also thank the Swedish International Development Cooperation Agency (SIDA) for its financial support of the Citizen Audit of the Quality of Democracy in Costa Rica.

Foreword

GUILLERMO O'DONNELL

In 1996, at the University of Notre Dame, I taught a seminar on democratic theory. The class discussed ideas on which I have continued working and that are discussed in my chapter in this volume as well as in some recent publications (especially O'Donnell 1999b, 2001, and 2003). In the last sessions of the seminar, we explored the question of whether it was possible to define different degrees, or levels, of quality of democracy and, eventually, how to proceed to this effect. One member of the seminar, Jorge Vargas Cullell, was a particularly active participant in the discussion. A year later, Vargas Cullell, who had returned to his native country, Costa Rica, called to inform me that he and economist Miguel Gutiérrez Saxe had formed a small team and secured funding for undertaking an *Auditoría Ciudadana de la Calidad de la Democracia* (Citizen Audit of the Quality of Democracy)[1] in Costa Rica, starting from ideas we had discussed in the Notre Dame seminar. They invited me to visit Costa Rica to discuss the outline of the project, as well as to meet with several political, institutional, and academic leaders of the country. In these meetings we persuaded ourselves that, although extremely complex and demanding, the project was both possible and potentially very valuable. I followed closely and advised those working on the audit, learning much from the careful and imaginative work that was done. Vargas Cullell's chapter in this volume contains a description of the motives, procedures, goals, and main findings of the Costa Rican audit, yet I suggest the interested reader access the audit's Web page (www.estadonacion.org.cr), where more and very interesting details can be found.

Since the inception of the citizen audit, the hope of the Costa Rican team, and, of course, mine as well, was that in addition to the value of the audit for Costa Rica, it would serve as an experiment that later could be applied, with the necessary adjustments, to other cases. That the audit would be carried out first in Costa Rica and by a highly qualified and hard-working team entailed an excellent methodological beginning. Costa Rica is a country with a long and proud democratic tradition, its politics are competitive but not very conflictive, and it is small and unitary—an ideal laboratory for experimenting with such a task. Hopefully, the lessons learned in Costa Rica (some of them distilled in Vargas Cullell's chapter) may be applied to more complicated cases, as are all the other Latin American countries, for various reasons. Furthermore, this learning can be applied not only to whole countries but also to various subnational units.

I must add that this story had a less felicitous continuation in my own country, Argentina. As soon as the Alianza parties won the national elections of 1999, I was invited by vice president Carlos Alvarez to carry out a citizen audit in Argentina. For several reasons I declined to direct the team that would have to be formed but agreed to be a consultant of it. Not long afterward, this incipient project was devoured, as were other more important things, by the chaos, internecine disputes, and utter incompetence of that government.

On the other hand, the Regional Office for Latin America and the Caribbean of the United Nations Development Program (DRALC-UNDP), which had been one of the main supporters of the Costa Rican audit, decided to explore the possibility of extending and adapting it to other countries. DRALC-UNDP invited the Costa Rican team to organize a workshop to discuss the extension of the audit, not only at the national but also at subnational levels. From this initiative resulted a workshop held in Heredia, Costa Rica, in February 2002 on *Desarrollo Humano y Calidad de la Democracia en América Latina*. Several DRALC-UNDP officers participated in this event, as well as a group of distinguished academics. Vargas Cullell, Gutiérrez Saxe, and Evelyn Villarreal contributed a report on the Costa Rican audit that provides the background for Vargas Cullell's chapter in this book. I presented a paper that, after revisions mainly motivated by the comments (also included in this volume) of the academics participating in the workshop, became my chapter in this book.[2]

I hope that this brief history helps to make understandable not only the origins of the present volume but also the meaning and limitations of my own contribution to it. My intention here is to present the reasons for undertaking a citizen audit of the quality of democracy and to offer theoretical background and empirical suggestions for its implementation. For this purpose I found it necessary to present a rather detailed examination of some aspects of democracy, especially its grounding (or, if you wish, its microfoundation) on a particular conception of the human being as an agent. Furthermore, because the Costa Rican audit bears some important resemblances to an important UNDP project, its *Human Development Reports,* while working on the present text I was struck by the important convergences that, precisely around the topic of agency, can be detected between the conception of democracy I propose here and the views of human development proposed by UNDP. In turn, these reflections, in addition to conversations with my colleague at Notre Dame, Juan Méndez, led me to explore the fundamental role of agency in both democracy and the main currents of human rights.

These are the main themes, as indicated by the title, of my chapter in this volume. As these themes are sufficiently complex (and some of them quite unexplored), I have left aside, or only briefly discussed, other important but less directly relevant topics connected to democracy. In case it is of interest to the reader, when I have dealt with these topics in other publications, I include the appropriate references.

One final point. The present volume is the expression of an increasing concern in various policy and academic circles: the happy fact of the recent emergence of numerous democratic regimes (specifically, in continental Latin America practically all countries currently have democratic regimes) cannot, and should not, conceal the fact that the workings and impacts of the respective governments and states evince wide variations. Variations that run from acceptable to rather dismal performances have, of course, important consequences, including for the many—too many—that, at least in Latin America, have received few if any benefits from democratization. From this perspective, attempts to gauge the quality of particular democracies are not only (as I learned in Costa Rica) fascinating intellectual exercises; they also may be useful guides for the concerted efforts that will be necessary for improving both old[3] and new democracies. All the contributors to this volume hope, then, that on the basis of this unique Costa Rican experience, this book will contribute to foster the increasing practical and academic concerns about the quality of democracy.

Bellagio, May 2004

NOTES

1. From now on the *Auditoría Ciudadana de la Calidad de la Democracia* will be referred to as the citizen audit.

2. UNDP is currently sponsoring an important project that is in some senses an offspring of the one commented upon here. *Desafíos de la Democracia en América Latina,* directed by Dante Caputo and of which I am a consultant, deals with the seventeen continental Latin American countries and aims to identify the main challenges and opportunities faced by these democracies (for further information see www.lademocracia.org).

3. See, for example, David Beetham et al., *Democracy under Blair: A Democratic Audit in the United Kingdom* (London: Politico's Publishing, 2002). The approach of this valuable work, however, differs in some important respects from the one adopted in the Costa Rican audit.

Introduction

OSVALDO M. IAZZETTA

Purpose of the Book

This book lays the foundation for a new vision of democracy in Latin America. It highlights issues that most current democratic theory has overlooked by confining discussion to the narrow limits of the political regime. The book employs the concept of citizenship as a "lever" for projecting democracy beyond the regime toward other spheres where political power is exercised. This vision does not ignore the political regime's centrality to democracy or the challenges that remain for Latin America in this area. Yet it suggests that facing these challenges requires thinking about the complex spaces in which democracy extends beyond the realm of electing rulers in a free public setting. Reflecting on these challenges, the book presents new considerations related to the quality of democracy.

Observation of the Latin American reality prompted the origin of this vision. In the region democratized regimes exist alongside states with strong authoritarian legacies and societies that are profoundly unequal—the most unequal in the world. Citizens in these countries face institutional obstacles to civil and political equality to a degree that might seem grotesque to a person living in a liberal democracy. Moreover, a number of these citizens (at times the majority) experience the effects of extreme social inequality, which undermines a basic premise of democracy: individual agency.

Such characteristics reveal, first, the limits of thinking of democracy as merely a political regime—something weightless, far-off and pure—as if the method for electing officials did not also require the institutionalization of civil and political equality and minimal levels of social equity for citizens to properly exercise their rights. Second, the situation has sparked changes in political agendas throughout the region. Today, efforts to win citizen rights are coupled with pressures for the democratization of the state and social opportunities. The people living in these countries—more than theoreticians—have discovered that democracy must be seen as a permanent, day-to-day conquest and an order that is perfectible through citizen action.

The aim of this book is to help formulate a revised concept of democracy and to add a new focus on the quality of democracy. Likewise, it is inspired by the goal of exploring new tools that allow us to evaluate the "democraticness" of democracy's components, to identify its strengths and weaknesses, and to signal areas of risk. In presenting these tools, the book attempts to show that a new vision of democracy exists beyond the world of pure ideas and that it can be explored through empirical research.

This aspect is not confined to a search for instruments that can be used to assess various dimensions of democracy. The effort also seeks to promote tools that citizens can use to evaluate their own democracies and generate public information about the problems and challenges they face. Accordingly, the book presents and discusses the experience of the Citizen Audit of the Quality of Democracy in Costa Rica.

While we hope to contribute ideas to the debate on democracy in Latin America, we also recognize the extraordinary theoretical and political complexity of the problems we wish to analyze. We are well aware that the answers proposed here are far from complete. The book is a point of departure, not arrival. The book's style is therefore open ended and at times tentative. It tries to present pros and cons related to various themes so that the reader can reflect on the various options and adopt his or her own position. For this reason, the book also presents an array of comments, written by distinguished scholars, about its main arguments and hypotheses.

Certainly the climate of citizen discontent with democracy that has spread throughout Latin America—caused by its institutional limits or its frequently poor economic and social results in recent years—has spurred this attempt at reflection. Fortunately, the phenomenon has not threatened democracy's permanence, but the prevailing mood is far less enthusiastic than in the years immediately following the fall of authoritarian regimes. This fact makes the challenge of perfecting democracy in its different dimensions—and of promoting greater identification with and commitment to democracy among citizens—all the more urgent and necessary.

In this climate of citizen discontent, the book chooses to advocate for more and better democracy. Latin America's future demands imaginative efforts that allow us to appreciate and defend democracy's accomplishments while continuing to push for the expansion of its horizons. The book advocates for better-quality democracies that can be effective tools for creating more developed and fair societies. At the same time it does not forget that democracy, as Amartya Sen has suggested, is based upon its own values and justifies itself independently of its relationship to economic development. The intrinsic relevance of the rights that democracy guarantees allows us to defend its existence without having to demonstrate whether or not it also encourages economic growth. Nevertheless, the book warns against the temptation of drawing false conclusions from the correct observation that democracy's normative superiority is a sufficient argument to justify its existence. It is difficult to defend a democracy that proves itself impotent in the face of social inequalities and a permanent lack of economic opportunities.

In recent years economic and social turbulence in Latin America has put citizen loyalty to democratic regimes to the test. While the situation reflects a tension that cannot be prolonged indefinitely, it also presents an important learning experience for Latin American societies, who must separate appreciation for a democratic regime from the socioeconomic factors that come with it. The current Argentinean economic crisis, unprecedented in the country's history, provides the flipside of a society that has grown more sensitive to the fate of its democratic institutions. This attitude stands in stark contrast to the past, when less serious crises succeeded in bringing down the same institutions that Argentineans seek to preserve today.

While this development is important, it would be wrong to trust Latin American societies to judge democracy independently from the way they fare under it. Although such support may tempt some leaders to try society's patience, leaders have also learned lessons—associated in citizens' imaginations with the legacy of the authoritarian past—that provide democracy with a new opportunity to perfect its performance in a free setting. This situation, observable in some countries around the region, must not turn into a chance for certain de facto powers and organized groups to abuse the tolerance of a now mature citizenry. Instead, it must be understood as an opportunity—and these are always limited in number—to correct democracy's path for the common good.

A Brief History of the Book and Its Structure

This book draws upon the reports and discussions that grew out of the workshop on the "Quality of Democracy and Human Development in Latin America," held in Heredia, Costa Rica, on February 1–2, 2002. It was organized by the State of the Nation in Sustainable Human Development Project in Costa Rica and the United Nations Development Program. The workshop focused on two documents: "Human Development, Human Rights, and Democracy," by Guillermo O'Donnell, and "Citizen Audits on the Quality of Democracy: Reflections on Their Civic and Academic Potential," by Jorge Vargas Cullell in collaboration with Evelyn Villarreal Fernández and Miguel Gutiérrez Saxe. This book reproduces both of these documents, which the authors revised after the workshop in response to the discussion as well as comments made by prominent Latin Americanists from Europe, the United States, and Latin America.

O'Donnell's chapter develops the argument for expanding democratic theory beyond the limits of the political regime. He bases this theoretical affirmation on the elective affinities that link democracy to human rights and human development and on the convergences that these three currents share by recognizing the human person as an *agent* carrier of rights. This assertion is central to our understanding of the new vision of democracy proposed in this book.

Next, the chapter by Vargas Cullell examines the novel experience of a citizen audit of the quality of democracy carried out in Costa Rica. In addition to describing the initiative, his reflections have the broader aim of exploring new tools for citizen participation and evaluation of democratic quality that might be of interest to other countries in Latin America and elsewhere. Thus, although the empirical references pertain to Costa Rica, we must not to be lulled into inaction by the idea of Costa Rican "exceptionality." The book encourages us to view this citizen audit as a laboratory whose borders extend beyond that country and to use it as a tool for critically assessing the potential of the region's democracies. It is worth clarifying, however, that the contributors to this book do not see Costa Rica's citizen audit as a blueprint for the entire region. As a *tool* for citizen participation and evaluation, it would require adjustment to the particularities of each country.

Along with the two main essays, the book includes responses from several distinguished Latin Americanists who wrote comments on the theoretical and methodological proposals presented by O'Donnell and Vargas Cullell. The editors are deeply grateful to each of these contributors. In some cases, the comments prioritize conceptual discussion of democratic theory; in others, they explore the viability and scope of different instruments for measuring democratic quality and citizen participation. While both concerns are present in most of the comments, their emphasis varies by author. Overall, the comments provide a plurality of viewpoints that may help other citizen audits to be undertaken.

Accordingly, we have organized the comments into three groups. The first set (Ippolito, Whitehead, Karl, Méndez, and Lechner) gathers texts that focus on the conceptual implications of extending the vision of democracy beyond the regime. The second group (Tavares de Almeida, Conaghan, Iazzetta, and Alcántara Sáez) consists of comments that join the discussion of some conceptual aspects while adding reflections on methodological issues related to measuring the quality of democracy. Finally, the third group (Coppedge, Mazzuca, and Munck) includes additional methodological comments on the concept of quality of democracy jointly with remarks on the achievements and limitations of the citizen audit in Costa Rica.

Rationale for the Book

Given the growing challenges and emergencies that afflict democracy in countries throughout Latin America, it might be argued that experiences such as the ones undertaken here are "luxuries" affordable only to countries with a long democratic tradition and not hindered by a poor economic performance. This book tries to reverse this impression and highlight the fact that tools like the audit can also be beneficial for democracies that are recent and/or are performing poorly. Moreover, the further democratization of Latin American democracies requires us to improve our political regimes, a task that remains unfinished in many countries in the region. Some, for example, still maintain obstacles to electoral participation; in others the administration of electoral processes is deficient. In addition, at the subnational level serious democratic restrictions exist, and in the last ten years several countries have curtailed civil and political liberties using different justifications.

On the other hand, the book reminds us that even incomplete democracy provides an institutional framework capable of guaranteeing a threshold of freedoms—freedoms that make it possible for citizens to protest, give expression to their struggles for rights, and create new, as yet unrecognized, rights.

In Latin America today, this is a particularly important matter. The democratization that took place in the last quarter of the twentieth century allowed the recuperation or installation (depending on the case) of rights—particularly political rights—that had been systematically denied under authoritarian regimes. At the same time, we should not ignore that the current democratic experience has coincided, in several countries of the region, with the deterioration of citizen rights that had seemed assured (especially social and civil rights) due to the impact of major economic and social crises and to policies that have dismantled entire areas of the state.

This paradox constitutes a dangerous source of impatience, feeding the temptation to judge as "useless" the minimum guarantees that still protect democracy. The setting encourages receptivity to messages that undervalue the rights guaranteed by democracy. Yet we must not forget that much of Latin America's political tragedy can be traced to circumstances in which some of those who could exercise their rights chose instead to slight them and were later destroyed by authoritarian regimes.

As O'Donnell notes in his chapter, the rights recognized under democracy—even those considered to be merely formal—not only protect citizens but *empower* them, offering them opportunities to struggle for new rights they currently lack. In effect, democracy is no more than a source of opportunities to enjoy rights, and the manner in which these rights are guaranteed and exercised will be decisive for broadening the horizons of the regime, the state, and society. Only the existence of democracy will allow us to correct its path since, as this book emphasizes, democracy itself contains the levers that allow it to be perfected and deepened.

In light of this situation, experiences like the ones evaluated in this book are important because they encourage the diffusion of new participatory tools that allow citizens to appropriate the opportunities that democracy offers on a day-to-day basis and to become closer to their institutions. Strengthening citizen participation and expanding the agenda for public discussion are complementary, mutually reinforcing tasks that indicate the quality of a democracy. Democracy will never be independent from a lively public sphere because the latter nurtures the former and provides the setting in which democracy can expand and enrich itself.

part I

Theoretical and Empirical Foundations

chapter 1

Human Development, Human Rights, and Democracy

GUILLERMO O'DONNELL

T his chapter is based on a central argument: a democratic regime (to be defined below) is a fundamental component of democracy, but it is insufficient for adequately conceptualizing what democracy is. This is true everywhere, but it has been made particularly evident by the study of new (and some not so new) democracies in the South and the East. Generally, mainstream political science limits itself to the study of the regime. This limitation offers the safe harbor of an obviously important and apparently well-defined field of study. Going beyond the regime is a risky enterprise; it could lead to a slippery slope that ends with equating democracy with everything one happens to like. One way to avoid this risk is to tie a strong rope onto a relatively firm foundation—the regime—and with its help cautiously descend into the abyss. Of course, not any rope will do. The one I have chosen comes from an often neglected but important aspect of democracy that is already present at the level of the democratic regime: a particular conception of the human being *cum* citizen as an *agent*. This is the grounding factor, the thread that we will follow. The hope is that it will help us provide a better understanding of democracy in Latin America and elsewhere.

Thus, what follows is democratic theory with a comparative intent. It is a first exploration. It relies on contributions from several disciplines, but it sees some phenomena from angles that are largely unexplored. For this reason this chapter is an incomplete piece of democratic theory. I basically argue about foundations and some of its consequences. I say little about other extremely important topics, such as who are the real political actors—individual and collective—in a given circumstance; or how governments and states exercise their power; or the domestic consequences of various dimensions of globalization.[1] Furthermore, even though the state occupies a central place in my analysis, because of space and time limitations my discussion of the state is rather elementary. I hope, however, that even at the cost of some parsimony the present incursion beyond the regime opens topics and angles of inquiry that are not only intellectually challenging but also useful for enhancing the quality and impact of democracies in the East and South.

When reflecting on the grounding factor of democracy—agency—I found that there are intimate connections between democracy, human development, and human rights.[2] In addition to highlighting these connections, I argue that they lead us to assess the differential quality of existing democracies, and I propose some criteria for dealing with this matter. My main point is that democracy, human development, and human rights are based on a similar (moral and, in democracies, legally enacted) conception of the human being as an agent. I also note that this same view can be found in several international and regional covenants and treaties, as well as in the United Nations Development Program's (UNDP) *Human Development Reports.* I further argue that this conception traces a perpetually moving horizon that prohibits considering human development, human rights, and democracy as static or unilinear phenomena, such as seeing human development as merely the increase in the availability of material resources or of aggregate utility; or reducing human rights to protection against physical violence; or, indeed, restricting democracy to the regime.

To my knowledge, the detection of this common grounding and the exploration of its consequences is close to *terra incognita.* One danger of entering largely uncharted territory is the possibility of getting lost in the many ramifications that appear. Although I have not fully avoided this danger, my inquiry is guided by the following questions: What is the common grounding of these currents? Why should we be concerned, aside from instrumental reasons (such as, for example, its presumable contribution to economic growth) with democracy and its quality? What are the conceptual parameters under which the question of the quality of democracy may be fruitfully posed? How can we establish a conversation among these three currents so that they might nourish each other and thereby foster in theory and practice the view of agency that the three of them share?

It may be helpful if I summarize at the outset the main lines of my reasoning.

1. Human development, human rights, and democracy share a common, morally grounded, view of human agency.
2. The enacting of agency requires the universalistic attainment of at least some basic rights and capabilities.
3. Because of their common grounding in a shared view of agency, the rights and capabilities postulated by these three currents overlap quite extensively.
4. It is theoretically impossible to identify precisely the set of rights and capabilities that would be necessary and jointly sufficient for generating an "adequate" level of human development, human rights, or political rights.
5. The above fact does not prevent—quite the contrary, it challenges us—to be as specific as possible concerning the rights and capabilities involved, as well as their mutual relationships.
6. The processes aimed at inscribing need-claims as legally enacted and backed rights are eminently political (and, consequently, conflictive).
7. Given the indeterminacy and historical variability of these processes, democracy is not only very important per se but also as an enabling institutional milieu for the struggles usually needed in order to inscribe need-claims as effective rights.

A corollary of these considerations is that we have good reasons for assessing differences and changes in the quality of existing democracies. In order to help the reader follow my arguments, I have included *propositions* that highlight the main conclusions reached as I develop my argument. I also include suggestions concerning the empirical assessment (or auditing) of the quality of democracy.

1. Preliminaries

The concept of human development that has been proposed and widely diffused by UNDP's *Reports* and the work of Amartya Sen was a reversal of prevailing views about development. Instead of focusing on aggregate measures of economic performance or utility, human development as conceived by UNDP and Sen begins and ends with human beings. The concept asks how every individual is doing in relation to the achievement of "the most elementary capabilities, such as living a long and healthy life, being knowledgeable, and enjoying a decent standard of living" (UNDP 2000a: 20). These are deemed basic conditions necessary "so that each person can lead a life of respect and value." From this point of view, not only is "human development . . . a process of enhancing human capabilities" (UNDP 2000a: 2); it also becomes the yard-stick with which other aspects of development are assessed.

Throughout its *Human Development Reports,* UNDP has become increas-ingly assertive in drawing an important corollary of this approach. The achievement of basic capabilities and their expansion is not just something to which human beings have a moral claim, or a goal that well-meaning indi-viduals may posit. More consequentially, achievement of basic capabilities is deemed to be a *right* of all who suffer, at least, deprivation of primary (or basic) capabilities. This is a human interest, the satisfaction of which can be legiti-mately claimed to be the responsibility of others, especially the state.

The assertion of these rights strikes me as a quite radical and, indeed, institutionally courageous move. To begin with, the existence of such rights is disputed, in and of themselves or because of their alleged impracticability, by influential currents in philosophy, ethical theory, and jurisprudence and is plainly ignored by most of political science. Furthermore, in the *Human Development Report* I have been quoting, this assertion comes together with a discussion of human rights, including their similarities and differences with the concept of human development. This convergence is not accidental. Once the achievement of some basic capabilities is defined as a right (say, to some basic standards of nutrition and health), then some of the human interests obviously entailed (say, to physical integrity) tend to be defined as no less than basic human rights.

These perspectives have some crucial elements in common: both begin and end with human beings, and both ask for what may be, at least, a mini-mum set of conditions, or capabilities, that enable human beings to function in ways appropriate to their condition as such beings. True, in its origins the con-cept of human development focused mostly on the social and economic context, while the concept of human rights focused mostly on the legal system and on the prevention and redress of state violence. Yet the 2000 *Human Development Report's* discussion of human rights, on one side, and the increas-ing attention of human rights scholars and practitioners to (broadly under-stood) social factors, on the other,[3] reveals an important convergence: both currents deal with bundles of rights and capabilities that, in Sen's terms, are valuable insofar as they allow individuals to freely choose functionings (what they actually do and are) appropriate to their condition as human beings—as agents, as I argue below.

You may have noticed that I have twice used the exceedingly vague term "appropriate." The only way to specify this term is to come up with a certain conception of the human being in terms of which the attribute of appropriateness is predicated. Following the argument I have developed up to this point, I have jumped into deep waters. In the first place, in terms of the logic of their arguments both the proponents of human development and of human rights must be unabashed universalists, at least in terms of the "basic" rights and capabilities they posit. Proponents of slavery, the inferiority of certain races, the innate inferiority of women, and the irreducible uniqueness of cultures, cynics of various sorts, governments that do not want to be assessed in terms of their records on human development and human rights, and the like strenuously deny this universalism. In contrast, human development and human rights authors and practitioners ask, What are the basic conditions applicable to every human being, irrespective of social, cultural, and biological conditions?[4]

Secondly, it is the job of the universalists to delineate—and face the sharp discussions that will inevitably follow—the conception that underlies their claim that at least a basic set of capabilities and human rights should be generally achieved. Later in this chapter I argue that this underlying element is a moral conception of the human being as an *agent*; that is, someone who is normally endowed with sufficient autonomy for deciding what kind of life she wants to live; has the cognitive ability to reasonably detect the options available to her; and feels herself to be, and is construed by others, as responsible for the courses of action she takes. Of course, an individual can abdicate these characteristics, or may choose courses of action (functionings) that are useless or even self-destructive, or, unfortunately, may be born, say, with a severe cognitive impairment. These are important issues, but not the ones that mainly concern human development and human rights.[5] The central issue, because it affects hundreds of millions of people, refers to situations that objectively (that is, well beyond the presumable preferences of those concerned) and severely hinder the probability of an individual becoming, after the biologically determined heteronomy of infancy, an agent. The problem, of course, is how to arrive, and by whom, at criteria that will allow us to gauge these matters.

Now I recapitulate my argument thus far with some propositions.

— 1. *The concepts of human development and human rights share an underlying, universalistic vision of the human being as an agent.*
— 2. *This vision leads to the question of what may be the basic conditions that normally enable an individual to function as an agent.*

I mentioned how difficult and, indeed, disputable is the first issue; the second one, although more practical and empirical, is no less complex. Yet before tackling these matters we need to add another dimension to our discussion—democracy.

2. Components of a Democratic Regime, or Political Democracy

After the preceding prolegomena, we must focus on the rock to which we will, later on, tie our rope. In a democratic regime elections are competitive, free, egalitarian, decisive, and inclusive, and those who vote also have the right to be elected—they are *political citizens*. If elections are competitive, individuals face at least six options: vote for party A; vote for party B; do not vote; vote in blank; cast an invalid vote; or adopt some random procedure that determines which of the preceding options is effectuated. Furthermore, the (at least two) competing parties must have a reasonable chance to make their views known to all (potential and actual) voters. In order to be a real choice, the election must also be free, in that citizens are not coerced when making their voting decisions and when voting. In order for the election to be egalitarian, each vote (or nonvote) should count equally and be counted as such without fraud, irrespective of the social position, party affiliation, or other characteristics of each.[6] Finally, elections must be decisive in several senses: (a) those who turn out to be the winners gain incumbency of the respective governmental roles; (b) elected officials, based on the authority assigned to these roles, can actually make the binding decisions that a democratic legal/constitutional framework normally authorizes; and (c) elected officials end their mandates in the terms and/or under the conditions stipulated by this same framework.

Notice that these attributes of democratic elections say nothing about the composition of the electorate. There have been oligarchic democracies—those with restricted suffrage—that satisfied the above conditions. But as a consequence of the historical processes of democratization in the originating countries[7] and of its diffusion to other countries, democracy has acquired another characteristic: *inclusiveness*, meaning that the right to vote and to be elected is assigned, with few exceptions, to all adult members of a given country. For brevity, from now on I will call *fair elections* those that have the joint condition of being free, competitive, egalitarian, decisive, and inclusive.[8] This kind of election entails that governments may lose elections and must abide by the results (Przeworski 1988). Fair elections are a specific characteristic of a *democratic regime,* or *political democracy,* or *polyarchy*—three terms that I use interchangeably. Elections may be held in communist and other authoritarian countries, or for the selection of the pope, or even in some military juntas, but only in a political democracy do elections meet all the above criteria.

In contrast with influential "minimalist" currents in political science,[9] however, I maintain that fair elections are not sufficient for characterizing a democratic regime. In democratic regimes elections do not refer to a onetime event but to a series of elections that continue, and are broadly expected to continue, into an indefinite future. In saying this I have defined an *institution*. Elections under a democratic regime are institutionalized: practically all actors, political and otherwise, take for granted that fair elections will continue being held into the indefinite future at legally preestablished dates (in presidential systems) or according to legally preestablished occasions (in parliamentary systems). This means that the actors also take for granted that some "political" rights (to which I refer below) will continue to be effective. Where these expectations are widely held, fair elections are institutionalized. These cases are different not only from authoritarian ones but also from those where, even if a given election has been fair, it is not widely expected that similar elections will continue to occur in the future. Only when elections are institutionalized do relevant actors adjust their strategies to the expectation that fair elections will continue to be held. Normally, the convergence of these expectations increases the likelihood that such elections will continue happening.[10] Otherwise, elections will not be "the only game in town," and relevant agents will invest in resources other than elections in order to access the highest positions of the regime.[11]

I have been referring to a *regime,* a term that demands definition. By regime I mean the patterns, formal and informal and explicit or implicit, that determine the channels of access to principal governmental positions; the characteristics of the actors who are admitted and excluded from such access; and the resources and strategies that they are allowed to use for gaining access.[12] Fair and institutionalized elections are a central component of a democratic regime because they are the only means of access (with the exception of high courts, armed forces, and, eventually, central banks) to the principal governmental positions.

But this still is not sufficient for characterizing a democratic regime. I stated above that in a democratic regime each voter has at least six options. We must also recall something quite often overlooked: all citizens have the right to try to get elected. The fact that she may or may not want to exercise this right is irrelevant in relation to the fact that, by having the right to be elected, each adult carries with her the potential authority of participating in governmental decisions. The important point with respect to the participatory political rights of voting and being elected is that they define an *agent*. This definition is a *legal* one; these rights are assigned by the legal system to most adults in the territory of a state, with exceptions that are themselves legally defined. This assignment is *universalistic:* it is attached to all adults in a territory, irrespective of their social condition and of adscriptive characteristics other than age and nationality. At the level I am discussing—a democratic regime—agency entails the *legal attribution* of the capacity to make choices that are deemed sufficiently reasonable as to have significant consequences in terms of the aggregation of votes and of the incumbency of governing roles. Individuals may not exercise these rights, yet the legal system construes them all as equally capable of effectuating these rights and their correlated duties (such as, say, abstaining from fraud or violence when voting, or acting within legally mandated limits in governmental roles). This attribution creates a space, or a dimension, of universalistic equality predicated on all those who meet the criterion of citizenship.

This attribution clearly entails the agency of all those to whom it applies— the citizens. This agency pertains to relationships referred to a regime based on fair and institutionalized elections. For the later discussion of this topic, notice that this is an attribution of agency by means of a *bounded universalism:* it applies to most adults in the territory of a state that contains a democratic regime. Normally, the universalism predicated by human development and human rights is *unbounded,* in that it extends across all sorts of states and regimes. Yet the bounded universalism of political rights has a distinct advantage. It clearly establishes an addressee for the respective rights: they can be claimed, via the legal system, against the state as well as against private individuals who may infringe on these rights. These are valid (that is, legally actionable) subjective rights (see section 4) that exist because of the very fact that these individuals are located in a territorially delimited state that includes a democratic regime.

Seen from this angle, political democracy is not the result of some kind of consensus, individual choice, social contract, or deliberative process. *It is the result of an institutionalized wager.* The legal system assigns to every individual manifold rights and obligations. Individuals do not choose them; at birth they find themselves immersed in a social web that includes rights and duties enacted and backed by the legal system of the state in which they live. We are social beings well before we make any willful decision,[13] and in contemporary societies an important part of that being is legally defined and regulated. What is the wager? It is that in a political democracy every *ego* must accept that practically every other adult participates—by voting and eventually by being elected—in the act of fair and institutionalized elections, which determines who will govern them for some time. It is an institutionalized wager because it is imposed on every *ego* independently of his will: *ego* must accept it even if he believes that allowing certain individuals to vote or be elected is very inappropriate. *Ego* has no option but to take the chance that the "wrong" people and policies are chosen as the result of fair elections.[14] *Ego* has to take this risk because it is entailed, and backed, by the legal system of a democracy; this is part of the fact that *ego* is a social being embraced and constituted by rights and duties enacted and backed, if necessary with coercion, by the state.[15] For *ego* this is, however, a tempered risk: she is assured that in future elections she will have a fair chance to try to have the "right" people elected.

We have found another characteristic specific to political democracy: it is the only kind of regime that is the result of an institutionalized, universalistic, and inclusive wager. All other regimes, whether they include elections or not, place some kind of restriction on this wager or suppress it entirely. New or old, beyond their founding moment contemporary democratic regimes are the result of this wager and are profoundly imprinted by this fact. We can now include a proposition.

— *3. A democratic regime includes elections that are fair and institutionalized, as well as an institutionalized, inclusive, and universalistic wager.*

At this point we should remember that the individuals in a state with this kind of regime have some participatory rights. In addition, it stands to reason that in order for individuals to effectively enjoy these rights, the state and its legal system must uphold other "political" rights, or guarantees. If fair elections are institutionalized, especially because it involves expectations of indefinite endurance, such elections cannot stand alone. Some freedoms that surround the elections and—very importantly—continue in force between them must also exist. Otherwise, the government could quite easily manipulate or even cancel future elections. According to an influential author, Robert Dahl (1989, 1999), the relevant political freedoms are those of expression, association, and access to pluralist information; other authors posit, more or less explicitly and in detail, similar rights. Like the participatory rights, the rights I am discussing at this moment are boundedly universalistic, in that they are assigned to practically all adults in and by the legal system of a state that contains a democratic regime.

We should notice, however, that the combined effect of the freedoms listed by Dahl and other authors cannot fully guarantee that elections will be fair, much less institutionalized. For example (taking into consideration freedoms usually omitted in these definitions), the government might prohibit opposition candidates from traveling within the country, or subject them to police harassment for reasons allegedly unrelated to their candidacy. In such cases, even if the freedoms listed by Dahl and others held, we would hardly conclude that the elections are fair. This means that the conditions proposed by Dahl and others are not sufficient for guaranteeing fair elections. Rather, these are *necessary conditions* that jointly support a probabilistic judgment: if they hold, then *ceteris paribus* there is a strong likelihood that elections will be fair.[16]

We may now discuss a matter that is ignored by most contemporary theories of democracy but has a close bearing on the topic of human development and human rights. The rights mentioned above are inductively derived. The listing of these rights is the result of a reasoned empirical assessment of their impact on the likelihood of fair elections.[17] This judgment is controlled by the intention of finding a minimal, or core set, of "political" freedoms, in the sense that the listing does not slip into a useless inventory of every right or freedom that might have some conceivable bearing on the fairness and institutionalization of elections. The problem is that since the criteria for inclusion of some freedoms and exclusion of others unavoidably result from inductive judgments, there cannot exist a theory that establishes a firm and clear line that would determine what I will call a *minimal sufficient set.* In the case of political freedoms, I mean a kind of set that would include only the necessary and jointly sufficient conditions for the existence of fair and institutionalized elections; this set, conversely, would exclude other freedoms that, even if they might be supportive of, are not necessary or sufficient for fair and institutionalized elections. Because the freedoms to be included and excluded in the set are inductively derived, however, there never will be generalized intersubjective agreement on the contents of the minimal sufficient set—we will forever dispute the freedoms are "truly" necessary and jointly sufficient for the exercise of political citizenship.[18]

Up to now I have discussed the external boundaries of the freedoms that surround, and make likely, fair and institutionalized elections—the issue of which freedoms to include and exclude from this set. But there is another problem, namely, the internal boundaries of each of these freedoms. All of them contain a "reasonability clause" that, once again, is usually left implicit in theories of democracy.[19] The freedom to form associations does not include creating organizations with terrorist aims; the freedom of expression is limited, among others, by the law of libel; the freedom of information does not require that ownership of the media is fully competitive, etc. How do we determine if these freedoms are effective or not? Surely, cases that fall close to one or the other extreme are unproblematic. But other cases fall in a gray area between the two poles, and these cases depend on inductive judgments about the degree to which the feeble, or partial, or intermittent effectiveness of certain freedoms supports, or not, the likelihood of fair and institutionalized elections. Once again, there is no firm and clear answer to this problem: the external and the internal boundaries of political rights are *theoretically undecidable.*[20] In other words, the minimal sufficient set of these freedoms is undecidable. This fact, however, should not lead us to deny that the freedoms that are reasonable candidates to belong to the minimal sufficient set are extremely important, and as such should be taken into careful consideration.[21]

A further difficulty is that the internal boundaries of freedoms such as the ones listed by Dahl, and of other rights and freedoms that also are potentially relevant to fair and institutionalized elections, have undergone significant changes over time. Suffice to say that certain restrictions on freedom of expression and of association that in the originating countries were considered acceptable not long ago would be deemed undemocratic today.[22] With this in mind, how demanding should be the criteria we apply to newly emerged democracies (and to older ones outside the Northwest)? Should we apply the criteria presently prevalent in the originating countries,[23] or the criteria used in their past, or, once more, make in each case reasoned inductive assessments of these rights in terms of the likelihood of the effectuation of fair and institutionalized elections? It seems to me that the latter option is the more adequate, but it sends us back squarely to the undecidability of the respective set of rights, now further complicated by their historical variability.

I conclude that there is, and there will continue to be, disagreement in academia and, indeed, in practical politics, concerning where to trace the external and internal boundaries of the freedoms that surround, and make likely, fair and institutionalized elections. This is not a flaw in the attempts to list these freedoms. These freedoms are very important per se and because of their relation to those elections; they are necessary conditions for enabling the rights of participation entailed by a democratic regime. As such these freedoms are worth listing. On the one hand, it can be empirically established that the lack or severe curtailment of some of these rights or freedoms (say, of expression, association, or movement) eliminates the likelihood of fair elections and, *a fortiori,* of their institutionalization. On the other hand, the inductive character of these listings, and the related problem of their external and internal boundaries, shows their limitations as theoretical statements. Consequently, instead of ignoring these problems, or artificially trying to fix the external and internal boundaries of these freedoms and rights, a more fruitful avenue of inquiry consists of thematizing theoretically the reasons and implications of this conundrum.[24] We are in a terrain that I gather is familiar to those who have reflected on human development and human rights in terms of attempts to find minimal sufficient sets for their respective concerns. After this discussion, it may be useful to list two propositions.

— *4. In addition to the characteristics noted in proposition 3, a democratic regime consists of some (boundedly) universalistic "political" freedoms. These rights are important per se and because they are necessary conditions for fair and institutionalized elections and for the continued effectiveness of the democratic wager.*
— *5. Because the external and internal boundaries of these freedoms are theoretically undecidable, there is no theoretical or intersubjectively general valid way of clearly and firmly establishing a minimal sufficient set of these rights.*

Let us now notice two conclusions we have implicitly reached through the preceding discussion. One is a definition of *political citizenship* as the individual component of a democratic regime. It consists of the legal assignment of the rights entailed by the wager—both some surrounding freedoms (such as of expression, association, information, free movement, and the like) and the rights of participation in fair and institutionalized elections, including voting and being elected. The second point is that in reaching this definition we have gone beyond the regime and run into *the state* in two senses: (a) as a territorial entity that delimits those who are the carriers of the rights and obligations of political citizenship; and (b) as a legal system that enacts and backs these rights and obligations. The democratic wager and political citizenship are, respectively, the aggregate and the individual sides of the same coin, and they jointly presuppose the state, both as a territorial delimitation and as a legal system. Furthermore, these aspects of the state have a double face. In one sense, they are necessary conditions for the existence of a democratic regime. In another sense, which I discuss below, they are characteristics of the democraticness of the state itself, not just of the regime. Now I include some propositions.

— *6. Political citizenship consists of the universalistic assignment of the rights entailed by the inclusive democratic wager, both some surrounding freedoms and the rights of participation in fair elections, including voting and being elected.*
— *7. A democratic regime (or political democracy or polyarchy) presupposes: (a) a territorially based state that delimits those who are considered political citizens; and (b) a legal system of that same state that within its territory assigns political citizenship on a (boundedly) universalistic basis, by means of various participatory rights and political freedoms.*

3. First Excursus on Assessing the Quality of Democracy

The present excursus, as well as the ones that follow, bear strong resemblance to the extremely valuable work done by the team of the Costa Rican Proyecto Estado de la Nación, especially their *Auditoría Ciudadana sobre la Calidad de la Democracia* (2001).[25] This is no accident, since I was inspired by their work and on several occasions I have discussed these matters in detail with the authors. The premise of the citizen audit, as well as of what follows here, is that the quality of democracy in given countries may be gauged by its different degrees of democraticness along several dimensions.[26] In the present excursus I limit myself to dimensions that are directly implied in my discussion so far.[27] I discuss other dimensions as I analyze other themes.

For the purpose of ordering my suggestions on this matter, I arrange sequentially several typical events about which we want to know:

With regard to elections as fair and institutionalized

In terms of citizens:
1. How many have a clear and presumably stable preference for a democratic regime over any other.
2. How many accept that the territorially bounded population of the state in which they live is the proper unit for defining the electorate.
3. How well informed they are about the parties, candidates, and issues of the election.
4. How interested they are about the parties, candidates, and issues of the election.
5. How much and in what ways they participate in political activities, especially those related to elections.
6. To what extent they use existing opportunities for expressing views concerning the discussion, decision, or implementation of public policies.
7. If policies and/or incentives exist for facilitating and eventually promoting the self-organization and political participation of poor and/or otherwise discriminated against sectors or categories of citizens.[28]

In terms of the electoral system:
1. If national elections are held with sufficient frequency to reflect major changes in public opinion, and if there are constitutional mechanisms that enable citizens to remove elected officials between elections.[29]

2. If there exists an independent, impartial, and adequately empowered and funded electoral commission.

3. If the electoral system does not overrepresent some constituencies and, if this is the case, to what degree.

4. If it significantly compensates for the disadvantages that some parties may suffer because they are not being supported by economically powerful groups.

5. If it has clear and enforceable rules for disclosing the contributions that political parties receive for electoral campaigns and/or for their continued functioning.

6. If it does not interpose high barriers to the creation and workings of political parties, with the exception of those that advocate violent means for political competition and/or for accessing governmental positions.

7. If it does not interpose difficult requirements for voter registration, especially those that may be hard to meet by poor and/or discriminated against individuals.

8. If every citizen is free to become a member of a political party, try to be nominated as a candidate for this party, and if nominated run for election.

9. If all parties and candidates are treated respectfully and impartially by state authorities.

In terms of political parties:

1. If their internal procedures, especially in terms of the appointment of their leaders and electoral candidates, are themselves democratic as well as open to the scrutiny of their affiliates and pertinent public institutions.

2. If they disclose, in proper time and form, the public and private support they receive and render proper accounts of the use of this support.

3. If they conduct their electoral campaigns respecting the civil and political rights of their opponents and in ways that do not entail or promote discrimination, bias, slander, or any type of bigotry.

In terms of elections themselves:

1. If voters are not intimidated or pressured in any way, and if their ballots are truly secret.

2. If there is free access to the polling places for representatives of political parties, election observers, and the media.

3. If the elections are conducted in an orderly and peaceful way.

4. If votes are counted fairly and the results announced expeditiously.

5. If those who turn out to be winners are proclaimed as such and in proper time take up their respective governmental roles.

6. If complaints about the elections are dealt with impartially and promptly.

7. If the election results are accepted as valid by the population at large.

With regard to the elected government

In terms of the executive:

1. If it acts with clear and consistent respect of the rights of the citizens and their associations and of the jurisdiction of other public institutions.

In terms of Congress:

1. If it acts with clear and consistent respect of the rights of the citizens and their associations and of the jurisdiction of other public institutions.

2. If it conducts its deliberations and makes decisions in ways that reasonably respect the right of every legislator to be heard (in plenaries and/or in commissions) and have his/her votes weighted equally.

3. If minority parties have a fair chance to have their criticisms and proposals considered and discussed, inside and outside of Congress.

In terms of the general workings of the government:

1. If it acts with clear and consistent respect of the rights of the citizens and their associations and of the jurisdiction of other public institutions.

2. If it offers clear, timely, and feasible opportunities for the citizens and their associations to express their views concerning the discussion, decision, or implementation of public policies.

I hasten to add that this is, so to speak, an innocent list. One reason is that it ignores trade-offs. In particular, the list is biased toward positively valuing citizens' opportunities for participation, thus enhancing—or at least facilitating—the popular component of democracy. In some policy areas, however (say, currency exchange decisions), there may be solid reasons against allowing that participation; or in other areas (say, foreign relations negotiations or some national security matters) the need for secrecy may be persuasively argued. In these cases I believe that the test of relative democraticness should focus on the kind of procedures and actors involved in the setting of these limitations,[30] as well as their amenability to challenge and revision.

The second reason for the innocence of the preceding list is that it overlooks the question of whether an electoral system is of better quality, or more democratic, if it tends toward majoritarianism or toward proportionality. Individuals who, according to any test we might apply, are solidly democratic would tend to prefer proportionality if they are of a strong liberal persuasion, while no less solid democrats who hold views derived from classic democracy or republicanism would tend to prefer majoritarianism.[31] I believe that ultimately this is an unsolvable problem. Assuming that the electorate is divided on this matter, the natural democratic answer is to have them vote. But if it is an election it has to be held under one or the other rule, and if it is a referendum, then the issue has been prejudged in favor of the majoritarians. This may be one reason why we often find hybrid electoral regimes that combine, sometimes in quite clumsy fashion, both kinds of rules. In view of this, I believe that an assessment of the quality of democracy should abstain from this issue.

Finally, you may have noticed an omission in the preceding list: it does not deal with some important aspects of the institutional format of democracies, especially regimes that are federalist or unitary and presidential or parliamentary (and various combinations thereof), nor with systems of judicial review versus constitutional courts. The reason is that, in the present state of our knowledge, I do not believe that any of these variations can be predicated as more or less democratic than the other;[32] furthermore, all of them may be assessed in terms of the items listed here and in further excursi.

4. Democracy and Agency

The preceding analysis of the regime is descriptive. We now enter a terrain where not only factual but also normative assertions are needed.[33] In particular, the theme of human agency, which I will discuss throughout the rest of the chapter, demands not only descriptive statements but also drawing the normative implications of its effectuation and, especially in the case of Latin America, its curtailment.

I begin by recalling that the democratic wager entails the (boundedly) universalistic attribution of agency. Let us now take a more careful look at political citizenship. It is a legally defined status assigned, as part and consequence of the democratic wager, to most of the inhabitants of a state that includes a regime consisting of fair and institutionalized elections. This status is mixed. It is adscriptive in that (excepting naturalization) it pertains to individuals by the sheer fact of their being born in a given territory (*ius solis*) or from a lineage (*ius sanguinis*). It is boundedly universalistic in that within the jurisdiction delimited by a state it is assigned on the same terms to all adults who meet the nationality criterion. It is also a formal status because it results from legal rules that in their content, enactment, and adjudication satisfy criteria that are specified by other legal rules, some of which are constitutional. Furthermore, political citizenship is public. By this I mean, first, that it is the result of laws that satisfy carefully spelled-out requisites of publicity and, second, that the rights and obligations it assigns to every *ego* imply, and legally demand, a system of mutual recognition among all individuals, irrespective of their social position, as carriers of such rights and obligations.[34] Finally, it is egalitarian: it generates a space of legally enacted equality in the attribution (and in the at least potential enjoyment) of political rights.

Now I turn to the democratic wager. Its inclusiveness is a recent achievement. For a long time in the originating countries, many social groups were excluded from voting, let alone being elected: peasants, blue-collar workers, domestic workers (and, in general, non–property owners and poorly educated individuals), blacks in the United States, Native Americans in the latter country as well as in many others, and women. Only during the twentieth century, and with regard to women as late as after World War II in many countries, did political rights become inclusive.[35] On their part, at various times countries in the South and East adopted inclusive suffrage; however, the variations of "tutelary" or "façade" democracies, and of course openly authoritarian regimes, that emerged there meant the denial of the democratic wager.

Everywhere, the history of democracy is the history of the reluctant acceptance of the inclusive wager—that is, the refusal to accept the universality of agency in the political realm. The history of the originating countries is punctuated by the catastrophic predictions and the violent resistance of privileged sectors of society opposing the extension of political rights to "undeserving" or "untrustworthy" sectors.[36] In the South and East, by means often more violent and comprehensively exclusionary, this same extension also has been resisted. What were the grounds for this refusal? Typically, the privileged classes argued for the lack of autonomy and responsibility—that is, lack of agency—of the excluded groups. Only some individuals (whether they were highly educated and/or property owners, a political vanguard that had deciphered the direction of history, or a military *junta* that understood the demands of national security, etc.) were supposed to have the moral and cognitive capabilities necessary for participating in political life. Only they were seen as sufficiently invested (in terms of education, property, revolutionary work, or patriotic designs) to have adequate motivation for responsibly making collective decisions. Of course, revolutionary vanguards, military *juntas,* and the like generated authoritarian regimes, while in the originating countries the privileged generated, in most cases, oligarchical, noninclusive democratic regimes for themselves and political exclusion for the rest.

As mentioned above, a central idea underlies the inclusive wager: agency. An agent is somebody endowed with practical reason: she uses her cognitive and motivational capabilities to make choices that are reasonable in terms of her situation and goals, of which, barring conclusive proof to the contrary, she is deemed to be the best judge.[37] This capacity confers upon the agent a moral dimension, in the sense that normally the agent will feel, and will be construed by relevant others as, responsible for her choices and for at least the direct consequences that ensue from these choices.

Surely, the literatures that deal with this topic from various angles offer a number of qualifications to what I have just stated. Yet the point I want to stress is that the presumption of agency is another institutionalized fact, one that in the originating countries is older and more entrenched than the democratic wager and fair elections. This presumption is not just a moral, philosophical, or psychological concept; it is a legally enacted one. The presumption of agency constitutes every individual as a legal person, a carrier of subjective rights. The legal person makes choices, and is assigned responsibility for them, because the legal system presupposes that she is autonomous, responsible, and reasonable—that is, that she is an agent.[38]

This view became the core of the legal systems of the originating countries well before the establishment of democracy. The institutionalized (that is, legally enacted and backed and widely taken for granted) recognition of an agent as a carrier of subjective rights was a long and convoluted process. It began with some of the Sophists and Stoics and Cicero, runs through Roman law and medieval legists,[39] was refined by natural law theorists, and was finally reappropriated and, as it were, politicized, in spite of their differences in other respects, by the great early liberal thinkers—especially Hobbes, Locke, and Kant, as well as a nonliberal, Rousseau.

I cannot recount this story here (see O'Donnell 2000). It suffices to note that it is the history of the formulation and progressive expansion of a view of the individual as a carrier of subjective rights, which pertain to each individual as such, not as a derivation (as in Aristotelian and other organicist theories) of the individual's position in a social hierarchy. These rights underlie what the classical legal theories called the *potestas* of each individual—his capacity to willfully and responsibly commit to duties he freely assumes and, correlatively, his right to demand the fulfillment of the duties of his counterparts. Historically, this conception found its main expression in contract law and in the progressive marketization of landed property (see, among others, Hamburger 1989). This institutionalization of agency occurred counterpointally to the expansion, in the originating countries, of capitalism and the state. On the one hand, the agent who validly commits his will is the same who "freely" sells his labor to the capitalist; on the other hand, the formally equalizing attribution of agency in the areas of contract and property and as common subjects to a ruler was a powerful instrument in the struggles of state makers against feudal powers, urban privileges, medieval corporations, and the Catholic Church (see Weber 1968). Until the liberal thinkers transposed this idea of agency into the political realm, the rights of individuals were basically limited to what in the continental tradition are called *civil rights,* those referring to "private" relationships among individuals. Furthermore, these rights were not extended universalistically: some social categories such as serfs or peasants, and women, were denied many of them.

The crucial facts for my discussion, however, are (a) the legal attribution of agency to an expanding number of individuals has a long history in the originating countries; (b) this attribution was elaborated in detail in diverse philosophical, moral, and—especially—legal doctrines well before the great liberal theorists transposed the idea of agency into the political realm;[40] and (c) later on this same view suffused the two great modern constitutions, those of France and the United States. Now I insert a proposition.

— 8. *In the Northwest the conception of the individual as an agent had, well before the universalistic extension of political citizenship, a long process of elaboration in religious, ethical, and philosophical doctrines. More importantly, this same conception was carefully elaborated, and progressively implanted at the rhythm of the expansion of capitalism and the modern state, as a legal doctrine that, in assigning subjective rights to individuals, attributed to them legally actionable agency.*

As many have argued, however, this construction of an agent carrier of subjective rights, because it omitted the actual conditions of the exercise of these rights, helped to reproduce extremely unequal relationships, especially between capitalists and workers.[41] Yet this construction contained explosive corollaries. First, if *ego* is attributed agency in certain spheres of life that are, for her and in the aggregate for the whole of society, extremely important (such as the labor contract or the sale of landed property), why should this attribution be denied in other spheres of social and political life, and who should have the authority to decide this matter? A second corollary proved no less explosive: since agency obviously entails choice, what actual options, or capabilities, are reasonably consistent with *ego's* condition as an agent?

The answer to the first question is the history of the further expansion of subjective rights, including the right of suffrage up to its present inclusiveness. In the originating countries, this history was written by manifold conflicts at the end of which, after having accepted massive death in war for their countries and exchanging revolution for the welfare state, the *classes dangereuses* were admitted into the inclusive democratic wager—they gained political citizenship.[42] While this happened, other processes continued in the originating countries. One was that the map of western Europe and North America was quite firmly drawn as a consequence of successful, and often cruel, state making (see especially Tilly 1985, 1990). Another was the further expansion of rights in the civil sphere, in the double sense that already recognized rights and duties were further specified and new ones were added.[43] These processes meant that, when sometime in the nineteenth century most countries of the Northwest adopted oligarchic, noninclusive democracy, an overwhelming part of their male population (and, albeit to a limited extent, females, too) already had been assigned a series of subjective rights that regulated numerous parts of their lives. These were not—not yet—the participatory rights of the democratic wager. They were civil rights—rights pertaining to "private" social and economic activities. These rights have been summed up as "civil citizenship" by T. H. Marshall.[44]

I want to stress that when full political inclusion became an issue, in the originating countries there already existed a rich repertoire of legally enacted and elaborated criteria concerning the attribution of agency to a vast number of individuals. Truly, the scope of these rights was, by our contemporary standards, limited. But it is also true that in the originating countries civil citizenship by and large preceded political citizenship and provided to it a rich supporting texture. These same processes furnished the historical background of the core idea of political liberalism: The government and the state must be limited and constitutionally regulated because they exist for, and on behalf of, individuals who are carriers of subjective rights enacted and backed by the same legal system that the state and the government must obey and from which they derive their authority.[45] I can now insert another proposition.

— *9. After a long and complex historical trajectory that in the countries of the Northwest first included the rather extensive achievement of (mostly male) civil citizenship, contemporary democracy is based on the idea of political citizenship, which in turn is based on the conception of an agency that is legally enacted and backed.*

In some countries this conception of agency describes quite well their historical experience, in which agency was first implanted in the sphere of civil rights and later expanded into the political sphere; in other countries, however, civil rights have never been effected for large parts of their populations. I discuss this matter further below, although here I note that these remarks have empirical implications. Some democracies may be conceived as having a central set of political rights that are surrounded, supported, and strengthened by a dense web of civil rights. Other democracies, in contrast, may exhibit (by definition of a democratic regime) these political rights, but the surrounding texture of civil rights may be tiny and/or unevenly distributed among different kinds of individuals, social categories, and regions. It seems to me that the differences along these dimensions, across cases and time, should have a strong bearing on the quality of democracy in each case and period.

Above I noted that even if initially restricted to civil rights, the idea of agency has explosive potentialities. In particular, an issue quite obviously raised by the presumption of agency is the capabilities (and, consequently, the range of options) available to each individual.[46] In the Northwest, the answer to this issue branched out in two directions. One focused on civil rights, especially, but not exclusively, in the (broadly defined) area of contract. A series of legal criteria were elaborated for voiding, redressing, or preventing situations in which there exists a "manifestly disproportionate" relationship[47] between the parties involved and/or where one of the parties may be construed—because of duress, fraud, mental incapacity, etc.—as not having lent autonomous consent to a contract or other legal relationship. These tutelary measures rest on a basic criterion of fairness, which in turn is a corollary of the idea of agency. Agents are supposed to relate to each other as agents, that is, without suffering for whatever reason lack of basic capabilities (a central theme of human development) or being subjected to decisive coercion (a central theme of human rights), which severely hinder their agency per se and/or in terms of the availability of a reasonable range of choices. In these circumstances individuals lack enough freedom to be construed as having willfully agreed to their obligations. We see that with regard to civil rights it has been recognized in multiple ways that agency entails choice, and choice entails the freedom to choose among alternatives that the agent has reasons to value. Through these legal constructions, the fairness requirement of creating a minimally level playing field among agents was added into the legal systems of the originating countries.[48]

The second direction in which the issue of agency and its relationship to capabilities branched out was the emergence of social rights.[49] Here again the value of the fairness component of agency stands out, albeit focused on social categories rather than on single individuals as in civil law. Through another long and convoluted process that I need not detail here, the newly accepted participants in the democratic wager exchanged their acceptance of political democracy for a share in the benefits of the welfare state. These benefits were not only material; through collective representation and other devices, these actors diminished their sharp de facto inequality with respect to capitalists and the state that Marx and others had pointedly denounced as existing behind the universalism of the legal systems. By means of welfare legislation, and with ups and downs in terms of the respective power relationships,[50] these views of fairness were incorporated into the legal system. Welfare legislation joined civil law in expressing the view that if agents are to be reasonably presumed to be such agents, then society, and especially the state and its legal system, should not be indifferent to, at the very least, cases where there exists severe deprivation of relevant capabilities. Preventive and remedial actions were consequently mandated, ranging from supporting basic levels of material conditions to various mechanisms of collective representation. Although they have been a mixed blessing,[51] these were democratizing changes: they increased the density of the legal texture that enacts and backs the very same agency that is entailed by democracy. It is time for another proposition.

— 10. *In the originating countries, the issue of the capabilities that actually enable agency was faced in terms of civil and social rights. The underlying view of these legal constructions is one of the fairness that, in terms of their available capabilities, is due to individuals who are construed as freely and responsibly choosing—that is, agents.*

I find quite remarkable (and, in fact, one of the negative consequences of the segmenting of disciplines that prevails in the contemporary academic world) that, to my knowledge, the story I have briefly told is largely ignored by democratic, human development, and human rights theories. This is regrettable insofar as these theories, and their practitioners, face the issue concerning if, and in what sense and to what extent, there should be at least a basic set of rights or capabilities pertaining to their respective concerns. We saw that this issue forcefully appeared in matters of, first, civil and, later on, social rights. There is much to be learned from this experience. One lesson lies in the agency and fairness arguments used for justifying the legal imposition of a more level playing field in a series of relationships, as well as in the criticisms and grim predictions that these attempts elicited. The second lesson, to which I will return, is that most of these rights were not just granted; they were conquered by means of manifold struggles by subordinated classes and sectors who faced discrimination; all of them ultimately aimed at inscribing their needs and claims as formally enacted and effectively implemented rights.[52]

Now I begin to develop an argument that is central to this chapter: The relationship between agency and capabilities in the political sphere is closely related to this same issue in connection with civil and social rights. Posing the issue of capabilities in the political sphere involves going beyond the universalistic assignment of the rights of political citizenship. It leads to the question of what conditions may allow the effective exercise of these rights.[53] In this sense, it seems to me mistaken to omit, as most political science theories of democracy do, the issue of the effectiveness of political citizenship when referring to individuals who are severely deprived of civil and social rights. True, in a democratic regime these same individuals are assigned the universalistic political rights we have examined. Yet looking exclusively at this side of the matter means eliding from democratic theory the very issue of agency and capabilities that private law and welfare legislation (as well as human development and human rights) could not ignore.[54] This assertion may be stated as a proposition.

— 11. *Agency has direct, and concurrent, implications in the civil, social, and political spheres because it is a moral conception, which in several aspects has been legally enacted, of the human being as an autonomous, reasonable, and responsible individual.*

This view of agency is not just one that has been enacted in some rich countries; it was also inscribed in the moral conscience of humanity by the French Declaration of the Rights of Man and of the Citizen; the Prologue and the First Amendment of the Constitution of the United States; the United Nation's Universal Declaration of Human Rights (1948); the International Covenant on Civil and Political Rights; the International Covenant on Economic, Social, and Cultural Rights; the Vienna Declaration on Human Rights; and several other international and regional treatises and covenants (including the Inter-American Convention on Human Rights), all of which have been ratified by a large number of countries.[55]

5. Democracy and the State

In the preceding sections we have gone beyond the regime. This demands that we consider the various ways in which the state is relevant for the study of democracy. To begin with, let us remember that in contemporary countries most rights and obligations are enacted and backed by a legal system. This legal system is a part of the state. Normally, the state extends its rule, most of it effectuated in the grammar of law, across the territory it encompasses. We saw that for a democratic regime to exist there must be a territorial delimitation of its citizens and some rights assigned to them. The state is not only a set of bureaucracies; it is also a legal system that is enacted and normally backed by the supremacy of coercion held by the state institutions over the territory they delimit.[56] This legal system embraces and constitutes *qua* legal persons the individuals in the state's territory. It follows that insofar as it upholds the democratic wager as well as a regime consisting of fair and institutionalized elections and some surrounding freedoms, the state and its system are democratic. Democraticness is an attribute of the state, not only of the regime (see O'Donnell 1999b and 2000).

Some authors consider the rights of association, expression, and the like as negative ones, but this view has been persuasively criticized.[57] One way or the other, the rights of voting and being elected clearly are positive. Furthermore, there is at least another right, implied by the former, that is also positive: the right to fair and expeditious access to courts. This right involves the expectation that some state institutions will undertake, if legally appropriate, actions oriented toward the effectuation of the above-mentioned rights as well as others (Fábre 1998). The denial of this expectation would mean that these rights are purely nominal. With this assertion we have again run into the state *qua* legal system that enacts and backs rights that, in spite of differences among authors as to which to list specifically, are widely agreed to be basic components or necessary conditions of political democracy. The point at this stage of my discussion is that in addition to the legal system, we have identified some institutions of the state that are directly related to a democratic regime. This allows me to complete the picture of a legal system: It is not just an aggregation of rules but properly a *system,* consisting of the interlacing of legal rules and legally regulated state institutions. In turn, a species of this genus—a *democratic* legal system—is one characterized by two features: (a) it enacts and backs the rights attached to a democratic regime; and (b) there is no institution or official in the state or in the regime (or, for that matter, in society) that is *de legibus solutus.* In an *Estado democrático de derecho*[58] everyone is subject to the legal authority of some other institution(s).[59] This legal system "closes," in the sense that nobody is supposed to be above or beyond its rules.[60] In turn, this characteristic is closely related (as the tradition of liberal constitutionalism recognized very early) to the protection of political and other rights; lacking this safeguard, there would exist some ultimately uncontrollable power(s) that may unilaterally cancel these rights. In a democracy rulers are supposed to be submitted to three kinds of accountability. One is vertical electoral accountability, resulting from fair and institutionalized elections, through which citizens may change the party and officers in government. Another kind of vertical accountability, of a societal kind,[61] is exercised by groups and even individuals who aim to mobilize the legal system to place demands on the state and the government in order to prevent, redress, and/or punish presumably illegal actions (or inactions) perpetrated by public officials. The third kind of accountability, horizontal, results when some properly authorized state institutions act to prevent, redress, and/or punish presumably illegal actions or inactions committed by public officials (see O'Donnell 1998a, 2003). Notice, however, that there is an important difference among these types of accountability. Vertical electoral accountability must exist by the very definition of a democratic regime, while the degree and effectiveness of vertical societal and horizontal accountability are variable across cases and time. These variations are relevant for assessing the quality of democracy; for example, the lack of a vigorous and self-assertive society or the impossibility or unwillingness of certain state institutions to discharge their authority over other state institutions (especially elected officials) are indications of a low-quality democracy.

We have reached another conclusion. Above I noted that there are three specific characteristics of political democracy not shared by any other kind of regime: fair and institutionalized elections, some participatory rights and "political freedoms," and an inclusive wager. Now we see that there are two other specific characteristics: (a) by implication of the definition of a democratic regime, a legal system that enacts and backs—at least—those same rights and freedoms; and (b) a legal system that prescribes that no person or institution is *de legibus solutus*.[62] While the first three characteristics of political democracy pertain to the level of the regime, the last two are located at the level of the state. We see that an exclusive focus on the regime is insufficient for an adequate characterization of democracy. We have abandoned democracy at the level of the regime and entered the more complex level of the state. These conclusions may be stated as a proposition.

— 12. *Democracy has five unique characteristics in relation to all other political types: (a) fair and institutionalized elections; (b) a set of participatory rights and political freedoms without which those elections would be meaningless; (c) an inclusive and (boundedly) universalistic wager; (d) a legal system that enacts and backs—at least—the rights and freedoms included in the definition of a democratic regime; and (e) a legal system that prevents anyone from being* de legibus solutus. *The first three characteristics pertain to the regime, the last two to the state.*

As implied by the example of courts, another aspect of the legal system is its effectiveness—the degree to which it actually orders social relations. This is a function of the interlacings of the legal system. For example, at one level, which we will call inter-institutional, a judge dealing with a criminal case would have no authority without the inclusion at several stages of the process of the police, prosecutors, defense lawyers, etc., as well as, eventually, higher courts and prisons.[63] Horizontally, I noted that in a democratic legal system no state institution or officer is supposed to escape from legal controls concerning the lawfulness of their actions. In a third dimension, namely, territorial, the legal system is supposed to extend homogenously across the space delimited by the state. In a fourth dimension, stratificational, the legal system is supposed to treat like cases alike irrespective of the class, gender, ethnicity, or other attributes of the respective actors. In all these dimensions, the legal system presupposes what Linz and Stepan call an "effective state" (1996: 37); in my terms, it is not just a matter of appropriate legislation but also of a network of state institutions that operate in the direction of ensuring the effectiveness of a legal system that is itself democratic. We will see that the weakness of this kind of state is one of the most disturbing characteristics of most Latin American countries. Before discussing this matter, we can add another proposition.

— 13. *The effectiveness of a legal system depends on the interlacing of its rules with a network of state institutions that, in a democracy, act with purposes and outcomes that are regularly consistent with an* Estado democrático de derecho *or, equivalently, a democratic rule of law.*

We have not finished our examination of the relationship between democracy and the state. Remember that through the assignment of various political rights, democracy construes citizens as agents. Remember, too, that agents are carriers of subjective rights that are legally assigned on a (boundedly) universalistic basis. Now I add that this legal system, beginning with its highest—constitutional—rules, establishes that citizens, as they make their voting decisions in fair elections, are the source of the authority exercised over them by the state and the government. Citizens are not only the carriers of rights; they are the source and justification of the claim to rule that states and governments articulate when making collectively binding decisions. Contemporary democracy hardly is *by* the people; but it certainly is *from* the people and, because of this, it should be *for* the people, too. Elected government officials quite obviously derive their authority from the citizenry. This is also true of all other state officials insofar as, in a democracy, they derive their authority from the highest—elected—powers of the country. Furthermore, the jurisdiction and obligations of those state officials are determined by the same legal system that, by prohibiting them from being *de legibus solutus,* subjects all public officials, elected and nonelected, to horizontal accountability. Finally, everyone, including those who are not political citizens (nonadults and foreigners) is also construed as an agent by the legal rules that regulate civil and social relationships.[64]

It follows that an individual is not, and should never be treated as, a subject—a supplicant of the goodwill of the government or the state. This individual—an agent carrier of a bundle of civil and eventually social rights, whether or not she is a political citizen—has a legally grounded claim to be treated with full consideration and respect and on an equal basis to everyone else who is treated with such consideration and respect.[65] Furthermore, this treatment must be based on the application of laws and regulations that are clear, knowable by the citizens, and enacted in ways that accord to democratic procedures.[66] In this sense, Robert Lane has argued that "By and large, democratic theory is reticent on how we are treated by the political, social and economic institutions that the theory addresses." However, a crucial aspect of democratic theory and practice is that "how we are treated is as important to us as what we get," including "who treats whom with dignity, with minimal procedural pain, and with sympathetic attention to the individual's sense of justice" (1988: 189).[67]

I believe that to the degree that state institutions effectively recognize these rights, they may be deemed more or less democratic, or at least more or less consistent with the duties imposed on them by democracy and its agency concomitants. Indeed, this is arguably the hardest face of democracy. In relation to fair elections and, normally, to the exercise of political rights, citizens are placed on a level of generic equality. In contrast, when dealing with state institutions individuals, whether citizens or not, are often placed in situations of sharp de facto inequality. They face bureaucracies that act on the basis of formal and informal rules that are seldom transparent and easily understandable and that make decisions (and omissions) that often have important consequences for their "subjects." It is a sad law of human nature that when individuals are placed on the more powerful side of sharply unequal relationships, they tend to forget that their right to exercise authority derives from those "below" who are carriers of rights that demand full consideration and respect.[68] This is a problem everywhere. It is more serious, and systematic, when the "subject" of these relationships is afflicted by severe and extended poverty and inequality. These ills breed social authoritarianism, including the way state institutions treat many of its citizens. This is, to my mind, another crucial dimension of the quality of democracy.[69] In Latin America, with its deep and persistent inequalities, this dimension is one of the most deeply flawed. Now I insert two propositions.

— 14. *Under democracy the state institutions have the duty (correlative to the rights of political and civil citizenship) of treating everyone with the full fairness, consideration, and respect due to an agent.*
— 15. *Although the tendency to deny these rights is structurally impressed in all vertical power relationships (especially if they are bureaucratized), deep poverty and inequality tend to accentuate this tendency.*

6. Second Excursus on Assessing the Quality of Democracy

In the two preceding sections we have covered broad ground. It is time to link some of the conclusions we have reached with the assessment of the quality of democracy.

With regard to the legal system

1. If it extends homogenously across the territory of the state.
2. If it extends homogeneously across various classes, sectors, and groups.
3. If it enacts rules that prohibit and eventually punish discrimination against the poor, women, foreigners, and various minorities.
4. If it deals in a respectful and considerate manner with indigenous communities and their legal systems.

With regard to the state and government

1. If there exists a state that exercises effective and legally bound control over its whole territory.
2. If there exist adequately authorized and empowered state institutions for the exercise of horizontal accountability, including in relation to cases of presumed illegal actions or inactions by elected officials.

With regard to the courts and their auxiliary institutions

1. If reasonably fair and expeditious access to courts exists, differentiated by kinds of courts.
2. If the courts recognize, and to what extent and in what kinds of cases, international covenants and treaties, including those on human, gender, childhood, economic, and indigenous social rights.
3. If there exist reasonably effective arrangements for access to the courts and the legal defense of the poor, illiterate, or otherwise legally deprived individuals and groups.
4. If the police and other security forces respect the rights of all citizens.
5. If individuals are not held in prison or subject to other ills in violation of basic rules of procedural fairness.
6. If the prisons are in adequate condition.

With regard to state institutions in general

1. If they treat everyone with fairness, consideration, and respect.
2. If they are regulated by rules that are clear, publicly available, and properly enacted.

3. If there exist prompt and effective mechanisms for the prevention, discontinuance, and/or redress of the violation of citizens' rights by state institutions.

As with the previous one, the present excursus merits some comments. One is that the preceding items may be rephrased negatively. This probably would furnish better empirical guidance in cases where flaws in these dimensions outnumber the achievements. A second comment is that it is obviously impossible to map all the ways in which state institutions interact with the population. The imaginative research conducted in the Costa Rican citizen audit, however, has shown a fruitful way to tackle this problem. This type of research starts from the assumption that the most interesting encounters are those in which state institutions typically face the poor, disadvantaged, and/or discriminated against and then chooses from among these encounters those that occur on the more "problematic frontiers" between state and society, and, by means of ethnographic observations and also "sitios centinela," studies these encounters in depth.[70] Surely, this method does not provide a full map of these interactions, but it does make it possible to locate typical situations and kinds of personal treatment that deserve close attention. This procedure may be usefully complemented by similarly close observation of situations that are known or presumed to be of satisfactory treatment.

7. Democracy and the Social Context

Many democratic theorists agree that in addition to the rights I have listed, the availability of free, pluralistic, and nonmonopolized or state-censored information is another necessary condition for the existence of a democratic regime. For example, among the attributes listed by Dahl is that "alternative sources of information exist and are protected by law" (1989: 221). Notice that this is not strictly an individual right. Having this kind of information is a social given, independent of the will of any single individual. It is a public good, characterized by being indivisible, nonexcludable, and nonrival (see Raz 1986, 1994). On the other hand, the availability of free and pluralistic information is the collective side of the coin of the rights of expression and association; they presuppose and produce each other.

The freedom of accessing free and pluralist information and its cognates, the rights of expression and association, spans over innumerable social sites well beyond the regime, as shown by the enormous attention paid to these sites in legal theory and practice. To be effective, this freedom presupposes two conditions. One is a social context that is congenial to the existence of a diversity of values, beliefs, lifestyles, and opinions. The other condition is—once again—a legal system that backs this diversity and, through it, the existence and continued transformation of a diverse social context.

Here we find another boundary problem. It is theoretically undecidable where and on the basis of what criteria we may trace a clear and firm dividing line between aspects of the freedom to express and obtain alternative information that are pertinent to political democracy and those that are not. For example, in a given case open discussion might be allowed about political issues, but these issues may be narrowly defined. If, say, the public discussion of gender or sexual diversity rights were censored, or if groups promoting agrarian reform were prohibited from accessing the media, we would have serious doubts about considering this freedom satisfied. On the other hand, in the not-too-distant past of the originating countries these restrictions were not considered problematic. As we saw with the boundary problems of other freedoms, this issue also poses a complicated comparative question. Would it be appropriate to apply to new democracies the criteria that the originating countries currently use, or should we accept more restrictive criteria such as those applied by the latter decades ago—or is there another alternative?

In order to deal with these matters we need to advance a bit more in our analysis. First let us go back to the political relationships demarcated by a democratic regime. We saw that in the sphere of the regime, individuals are construed as agents—they are political citizens who can vote and try to be elected. In order for voting to be a real choice, it stands to reason that citizens need a significant amount of free, plural, and competitive information. In addition, if, for example, Jane decides to try to get elected, she will need to mobilize some of her rights, such as expressing opinions and associating with parties and other citizens. These are rights that each person may or may not decide to utilize. Peter may not care whether these rights exist or not, and he may even believe it is wrong that other individuals have and eventually use these rights. Yet we saw that in a contemporary—that is, inclusive—democratic regime, the wager assigns these rights universalistically, independent of the preferences of Peter.

This reasoning relates to an argument that Joseph Raz (1986, 1994) has fruitfully developed. The effectiveness of rights such as the ones I have enumerated is a public good because "The interest of individuals in living in an open society is not confined to those who desire to benefit from it as producers or consumers of information or opinion. It extends to all who live in that society, for they benefit from the part of others in the free exchange of information and opinion" (Raz 1986: 253).[71]

Raz goes on to argue that this is the main reason why these rights are constitutionally entrenched. Whether we agree or not with this particular point, it is clear that Jane's rights would be ineffectual if a social context congenial to her purposes (say, one that does not discriminate against women entering into politics) did not exist. Without the public good of a diverse social context, the effectiveness of political rights is seriously hampered. When such a social context exists, it benefits everyone, even those who do not recognize its worth.

There is another point I want to stress because it connects with the *problématique* of human development and human rights. Agency, in Sen's conceptualization, entails having a capability set, defined as "the set of functioning vectors within his or her reach" (1985b: 20–21). These "capabilities are one way of characterizing positive freedom, and they can be seen as rights—positive rights to do this or to be that" (1985a: 16). An adequate capability set allows the individual to choose from among various valued functionings; according to Sen, this is the positive freedom to decide, with reasonable autonomy, knowledge, and responsibility, the course of one's life—in my terms, to be properly an agent.

There are many valuable lives that can be chosen, but each of us can only opt for one or very few of these lives. Agency and the freedom to choose functionings is at the root of social diversity.[72] That manifold others have lived and are living lives different than mine greatly enriches me.[73] Furthermore, that these others are agents engages my moral duty of accepting and even celebrating, not just tolerating (except special cases that a democratic legal system carefully legislates), that they have chosen lives other than the one I live.[74] The aggregate result is a social context that so positively values diversity that it inscribes the respective rights in its legal system. Furthermore, such a social context, populated by legally backed plural agents, offers the public good that authoritarian rulers most strive to suppress: the possible emergence of a public sphere of free and public discussion and deliberation about matters of general interest.[75]

We see now that what I have been calling "political" rights (expression, association, movement, and others) are actually segments of broader and older civil rights. These rights are effected in multiple locations of society, not only in the regime. In fact, we saw that in the originating countries many civil rights were effected well before its political segment. These are the same rights; they pertain to agents who need these rights (or, seen from the angle of human development, these capabilities) in order to freely choose the functionings they deem valuable. Individuals have the right to at least a basic set of rights and capabilities (social, civil, and political) so they can achieve functionings that are consistent with, and consequently enabling of, their agency.[76]

We have approximated some conclusions. One is that if my life is enriched by a diverse social context (and, indeed, if I am able to recognize this crucial fact of social life), then it is in my interest that all individuals, or as many as possible, have the necessary capabilities to freely choose their own functionings under the conditions established by a democratic rule of law. Second, it is also in my interest that these rights are inscribed in the legal system, thus clarifying and entrenching them against hostile views.[77] Third, the social aggregate of these individual rights, when broadly and effectively enacted, becomes the public good of freedoms that can be generally enjoyed and that surround and make possible a democratic regime. Fourth, if these rights are truncated (for example, if they are poorly implanted), the diversity of the social context is impoverished and, with it, the possibility of the emergence of the rich public sphere characteristic of a democracy of high quality.

These conclusions about democracy lead directly to human rights and human development. Pointing out and trying to remedy severe deprivations in these areas is not just a praiseworthy act of solidarity; it is a consequence of the moral duty of each agent to treat all others as such agents.[78] Furthermore, in several spheres of social life, treating every *alter* as an agent is a legal obligation; I already noted this obligation in what pertains to relations among political citizens, in many civil relationships, and in the encounters between state institutions and all individuals, citizens and noncitizens alike.

Let us go back to Jane, who has chosen among her functionings to become active in politics. Very likely, she would not have made this choice if she foresaw that it would bring upon her physical violence and/or severe material deprivations. If this were the case, Jane would not have considered entering politics to be within her capability set. Furthermore, in deciding to enter politics, she is taking for granted that there will be institutionalized places (the political party she joins, or the social movement she supports, or maybe just the public park where she addresses the passersby) where she can exercise her rights of expression, association, and movement. Those of us who have lived under authoritarian rule know this is exactly what one cannot take for granted. Clearly, Jane's agency would be curtailed if she did not count on these freedoms; her agency would be similarly curtailed if she could not choose this functioning because she suffers from severe material deprivations—"the autonomous agent is one who is not always struggling to maintain the minimum conditions of a worthwhile life" (Raz 1986: 155).

Jane, who does not suffer these deprivations, enters politics. There she encounters other citizens to whom the inclusive wager has assigned the same rights and duties she possesses. She can try persuasion, bargaining, or any other means for garnering votes; but she is prohibited, as are the other candidates, from using or threatening violence and, if she succeeds in getting elected, of accepting bribes and, in general, ignoring the legally defined rights and duties of her office. Throughout, Jane is a discursive being: she processes and conveys information and opinions. In doing this, she relies upon, and utilizes, various sources of information. She is benefiting from, and reinforcing, a diverse social context.

Yet Jane may not prefer to engage in directly political activities. She may want to become active in a union, a neighborhood association, a club, or some other organization. In any of these endeavors, Jane has the right to expect respectful and fair treatment, including that her views are given considerate hearing—an agent is an agent everywhere. Some social locations, however, such as a business corporation, or a university, or UNDP, may raise the kind of trade-offs I mentioned concerning the workings of a state's institutions. I refer to considerations of expediency or efficacy that may prevent the democratization of the respective entities. But even in these cases, Jane has the right to demand (as legislation and jurisprudence, especially in the originating countries, has progressively but still insufficiently recognized) effective recognition of her civil rights, as well as of those that, as part of the evolution of rights I depicted in section 4, have become known as labor rights.

One way or the other, Jane is lucky. Not only does she have the required capabilities to be an agent, but she lives in a diverse social context. Not every democratic regime, however, is joined by an appropriate degree of democraticness of the state, or with a social context that furnishes to all at least a minimum of human rights and human development capabilities, or with a social context that is broadly diverse. These caveats send us in the direction of looking at contemporary Latin American democracies. Before dealing with this topic, however, I must further elaborate on the role of the social context in democracy, which I undertake after inserting two propositions.

— 16. *The effectiveness of the rights of political citizenship requires a social context that includes varied, nonmonopolized, and non-state-censured sources of information. This availability, which is a component of a diverse social context, is a public good supported by a democratic legal system and the congenial performance of state institutions.*
— 17. *More generally, the existence of such a social context plus the broadly available "political" freedoms, insofar as they imply multiple agents freely choosing their functionings, is a nurturing social aspect of the very same agency that is entailed by democracy.*

In order to further clarify the relationship between democracy and a diverse social context, I will first reason *a contrario*.[79] It seems clear that a democratic regime could not exist in a country where information is monopolized or broadly censored or where many kinds of opinions and associations are prohibited. In such a social context, not enough information would exist to enable meaningful voting, and even if the rights of expression and association were formally enacted, the freedom to decide what to express and with whom to associate would be de facto cancelled. Positively, this reasoning shows that the rights of expression, association, movement, and the like have two faces.[80] The individual one I have already discussed. The other face is that the effectuation of these rights is also a social fact; it feeds from, and at the same time generates, a social context the diversity of which expresses—jointly with various cultural, religious, artistic, and other values and practices—the very effectuation of those rights. I argued that political rights are necessary conditions for a democratic regime and that these rights are actually segments of broader, and older, civil rights. Now we see that these same rights—both their political and civil sides—have a social dimension: they cannot exist outside social institutions, values, and practices. These are necessary milieus for the existence of these rights, which in their social expression I have called freedoms. On the other hand, these milieus are generated and reproduced by the effectuation of those rights. This social (or, if you wish, collective) side of rights is the complement of political rights: both sides of the coin are necessary conditions for the existence of a democratic regime.

Notice that if the preceding reasoning is correct, we need to assess the democraticness of the social context or, more or less equivalently, its congeniality with democracy. Insofar as a congenial social context is both a necessary condition for democracy and an expression of the exercise of political and civil rights, we can reasonably hypothesize that there will be important reciprocal influences between the quality of a democracy and the characteristics of its social context. In particular (as it would be assessed by means of the items suggested in the first excursus), if citizens broadly utilize their civil and political rights and solidly support democracy, then the social context will tend to be diverse and congenial to democracy; conversely, such a social context will tend to foster such attitudes and practices in citizens. There is an obvious circularity in the preceding sentence, but it is useful because it restates the mutual imbrications of the individual and social sides of political and other rights.

Finally, a diverse social context is extremely important not only for the effectuation of the political rights linked to a democratic regime. Such a context is also the social space where citizens (and, in general, inhabitants) exercise the rights and powers they have not transferred to the state or temporarily "loaned" to elected officials (Jorge Vargas Cullell, private communication). This is a *public* exercise, insofar as it entails, protected by a congenial social context and by the rights it recognizes, addressing others about matters that are, or are deemed by the addressors to be, of joint concern.

8. Third Excursus on Assessing the Quality of Democracy

Some of the items relevant to the preceding discussion I have already listed. On the other hand, some of the items that follow need further justification, which I attempt below.

With regard to the social context

1. If, in general—and as assessed, among other means, by public opinion polls, legislation, court decisions, and the media—a diverse social context exists, with special attention to indications of discrimination or intolerance.
2. If various media convey diverse information, opinions, and analyses about public matters, and if this information, opinions, and analyses may be deemed autonomous of interests or pressures of the state, the government, and/or various private interests, including economic ones.
3. If in associations other than directly political ones, rights of participation exist, or if at least the civil rights (and, eventually, the labor rights) of their members are upheld.
4. If adequate freedoms and guarantees exist for the exercise of various actions of societal accountability.
5. If, in general, there is a climate of opinion that rejects all types of bigotry and discrimination.

9. Contemporary Latin American Democracies

In contemporary Latin America many countries satisfy the definition of political democracy I propose above. They share two characteristics: they hold fair, institutionalized, and inclusive elections; and their citizens enjoy some political rights, especially freedom of opinion, expression, association, and movement and access to a reasonably free and pluralist media. While some Latin American countries presently have this kind of regime, there are variations as to the degree to which the above-mentioned attributes hold. There also are significant variations as to the degree to which the state and its legal system cover the whole territory of these countries.

In terms of these factors, a classification of contemporary Latin American regimes would look as follows:[81]

1. Countries where the regime and state characteristics of democracy are satisfied.
    —Costa Rica
    —Uruguay
    —Chile (Although the "authoritarian enclaves" inherited from the Pinochet regime raise important caveats about placing Chile in this group [Garretón 1987; Valenzuela 1992].)
2. Countries that may be classified as political democracies or democratic regimes. The pertinent characteristics are satisfied at the national level, but there are significant discontinuities in terms of the reach of the legality of the state in several regions, including the nondemocratic characteristics of some subnational regimes.
    —Argentina
    —Bolivia
    —Brazil
    —Colombia (Colombia may deserve special classification due to the extraordinary lack of reach of the state and its legal system over the territory, as well as the systematic violence that has been applied against candidates of leftist parties.)[82]
    —Dominican Republic
    —Panama
3. Countries that may be classified as "conditional political democracies." In addition to sharing the characteristics of the preceding group in terms of the limited reach of state legality, it is not presently certain (albeit for different reasons in each case) that fair elections have been institutionalized.
    —Ecuador
    —Guatemala (With the additional caveat that the armed forces are, although not formally as in Chile, an important authoritarian enclave.)
    —Mexico
    —Peru
    —Venezuela
4. Countries that may be classified as "electorally based authoritarian regimes." Although they have held elections, these elections have not been fair (especially in their decisive dimension) and do not seem to be institutionalized.
    —Paraguay
    —Haiti

As can be seen in table 1, there was a big drop in the acceptance of "democracy [as a kind] of government" in the relatively short period of 1995–2001—an average fall of no less than eleven percentage points. Consistent with the classification above, we also see the high level of support in the two unqualified democratic regimes, Costa Rica and Uruguay,[83] as well as a significantly lower level of support in Chile, where the restrictions to democratic politics generated by the authoritarian enclaves may have been a factor. Notice, too, the extremely low levels of support in large countries such as Brazil (30%) and Colombia (36%), as well as in El Salvador (25%) and Panama (34%), jointly with the sharp drop in support in Argentina (−18), Colombia (−24), El Salvador (−31), and Panama (−41). The data from other countries are difficult to interpret because of their very recent democratization (Mexico) or redemocratization (Peru) or the uncertainties raised by the peculiarities of their present regime (Venezuela). But the low level of support for democracy, and especially its sharp drop in most countries between 1995 and 2001, is

Table 1   Proportion of respondents agreeing with the statement "Democracy is preferable to any other kind of government."

Country	1995[a]	2001	Difference
Argentina	76	58	−18
Bolivia (1996)	64	54	−10
Brazil	41	30	−11
Chile	52	45	−7
Colombia (1996)	60	36	−24
Costa Rica (1996)	80	71	−9
Ecuador (1996)	52	40	−12
El Salvador (1996)	56	25	−31
Guatemala (1996)	51	33	−18
Honduras (1996)	42	57	+15
Mexico	49	45	−4
Nicaragua (1996)	59	43	−16
Panama (1996)	75	34	−41
Paraguay	52	35	−17
Peru	52	62	+10
Uruguay	80	79	−1
Venezuela	60	57	−3

Source: Data from Latinobarómetro, 1995, 1996, and 2001.
[a] Except when otherwise indicated, data was collected in 1995.

worrisome. This feeling is reinforced by the responses received to another question in the same survey: "How satisfied are you with the way democracy works in your country?" Costa Rica and Uruguay received the highest scores, with (a not too encouraging) 40% of responses being positive. In all the other countries surveyed (which were the same as those in table 1), the unsatisfied responses were above 60%, with Brazil and Argentina scoring a massive 80% and Colombia 90%.

Seen from the angle of popular opinion, democracy is not doing well in Latin America. An important reason is that too often the image of democratically elected governments is that they are incapable of or unwilling to deal with basic development issues as well as social equity and even violence. Underlying these images is the sad fact that in the past two decades the state has weakened tremendously, and, in some regions of these countries, it has virtually evaporated. Economic crises, high inflation, the antistatist fury of most economic adjustment programs, pervasive corruption, and clientelism have concurred to generate an anemic state.[84]

This anemia also appears in the legal system. In fact, in many Latin American countries a democratic regime coexists with an intermittent and biased rule of law. Simply put, the legality of the state does not extend to vast regions of the countries (and parts of their cities, too) where other kinds of law, basically variations of mafia law, are actually operative. Furthermore, even in the regions reached by the legal system, it is often applied with discriminatory biases against various minorities and even majorities, such as the poor and women. This truncated legal system generates what I have called a "citizenship of low intensity."[85] By this I mean that everyone has, at least in principle, the political rights that pertain to a democratic regime. Yet many are denied basic social rights, as suggested by the widespread poverty and inequality I do not need to document here. These people are also denied basic civil rights. They do not enjoy protection from police violence and various forms of private violence; they are denied fair access to state agencies and courts; their dwellings are raided arbitrarily; and, in general, they are forced to live a life not only of poverty but also of recurrent humiliation and fear of violence, quite often perpetrated by the same "security forces" that are supposed to protect them.[86] These people, whom I will call the *popular sector*, are not only materially poor; they are also legally poor.

Still, as it is true by definition in the countries I have classified as political democracies, at least in national elections these same people vote without physical coercion, their votes are counted fairly, and in principle they can use the rights of expression, association, movement, and the like. This is a situation in which the political rights that surround and make possible a democratic regime are effective, while at the same time social rights and, no less harmfully, many civil rights are denied to many—a majority, in some countries.

One aspect of the poor territorial coverage of the legality of the state is that in some countries there are regions where local elections are not fair. These regions are controlled by subnational authoritarian regimes.[87] These "brown" regions send their representatives to the national political institutions of the regime, thus permeating it with less than democratic actors, interests, and strategies. These problems are shared by many new and some not so new political democracies in the contemporary world. This situation is historically unique in terms of the experience of the originating countries. In these countries the historical pattern of acquisition and extension of various kinds of rights differed significantly from what we observe in most new democracies, Latin America included.

What does democratic theory have to say about this? Unfortunately, not much. In large measure this is because most theories of democracy have been formulated within and based upon the historical experience of the Northwest. These theories leave implicit that, as we already saw, in this region civil rights were reasonably effective and extended throughout society before the adoption of the inclusive wager and the universalization of political rights. In addition, these theories assume that the legality of the state extends homogenously throughout its territory and that, consequently, not only the national but also the subnational regimes are democratic.[88] Unfortunately, these assumptions do not fit the historical trajectory and present situation of most of Latin America.

Among the originating countries I note one basic variation. Great Britain, France, Scandinavia, and others roughly followed T. H. Marshall's sequence of the extension and expansion of rights—first the quite extensive achievement of civil rights, then of political rights, and finally of social rights (Marshall 1964). In Prussia/Germany, however, first civil rights were achieved, then social rights, and only later political rights. Yet in both sequences civil rights were quite effectively and extensively implanted before the achievement of other kinds of rights. This is more true with respect to men than to women and some minorities, an issue I will return to below.[89]

With some caveats that need not detain me here, the Northwestern sequences roughly apply to Costa Rica, Chile, and Uruguay. Costa Rica and Chile basically followed the Marshallian pattern of civil-political-social rights, although under Pinochet, Chile experienced a sharp regression in terms of the latter. Uruguay, with its early welfare state, achieved almost simultaneously social and political rights. One way or the other, the patterns in these countries are similar to the ones in the Northwest in the sense that, especially in the urban sectors, there existed a reasonably high degree of implantation of civil rights prior to the achievement of social and political rights. Indeed, despite the authoritarian interruptions suffered by Chile and Uruguay, these three countries are the longest-standing political democracies in Latin America. Furthermore, in terms of their present workings, with the already noted caveat of the *Pinochetista* legacy in Chile,[90] these three cases most closely approximate the typical patterns of functioning of the Northwestern regimes.

This was not the route followed by the rest of Latin America. Rather, the modal pattern has been as follows. First, some social rights were granted, although they were more limited than in the Northwest and, in the past two decades in most countries, have been sharply reversed. Later, political rights were acquired by means of past or recent processes of political democratization. Finally—and this continues even today—civil rights were implanted in a biased and intermittent way. This is the populist pattern followed by Argentina, Bolivia, Brazil, Ecuador, Mexico, and Peru.

Colombia and Venezuela differ because of their early, nonpopulist democratization, which meant the achievement of political rights in the first place. However, these countries share with the populist ones the fact that civil rights have not been significantly extended either before or after the achievement of political rights. In turn, Ecuador has alternated between authoritarian and oligarchic democratic regimes of various kinds. Now I summarize the preceding discussion as follows.

— 18. *In contrast to the originating countries, in most of Latin America (and in terms of population, for a large majority of this region), political rights were gained, or have been recovered recently, before an as yet unachieved generalization of civil rights. In turn, depending on the trajectory followed by each country, social rights were granted before or after political rights. In all cases these rights were rather limited, however, and recently in many countries they have been sharply reversed.*

— 19. *In these same countries, the penetration and effectiveness of state legality has been partial and intermittent. Furthermore, even under democratically elected governments the "brown" areas—those not covered by state legality— have grown, in some countries extensively.*

Consequently, an image of contemporary Latin America tells us the following: (a) in many countries, as a correlate of the inauguration of democratic regimes, the universalization of political rights has been achieved; (b) only a limited and biased implantation of civil rights has been attained, however; furthermore, for large segments of the respective populations these rights have barely expanded, if at all, during the presently existing political democracies; (c) in most cases, there has also been a regression in social rights, which, in addition, has occurred from a baseline that, compared with the Northwest, was very limited; and (d) with the exception of Costa Rica and Uruguay, the support for democratic regimes is low and has significantly diminished during recent years.

I insist that in terms of the historical trajectories of democracy this is a rather unique pattern. In spite of the fact that a long-standing democracy, India, should have alerted theorists of this uniqueness, many existing theories of democracy are ill-prepared to deal with this kind of situation. In particular, a narrow focus on the regime may be permissible[91] when it can be assumed that the effectiveness of civil and social citizenship is not particularly problematic. However, when these dimensions of citizenship are intermittent and unevenly distributed, as they are in Latin America, taking them into careful empirical and theoretical consideration is crucial, even for understanding the actual workings of the respective regimes.

Of course, severe deficits in civil and social rights do not afflict everyone in Latin America. Many members of the high and middle classes (intellectuals included) are better off under political democracy than under authoritarianism, if not all of them economically. This bifurcation of social conditions is not new for Latin America, but it is disturbing that in many of these countries it has worsened under political democracy. In spite of this, I suggest that a possible solution to this situation consists of using the reversal of the historical sequence as a springboard for expansion of the rights presently lacking. That is, instead of claiming, as some are doing currently, that the political rights of democracy are "purely formal," they can be used for conquering other rights. This is what the feminist and some minority movements have done in the Northwest—use political rights as a basis for struggling for civil and social rights. This strategy has been anything but linear; it does not lend itself to the more sequential (male) processes I depicted above. Rather, it has consisted of a long moving back and forth, from and to political rights to social and civil ones. This is a dialectic of empowerment in one sphere of rights in order to push for conquests in other spheres (see also UNDP 2000a: 8 and 2000b). This possibility, which originates in the availability of political rights, is denied by authoritarian rule; however, it is uniquely offered by democracy through the political rights it enacts, even for those who suffer truncated social and civil rights.

Of course, deep poverty and inequality, and the patterns of social authoritarianism and exploitation that are built on them, are formidable obstacles to the unfolding of this dialectical process.[92] In this respect I have an admittedly insufficient and at best medium-term suggestion: place more emphasis than it has been the case until now in Latin America on struggles for the expansion of civil rights. The reason is that, probably even more than in the Northwest, whatever civil rights are gained may become an important lever for further political democratization and human development. Civil rights not only protect, they empower; they provide opportunities to act for attaining further rights. Civil rights thus make it possible (but I grant, just possible) for various collective and individual actors to autonomously define their identity and interests. The main facilitating factor of these struggles is furnished by the political rights—expression, association, movement, and the like—that a democratic regime must sanction and to a respectable extent (lest it lose its democratic character) uphold. Furthermore, successful extensions of civil rights initially based on the utilization of political rights tend to reinvigorate the latter; this in turn opens avenues for further struggles for other rights, including social ones. As UNDP (2000a), among others, has insisted, these rights—political, civil, and social—may be analytically separated, but in practice they presuppose each other. Usually advances in any of them make it possible for other rights to move in the same direction. Advances in civil rights, social rights, or political rights are valuable per se and because they are springboards for the conquest of other rights.

It seems to me that the convoluted process sketched above is the only path open to Latin America. It is a path open only under democratic conditions, but I do not believe that authoritarian ones will lead to better outcomes. That traversing this route will not be easy is shown, among other indications, by the fact that the public agenda in Latin America has been monopolized by economic policy issues (defined in a very technocratic and socially regressive way, in addition),[93] corruption scandals, and various kinds of violence. Additionally, governmental reactions to social violence often go in the direction of further curtailing the civil rights of the popular sector. The deprivations provoked by the lack of civil and social rights scarcely reach the public agenda, except as problems to be dealt with by the police or through temporary—and humiliating—handouts of some goods to segments (often clientelistically selected) of the popular sector.

It may be argued that the dispossession of the popular sector of basic civic and social rights is the same old story of Latin America. There is a new element, however. In the countries that fit the definition of political democracy, the popular sector now has political rights: they can assemble, express opinions and demands, and affiliate with political parties and social organizations. Their rights are important, because, in spite of social authoritarianism and manifold mistreatments, they may determine that these political democracies are not fake.

I am afraid that, in terms of human development and human rights, little progress has been achieved in Latin America under the existing democratic regimes.[94] This statement merits two caveats, however. One is that in some dimensions of social welfare (such as literacy, schooling, and infant mortality) some countries have improved their situation. But I do not know to what extent these changes are due to secular trends or to the impact of democratically elected governments. The second caveat is that at least in the aggregate and in the medium and long run, political democracy does seem to make a difference. Adam Przeworski and his collaborators undertook a massive study that included all the countries in the world for which there were some reasonably available data. They dichotomized these countries as either democracies (according to the kind of minimalist criteria I referred to in section 2) or authoritarian ones. On this basis, they asked if these regime types could account for various outcomes along a series of dimensions. Some findings were negative (for example, the rates of economic growth of countries that include democratic or authoritarian regimes are very similar), but other findings are significant and, indeed, worth noting. In particular,

> [D]emocracies have lower birth rates and lower death rates. Women in democracies have fewer children. More children survive to adulthood. As adults, they live longer, years longer. . . . The observed differences in infant mortality are larger. . . . And the effect of regime on life expectancy is astonishing: The observed difference is enormous at each income level. (Przeworski et al. 2000: 264)

Furthermore, "average infant mortality is much higher under dictatorships." In turn, "educational expenditures," which are higher in democracies, "sharply decrease mortality under both regimes," and the same happens with health expenditures, which under democracies are more than double that under authoritarian regimes—3.3% and 1.5% of gross domestic product (GDP), respectively (ibid., 237–39). Finally, "The effect of political regimes on the lives of women is glaring . . . under dictatorship women engage in gainful activities outside the household as frequently as under democracy. But in addition they bear many more children, see more of them die, and are themselves more likely to die" (ibid., 265).

Democracy does seem to make a difference in terms of various dimensions directly connected to human development (this research did not look at indicators directly relevant to human rights). At least as yet, however, these beneficial consequences are not visible in Latin America; furthermore, in some of the dimensions mentioned by Przeworski et al. (2000), regressions seem to have occurred.[95]

Clearly, we confront a tall order in trying to overcome these deficiencies. Of course, the popular sector can hardly succeed alone. At the very least, it needs a friendly state, rather than the enemy it often is. Efforts to reform the state into one that is not only more efficacious but also more congenial to the agency of everyone are badly needed. This is true not only of state institutions but also of its legal system, for two reasons. One is that some rights still need to be inscribed, as demonstrated by existing discriminatory rules against women and various minorities as well as by police and judicial practices that foster gross violations of human rights and due process. The second reason is that many of the preexisting and new rights need to be implemented; the citizens of Latin America know too well about laws that are no more than a piece of paper. In order to overcome this legacy, not only better laws and courts are needed. As we saw in section 5, also necessary is a network of state institutions, both national and subnational, that is committed to implementing not just any law but a *democratic* rule of law.

Up to now I have not said much about another huge challenge facing Latin America: overcoming at least the most pressing human development needs of the popular sector. This is due to my belief that in order for these needs to be met, the enjoyment of political rights and important advances in civil rights are very important. Otherwise, the policies against poverty and inequality will continue being captured and distorted by ingrained practices of clientelism and paternalism. Democracy and its rights are important—probably, they are necessary conditions—for advances in human development that are not easily reversible and/or submerge the popular sector in further clientelistic dependency. Perhaps, during the convoluted process I have sketched, social agents emerge that are capable of designing, or supporting, alternatives that we cannot presently envisage.[96] For this to occur, we should remember that under the democratic regimes that presently exist in Latin America political rights are the only ones that the popular sector more or less fully enjoys. If, as I argue above, political democracy and its rights are public goods, it is our moral and political duty to help the popular sector use the levers of these rights for the conquest of other rights; any achievement in these matters sharpens the "weapons of the week" for their uphill struggles.[97]

10. Convergences and Overlaps

"No one . . . can fully enjoy *any* right that he is supposed to have if he lacks the essentials for a reasonably healthy and active life" (Shue 1996: 7, italics in the original). Consequently, "[I]t would be inconsistent to recognize rights referred to life or to physical integrity when the means necessary for the enjoyment and exercise of these rights are omitted" (Vázquez 2001: 12, my translation). These remarks are sadly obvious. Whether it is human development, human rights, or political rights, these remarks refer to the capabilities that enable, or disable, agency. For exactly the same reasons we saw when discussing political rights, it is theoretically undecidable what would be a sufficient minimal set in terms of human development and human rights. Where and on the basis of what criteria could we draw a firm and clear line above which agency may be reasonably construed as enabled in terms of human development or human rights? As with political rights, there is not, and never will be, clear and firm generalized intersubjective agreement about a minimal sufficient set for the respective rights or capabilities. And, as with political rights, instead of artificially trying to set the respective external and internal boundaries for human development and human rights, the appropriate procedure is to analyze the reasons for and consequences of their undecidability.

Before moving in this direction, I illustrate my point with a couple of examples of the vacillations and ambiguities that provoke attempts at fixing those boundaries, from minimalist listings that are criticized as manifestly insufficient, to long listings that are criticized as including practically every good thing one might want for human beings.[98] These problems are observable even within the same author's work. Here I mention two authors who are deservedly influential in their respective fields. Henry Shue asserts that there are some "strategically critical rights" that are necessary "for the enjoyment of all other rights" and consist of "security, subsistence and liberty" (Shue 1996: 197, 20, and passim). As Shue develops his analysis, however, he adds a series of other rights that he sees as also necessary for a sufficient set (ibid., 65 and passim).[99] On the other hand, in terms of human development Martha Nussbaum moves in the opposite direction. She begins with a complex list of "central human functional capabilities" (Nussbaum 2000b: 12).[100] Surely aware that this list is rather unwieldy, Nussbaum "minimalizes" it by asserting that there are two capabilities ("practical reason and affiliation") that are even more central, "since they both organize and suffuse all the others, making their pursuit truly human" (Nussbaum 2000b: 79, 82).

In spite of these vacillations, these and other authors imply two points with which it would be hard to disagree. One is that the minimalist versions of these lists are insufficient for fully guaranteeing the goods posited by human development, human rights, or democracy; one can always name another right or capability that may be persuasively argued as also necessary for enabling agency in any of these three dimensions. The second point is that the extended lists presented by Shue and Nussbaum (as well as, for that matter, UNDP) include rights and capabilities that are extremely important.[101] Another point usually made is that the rights and/or capabilities of these lists are "equally fundamental" (UNDP 2000a: 12 and passim for this and similar expressions). Yet this is the problem, in part because it risks leaving us without practical and analytical guidance, and in part because it offers an easy target for those who deny the relevance and/or conceptual import of the very *problématique* of human development, human rights, and a theory of democracy that goes beyond the confines of the regime. Another problem with these listings of "equally fundamental" goods is that they may be quite discouraging. Where should we begin, if so many people are deprived of so many closely interconnected rights and capabilities?

At this moment it should be clear why I undertook a rather detailed discussion of political rights. I aimed at justifying two assertions: (a) the minimal sufficient set of these rights is theoretically undecidable, and (b) these rights (of expression, association, movement, and the like) are segments of broader and older civil rights.[102] I also argued that these rights pertain to all human beings insofar as we re-cognize them as agents, and agency rights in the political sphere can hardly be effected if individuals lack the "basic" capabilities related to human development and/or the "basic" rights related to human rights' approaches.[103]

Perhaps I should take a moment to insist on the common grounding of democracy, human rights, and human development: They share, as the very foundation of their respective views, a moral conception of the human as an agent, and the three of them posit that this human condition originates not only moral claims but also universalistic rights, however undecidable may be the minimal sufficient set of these rights. A being endowed with practical reason has the right to be respected as such a being; she also has the right to the social provision of the conditions necessary for freely exercising the cognitive, moral, and sociability aspects of agency. Submitting this individual to, say, physical violence, or to the privation of basic material needs, or ignoring her political citizenship are all severe denials of her agency. This view has been explicit in the tradition of human rights. With regard to democracy, I have substantiated that even when looking at one of its aspects, the regime, we can see that agency is strongly—albeit implicitly—entailed. In relation to human development, its concern with capabilities can only be understood as they enable functionings that are adequate to agency. This grounding and its universalism has been explicit in the work of Sen and becomes clear in the crisp statement with which the 2000 *Human Development Report* begins: "Human rights and human development share a common vision and a common purpose—to secure the freedom, well-being and dignity of all people every-where" (UNDP 2000a: 1, italics added).

All these rights and capabilities associated with democracy, human rights, and human development directly pertain to, and enable, agency.[104] This is the nexus of these three currents. This is precisely why each, or a combination of two of them, may "push" toward the attainment of the other(s), or at least create opportunities for their attainment. We saw that in the originating countries the early achievement of civil rights (which contained important bundles of human rights), followed later by the conquest of political rights, greatly facilitated the attainment of social rights (which in turn contain significant elements of, and at the same time foster, human development). Yet, as we saw with Latin America, there are no historically or mechanically predetermined sequences in these matters. Another example of this is some East Asian countries—especially South Korea and Taiwan—that exhibit a sequence that differs both from the originating countries and Latin America. These countries first achieved a rather high degree of human development and only later attained quite extensive civil and political rights. In part because the common grounding among these three currents has not yet been adequately discussed, we know too little about the causal relations by which achievements in one or two of these dimensions push or at least create opportunities for advances in the other(s). But in light of their common grounding and the insights provided by sweeping historical generalizations such as the one I have just undertaken, I believe that it can be asserted that there exists, in Weberian terms, a strong elective affinity among these three currents.[105]

Furthermore, as with political rights, the rights and capabilities implied by human rights and human development can only be derived inductively. Consequently, their minimal sufficient set[106] also is theoretically undecidable. On the other hand, and also as we saw with political rights, each of the capabilities and rights that seem reasonable candidates to be considered "basic" for human development and/or human rights are extremely important and as such should be empirically considered and theoretically thematized.

11. Struggles, Past and Future

The simultaneous undecidability and great importance of the rights and capabilities I have been discussing is, admittedly, a conundrum. One possibility, as I did with some examples in relation to political rights, is to proceed *a contrario,* identifying conditions of such deprivation that there can be little doubt concerning the denial of agency in terms of human development or human rights. This is a useful step; yet it is a negative determination that does not tell us at what point the options for agency may be positively satisfied. Furthermore, the relevant criteria for human development, human rights, and democracy have changed greatly. We saw that even in the originating countries this historical variability creates vexing problems in establishing a minimal sufficient set of these rights; obviously, it would be even harder to determine this set for countries that command far less resources than the former.

All this surely bothers a geometric mind. We can advance some steps, however, by elaborating on some recent contributions. Sen has made the interesting observation that even in relation to theories of a conservative bent,

> It may be useful to ask why it is that so many altogether different theories of the ethics of social arrangements have the common feature of demanding equality of something. . . . It is also of considerable pragmatic interest to note that impartiality and equal concern, in some form or other, provide a shared background to all the major ethical and political proposals . . . which continue to receive argued support and reasoned defense. . . . If a claim that inequality in some significant space is right (or good, or acceptable, or tolerable) it has to be defended by reason . . . [when this is the case] the argument takes the form of showing this inequality to be a consequence of *equality* in some other—more centrally important—space. (1992: 17–21, italics in the original)[107]

This is a contemporary achievement. For a long time many theories postulated intrinsic human *inequality;* as I noted in a different but convergent context, serfs, workers, women, and many others were deemed to lack agency and hence to be intrinsically inferior to their "superiors." I surmise that the tendency noted by Sen of all sorts of contemporary ethical theories to base themselves on some dimension of human equality is a reverberation of the historical process of extension of the attribution of agency to manifold social and political sites. In spite of the many horrors of the past century, this increasing indisputability that all humans are in some fundamental sense equal is a huge achievement. As a consequence, the universalistic view of agency postulated by human development, human rights, and democracy is not, in the contemporary world, an odd and isolated argument. In addition, I do not think that the universalistic equality that these currents postulate can be defeated by the extreme cultural relativism presently in vogue in some quarters.[108] Even in countries where, as in Latin America, this equality is factually denied in many ways, the equalizing view of agency entailed by their democratic regimes and legal systems is already there, amenable to being mobilized for the conquest of the many rights still lacking; this is no more and no less than a possibility that may be effected by purposive political action.[109]

The preceding assertions gloss over the philosophical and ethical discussions that center on equality and its trade-offs with liberty. These are extremely important issues that will forever engage theoretical discussions and political conflicts. I cannot deal with this matter in the present text. Furthermore, here I have in mind situations that are, in an important sense, previous to those discussions. In the Northwest these discussions usually deal with the question of which principles of liberty and/or equality should regulate the allocation of social goods once everyone, or most, has attained a basic level of rights and capabilities.[110] In the situations I am referring to here, however, the main issue refers to those individuals—and there are many—who have not attained these basic rights and capabilities. This poses a sad but, in terms of the issues involved here, simpler question: Do good reasons exist—before the predicaments of liberty vs. equality under affluence are sharply posed—for asserting a universalistic right to the attainment of a basic level, or set, of rights and capabilities? I believe that these reasons do exist and that their grounding is agency. These reasons refer to a primary aspect of fairness—not full equality, but basic equalization. By *equalization* I mean the right of everyone to at least two things: (a) as we saw when dealing with state institutions and now more generally, to be treated with the fairness and consideration due to an agent; and (b) to attain and, if necessary, enjoy the social provision of a floor consisting of basic rights and capabilities that enable agency or, at the very least, not to suffer deprivations that clearly hamper agency.[111]

Above this level we can, and should, have complicated disputes; yet whatever the answers to these disputes, the question remains as to whether there are not only moral duties to provide but also positive rights to claim basic agency-enabling rights and capabilities.

I will return to this point after noting another contribution by Sen. He argues that democratic "political and social participation has *intrinsic value* for human life and well-being," as well as "*instrumental value* in enhancing the hearing that people get . . . in their claims to political attention (including claims of economic needs)" (1999a: 10, italics in the original). Sen further elaborates that democracy has *constructive value* because

> Even the idea of "needs," including the understanding of "economic needs," requires public discussion and exchange of information, views, and analyses. . . . Political rights, including freedom of expression and discussion, are not only pivotal in inducing social responses to economic needs, they are also central to the conceptualization of economic needs themselves. (1999a: 11)

We may relate these observations to my discussion of the theoretical undecidability of the set of rights pertaining to democracy. In relation to this topic Jeremy Waldron comments that

> Any theory of rights will face disagreements about the interests it identifies as rights, and the terms in which it identifies it. . . . In addition, theories of rights have to face up controversies about the forms of duty that they ground and the forms of moral priority they establish: absolute duties, prima facie duties, lexical priorities, weighted priorities, agent-relative side constraints, agent-relative prerogatives, and so on. (1999: 225, 226)

The content of rights, their degree of specificity, the scope of their reach, the relative priority of some rights over others, and other issues of this kind are and will be forever disputable—there are too many views and preferences, too many theories of what is just and/or fair, and too many social interests and positions for any of these issues to be clearly and firmly settled. This is a fact of social life. It should not be denied or regretted; it is a consequence of human agency and the diversity of life projects, views, interests, and social locations it sustains.

This fact is compounded by a practical problem that has been stressed by another recent contribution:[112] implementing rights, practically any right, requires complicated institutional arrangements, and these arrangements cost money, usually provided by taxes. Not only because of bias or neglect, some rights are not enacted, others are weakly or selectively implemented, and others are only partially implemented. Rights are not static; they "are constantly expanding and contracting under the impact of legislative and adjudicative action" (Holmes and Sunstein 1999: 104). Holmes and Sunstein focus on a rich country—the United States—when describing selectivity in the enactment and implementation of rights that result from various institutional and economic constraints; of course, these constraints are more acute in weaker states. Now I recapitulate the preceding discussion by means of some propositions.

— *20. In any given historical circumstance, it is eminently disputable what rights, with what intensity, with what scope, and with what priorities are enacted and implemented.*
— *21. This fact is in part due to institutional and economic constraints, but it also results from the social diversity entailed by agency and the manifold views, lifestyles, and interests it generates, both (statically) at any given moment and (dynamically) as those characteristics unfold and change over time.*

What is the answer to these problems and restrictions? Quite simply, democracy. The crucial issue is who decides, how, and on what grounds which rights are enacted and implemented and with what intensity and scope while other rights are not inscribed or remain *letra muerta*. Even if grounded in universal characteristics of human beings, what claim-needs become rights, to what extent they are implemented, and in what trade-offs with other rights and obligations is a social and political construction. A very important matter is who concurs to this construction and how (including, indeed, those claim-needs that do not succeed in being inscribed as rights).[113] The mutual agency recognitions demanded by political citizenship are crucial here.[114] This is a space for political participation, backed by the rights attached to a democratic regime. It is in this space that, at least in the originating countries, many need-claims of workers, peasants, women, and others were transformed into actionable rights, thus furthering democratization against the sometimes stiff resistance of the privileged.[115] I noted that currently, however, the struggles in the originating countries around needs, claims, and rights presuppose that almost everyone is above a basic floor of rights and capabilities. Indeed, this is not the case in Latin America and other regions of the South and East. This lends special urgency and dramatism to arguments and struggles about which rights should be enacted and implemented in these countries. The very possibility of agency is often at stake there. I also noted that in some countries, whether by means of authoritarian repression or because of severe deprivations suffered by the popular sector, their need-claims scarcely reach the public agenda. This is a reflection of the inequality of these countries. Few issues get onto the public agenda other than those that interest the dominant sectors and classes, except concerns for "public security," which often entail the criminalization of poverty and, with it, further regressions in the civil rights of the popular sector.

Paradoxically, it is in the countries where broad public discussion about need-claims is most needed that it is more difficult to incorporate these issues into the public agenda. The resulting deafness of the agenda is an indication of the low quality of these democracies—it strongly suggests that many of those who are political citizens lack basic social and civil rights and capabilities. I argued above that the answer to this situation is more, better-quality democracy. The rights of political citizenship plus whatever civil rights do exist in a given case, in addition to appropriate political alliances (see O'Donnell 1998b), are the initial levers for this surely long and arduous task. Curiously, perhaps, the main theme of this task is the very issue I argued is theoretically undecidable: what would be "a decent social minimum" (Nussbaum 2000a: 125) in terms of a basic set of human development capabilities and human rights? Furthermore, if a country is poor and has an anemic state and a truncated legal system, which sequences and trajectories would be adequate for the achievement of that minimum?[116]

As should be clear by now, we cannot know in advance the answer to these questions. It would be a presumptuous intellectualistic fallacy to try to predetermine what *menu* of rights will or should be demanded by what deprived groups, sectors, or classes in a given country and period. All we can do, I believe, is try to clarify these issues and insist on the potential importance of the—few, but as I have argued, not insignificant—rights that political democracy entails. For these purposes, furthermore, we do know two helpful things. One is that, as we saw in relation to these rights, we can derive, inductively and *a contrario sensu,* conditions that beyond a reasonable doubt hamper agency, whether it is defined in terms of human rights or human development. Being subject to physical violence, the recurrent fear of violence, hunger or malnutrition, serious preventable diseases, or severe inherited incapacities are, among others, strong candidates for being considered deprivations of basic rights and capabilities.

We have reached a point I want to stress. In relation to political rights, the undecidability of their minimal sufficient set did not deter us from identifying some rights (such as expression, association, and movement) about which we can confidently make an empirical, inductively derived, causal proposition: *If these rights are lacking, or if they are severely curtailed, then* a democratic regime and its component of political citizenship do not exist. In the same sense, the impossibility of determining a minimal sufficient set for human development and human rights should not deter us from establishing conditions that, on the basis of available knowledge,[117] allow us to confidently assert that they severely hamper the agency of those suffering these conditions. Furthermore, most of these conditions probably would have to be asserted *a contrario,* at least until we have more and better knowledge. For example, in terms of human development, physicians and biologists know quite well the minimal nutritional requirements of various social categories (pregnant and nursing mothers, children at various ages, manual laborers, etc.), as well as the tragic consequences that deprivation of the respective requirements bring for their victims and their offspring.[118] In terms of human rights, for example, we can identify practices of domestic violence, police torture, or other severe mistreatments that clearly deny agency. Fortunately, currently there are many institutions—public, private, and international—gathering all kinds of relevant data; perhaps the time has come for some institution (maybe UNDP?) to take the lead in coordinating the sharing and harmonization of these data.[119] The second thing we know is that it is not just isolated individuals who are suffering this deprivations and needs; these are *social matters,* to be dealt with in terms of the acknowledgement of collective and public responsibilities.[120]

On the basis of evidence of these kinds of deprivations and their consequences, a strong argument may be made that a country's resources should be primarily allocated to overcoming them. We can be guaranteed that alternative arguments will be made, such as, for example, allocating most of these resources to improve health and education services for the middle sectors so a better-trained and healthier workforce will improve economic growth rates, which presumably will also benefit those who suffer severe deprivations. Furthermore, these are *political* questions, informed by different values, ideologies, and social locations and by more or less implicit theories about the workings of a given society and, presently, increasingly also about the workings of the whole world. These discussions define what are the "real" (that is, socially defined) needs that a country faces, ignores, and represses. Politics, democratic politics included, is as much consensus as it is conflict. Pushing some issues onto a public agenda that closely reflects existing social inequalities, arguing that some needs are positive rights, and debating about the relative priorities of various kinds of rights are all conflictive matters—the more so the more unequal a society is and the more accustomed its dominant sectors and classes are to their privileges.

At this point an intersection among democracy, human development, and human rights may be highlighted: Except perhaps for some truly exceptional individuals, the effectuation of political rights requires that at least some basic human capabilities and human rights have been achieved;[121] conversely, the struggles for achieving those rights and capabilities benefit from the universalistic rights and potential empowerments furnished by political democracy. It could be said that I have just stated an unbreakable vicious circle, but an alternative view is the dialectical one I sketched in section 9. This view recognizes democracy's peculiar dynamics and historical openness. The always possible extension or retraction[122] of political, social, and human rights and—encompassing them all—the issue of the capabilities that enable agency are the field on which, under democracy, political competition has been and will continue being played. This is the main reason why variations and changes over time in the quality of democracy are consequential, both as a result and as a propeller of struggles for human development and human rights.[123]

Truly, we saw that a democratic regime may coexist with severe human development deprivations as well as with the curtailment of important civil rights; furthermore, pending future and much needed research, we cannot say that a democratic regime in any strict sense *causes* advances in human development or human rights. Yet these three currents have a strong elective affinity:[124] Because they are based on the same view of the human being they, so to speak, invoke each other. For example, historically advances in the material conditions of the popular sector made it much more difficult for those in power to resist their demands for political citizenship; the extension of the latter provided to women and some minorities an important springboard for acquiring civil and social rights; the broad effectuation of civil rights furthered the conquest of social and political rights; the availability of political rights has prevented famines, which happen quite often under authoritarian rule; etc. These are just examples; these and others that may be brought to bear suggest that under the metaphor of elective affinity lies important empirical relations. I believe that the driving force of these relations is ultimately moral—the recognition that an agent should not be deprived of *any* of the basic rights and capabilities, however theoretically undecidable, postulated by these three currents. These currents have different intellectual origins, different moments of emergence, different institutional settings in which they are practiced, and different disciplinary specializations and literatures. I insist, however, that they all are based on the same conception of the human being. This is why they tend to converge in their theoretical and—hopefully, increasingly—in their practical concerns.[125] They have a strong elective affinity because they see the human being as an agent carrier of rights that define, and support, his/her very distinctiveness as a human being. As a consequence of both the above-noted differences and this basic agreement, students and practitioners of each of these currents do well to focus principally on some aspects of those rights; on the other hand, the three currents have much to gain, practically and theoretically, carefully exploring the overlaps that their common grounding unavoidably (and, indeed, fortunately) generates. This is, I believe, a much-needed conversation, to which I hope this volume will contribute.

12. Fourth Excursus on Assessing the Quality of Democracy

From the preceding section it follows that an assessment of the quality of democracy should not be indifferent to the extent to which some basic aspects of human development and human rights have been achieved, nor to the number and social characteristics of those who are deprived. Simply put, severe deprivations in these matters mean that except for exceptional individuals, their political agency is disabled. Insofar as democracy entails political citizenship, including its participatory rights, it includes the expectation that everyone is at least above a floor of basic human capabilities and human rights that enables them, if they wish, to exercise their political citizenship.[126]

For the reasons stated in the preceding section, I include some examples of the relevant human development and human rights dimensions with no claim that they constitute a complete listing.

With regard to (basically) human development

1. Number, percent, social position, gender, age, and geographical location of individuals lacking minimally adequate food intake, shelter, clothing, health services, and drinkable water.
2. Number, percent, social position, gender, age, and geographical location of individuals affected by lack of access to health services, by preventable diseases, and by inherited or acquired disabilities due to any of the deprivations listed in the present items.
3. Number, percent, social position, gender, age, and geographical location of full and functional illiterates and rates of enrollment and desertion at various educational levels.
4. Number, proportion, social position, gender, age, and geographical location of individuals who are unemployed or working in informal sectors of the economy that do not recognize basic civil and/or labor rights such as the ones listed above.

With regard to (basically) human rights

1. Number, social position, gender, age, and geographical location of individuals who are and/or have been victimized by physical violence, including domestic and police-perpetrated violence.
2. Number and geographical location of various crimes, especially homicides and armed robberies.
3. If foreigners are assigned the same civil and social rights as citizens, if at least at the local level they can participate in political affairs, and if they are treated by state agents and citizens with due consideration and respect.

The above are just examples, but their very listing recommends some practical criteria. Even though it is no small task to gather (or, when available, to organize) the kind of data implied by the previous excursi, they pertain quite naturally to an inquiry into the quality of democracy. Instead, the data implied by the items listed in the present excursus are the main empirical field of institutions working on human development and on human rights. These institutions, especially if persuaded of the intimate connections that exist between their concerns and democracy, may be amenable to share their data with those who wish to assess the quality of democracy. The latter, of course, should be willing to share their own data with those institutions.

13. Some Precisions on the Quality of Democracy

At this point, after the final excursus, I summarize my views about the conceptualization of the *quality of democracy.* By this I mean *different degrees of democraticness,* referring to the items (or as the Costa Rican citizen audit proposes, standards) such as the ones I have proposed here. These items may be seen as vectors that tap dimensions that, depending on the data feasible for each, may be arranged in some scale or ordering.[127] The distance to the level established by the respective standard or, eventually, from a "bottom" indicating the absence of the given factor or dimension would establish (or allow a reasoned assessment of) the relative democraticness of that dimension. The overall result would be a series of vectors[128]—of course, some of them better measured than others—of relative democraticness. In turn, the relationships among these vectors should not be presupposed; rather, it is an empirical matter for the study of which the disaggregation of the vectors (and their component variables) is a necessary step.[129] As the citizen audit has skillfully done in Costa Rica, and with the experience derived from this innovative experiment, similar assessments in other countries (or, for that matter, regions or cities) would provide much new and useful knowledge about the workings—both achievements and failures—of a given democracy. Furthermore, with good methodological care important aspects of these data may be comparable across cases.

I must now make explicit a personal bias: The more democraticness one finds, the better. This does not ignore, as I already mentioned, that there are trade-offs, nor that seldom if ever all good things come together. But still I believe that *in dubio pro democracy;* that is, trade-offs against a given democratic dimension ought to be carefully justified. Furthermore, these justifications must be given publicly, a fair chance for public debate should be offered, and the decision to accept the trade-off must be made by legally authorized institutions proceeding according to democratic rules[130] (or, as with the examples I presented above of making some foreign currency or national security decisions, by institutions that have been properly authorized to this effect and whose authority can be challenged by democratic means).

Now I must qualify my assertion that *in dubio pro democracy*. I believe that this is a valid general yardstick, but it does not preclude the theoretical and, indeed, eminently political discussion about two questions: How much democracy, and democracy where? In relation to these questions, a radical democrat will want to advance homogenously in all the vectors of democratization, while, at the other extreme, a conservative democrat will prefer low, or even zero, levels of advancement in some of these vectors.[131] The personal bias I have confessed does not aim at precluding this issue, which is at the very core of what democratic politics (and, in fact, politics in general) is about. To what social spheres beyond the regime should democratic mechanisms of decision making and the principle and rights of citizenship extend? What costs in terms of trade-offs with other social goals are we willing to pay for advances in democratization? Should democratic mechanisms and principles of citizenship be extended to, say, the internal workings of political parties, trade unions, and business associations, but not to, say, business corporations, universities, international organizations, and families? Can there exist a reasonably consistent and broadly accepted criteria concerning where to apply and where not to apply those mechanisms and principles? And, perhaps even more puzzling, who, and with what decision-making processes (democratic or otherwise), should decide this kind of issue?

Dealing satisfactorily with these themes demands as yet unwritten theories of democracy.[132] Furthermore, I take it that these theories would have to take into consideration that we may be dealing with the ultimate undecidable, the final distillation of all the other undecidables. A conception of democracy that claims to be consistent must be grounded, as we saw above, in the conception of agency as it is entailed by a democratic regime and its universalistic wager. The theoretical undecidability of political and other rights gives democracy its peculiar dynamics and historical openness. As a consequence, sincere democrats of various persuasions will forever debate where, how, and why the boundaries of democracy (and, indeed, of politics in general) should be located. The content of these debates will not be determined by theoretical arguments alone; they will be strongly influenced by ideological, practical, and prudential considerations, such as the resources and the degree of inequality of the country, the international context, and the political alliances that support the given positions. Obviously, these matters are well beyond the present text. Yet two important points can be made. One is that an audit of the quality of a given democracy should be useful to everyone, including those who believe that advances in some of its vectors are undesirable. The audit generates public information for the use of citizens who may validly disagree as to how much democracy and in what social locations they prefer.[133] The second point is that, as you may have noticed in excursus 3 (as well as in the standards of the audit discussed in Vargas Cullell's chapter in this volume), I do not assume that democratic mechanisms are adequate for all social institutions. In this chapter, however, the discussion of agency as existing in all social spheres, not just the regime, has supported the expectation that in nondemocratic social institutions the civil and labor rights of their members are respected— because agency is *always* involved, the absence of democratic mechanisms or of citizenship in a given social situation does not justify despotic or arbitrary rule.

Now I include some comments on the various levels implied by my suggestions about the items, or standards, with which the quality of democracy may be assessed. I take it that the regime, as well as the attitudes and opinions of the citizens toward democracy and some general aspects of politics (excursus 1), are not problematic topics to be assessed.[134] On the other hand, the discussion of the democraticness of the state institutions and the legal system (excursus 2) took us beyond the regime-centered views current in mainstream political science. I hope I have shown, however, that this is an extremely important aspect of democracy; consequently, in spite of difficulties in collecting date, I am persuaded that every effort should be made to gauge this level, too.[135] In turn, based on the argument that certain characteristics of the social context are (at least) a necessary condition of democracy, and that variations in those characteristics presumably have a strong positive relationship with the quality of democracy, in excursus 3 I include some items geared toward assessing some of those characteristics. Finally, the crucial connection that I argued exists among democracy, human development, and human rights led me to excursus 4. With this level I trespassed current conceptions of democracy even further than I did with the state. I believe, however, that my discussion of the various aspects of citizenship, as well as of the common grounding on agency of these currents, justifies the inclusion of this level in an assessment of the quality of democracy; in particular, the deprivation of basic conditions (once again, however theoretically undecidable) of human development and human rights means, as I have argued, the factual disabling of political citizenship. Obviously, the items of excursus 4 can also be specifically assessed in terms of human development or human rights. This does not sound problematic to me. Due to the strong elective affinities among these currents, such assessments should not be seen as incompatible or competitive with those that an audit of the quality of democracy may also make;[136] rather, looking at human development and human rights *also* from the angle of democracy would both express and reinforce these affinities.

14. Epistemic Notes on Assessing the Quality of Democracy

In the "Decalogue" of the audit of democracy I prepared for the March 2001 San José workshop (reproduced in Proyecto Estado de la Nación 2001: 35–36), I argue that a proper procedure for assessing the quality of democracy would combine "internal" and "external" approaches. By the latter I mean that a combination of expert and politically aware citizens establishes the basic defining characteristics of a democratic regime as well as aspirations, or standards, that may be reasonably posited in terms of improving the quality of a given democracy.[137] On the other hand, an audit of this kind should invite the citizens themselves to voice their views, both in terms of the failings and achievements of their democracy and of the aspirations they hold for it. Of course, this side of the audit is difficult to gauge empirically; fortunately, it inspired the imaginative methodological combinations and the extensive research efforts of the Costa Rican citizen audit.

The rationale for this double approach should be quite obvious. On the one hand, a purely external view easily risks being too abstract, too technical, and/or too distant from how the citizenry evaluates its own democracy. On the other hand, a purely internal approach, especially in countries where democracy suffers serious deficiencies, risks gathering opinions mostly from people who are poorly informed and/or are expressions of the adaptive preferences of severely deprived individuals.[138] This is why the Costa Rican audit claims that it is not a theoretical (or academic) exercise oriented toward formulating, testing, and revising theoretical propositions. It is an exercise in evaluation—properly, an audit. Yet this exercise is not raw empiricism; it is theoretically informed by concepts about what are a democracy and its several dimensions. This initial theoretical—or external—moment leads to an internal one, which consists of gauging, with as much detail and care as possible, how citizens view the democracy existing in their country. In turn, in a third stage these views return to the citizen audit and are assigned conceptual locations that, as noted, are theoretically guided.[139] After this stage of incorporating and conceptually locating the "internal" information, it is analyzed in terms of its distance in relation to criteria, or standards, that theory and comparative observations suggest are in principle feasible and desirable features of a democracy of good quality.[140]

These complicated but indispensable movements (to and from internal and external views, and to and from empirical data and theoretically informed concepts) prohibits, as already noted, the audit from being considered a theoretical or academic undertaking and product per se.[141] It is, as the authors of the Costa Rican audit correctly argue, an instrument with which the citizens evaluate their own democracy.[142] In fact, the audit is an attempt to enrich the public sphere and a contribution toward expanding the restricted public agenda that afflicts many countries. For this reason it is crucial that, after the steps I have described, the main results of the audit "return" to the citizenry by means that are widely available and easily understandable.[143]

These are the ideas on which, inspired by the Costa Rican audit, I based my "Decalogue." After writing it I came across a text by Sen that I found extremely useful. In this text Sen discusses a problem that by now it should be clear is homologous to the one I am dealing with here: how to assess, in terms of their capabilities and functionings, the "real interests" of individuals. Sen also reaches the conclusion that both internal and external perspectives are needed. As to the former, Sen observes that due to a variety of reasons individuals may be subject to "objective illusions"—beliefs "that are formed on the basis of a limited class of positional observations," and although they have "some claim to being objective in their own terms," they are in fact mistaken. Sen's main examples concern beliefs about the relative sizes of the sun and the moon, but they easily could be extended, as he does in other contexts, to the characteristics of a given society. On the other hand, Sen notes that from the external point of view there can never be truly objective knowledge. It is always a "positional objectivity," due to unavoidable "parametric dependence of observation and inference on the position of the observer;" this can be alleviated but never eliminated by "transpositional assessment[s]—drawing on but going beyond *different positional observations*" (Sen 1993: 130, italics added).[144] All knowledge is perspectival, as it "takes place within the framework of contemporary standards and beliefs" (Hamilton 1999: 527).[145] Yet the external point of view is indispensable for "evaluat[ing] issues like well-being and the standard of living as outcomes . . . [as these matters are] tested in the light of additional information and different positions" (Hamilton 1999: 530, commenting on Sen's views).

It is clear that neither an internal or an external perspective suffices for assessing human interests. In part for this reason, Sen implies (and Hamilton 1999 concurs) that there is not, and there never can be, a firm and generally intersubjectively agreed upon theory of human interests, basic or otherwise. This is another theoretical undecidable; more precisely, it is another facet of the undecidability that we first found when discussing political rights and then reencountered several times throughout this chapter.

On the other hand, the views of these authors do not lead them (and mine does not either) to value relativism; all of us are discussing very real human interests—and consequent rights—that pertain to the agency that is a universal attribute of every human being. Furthermore, Sen argues, as does the Costa Rican audit, that the internal and external perspectives should engage in a dialogue during which, while learning much from the internal side, the external perspective may dispel some of the objective illusions of the former. Because of the need for this interactive process, Sen asserts, as we saw, the more than instrumental value of democracy and within it the crucial "role of practical reason in public discourse" (Sen 1995, 1999b; see also Nussbaum 2000b). Obviously, for this to happen it is helpful that everyone has the political rights attached to a democratic regime, even if some suffer severe deprivation of other rights.

15. Some Conclusions

There are rights that, at least in terms of their formal validity, are not problematic. Under a democratic regime, the rights of political participation as well as those of expression, association, movement, and the like must exist by definition of that regime. Furthermore, the historical core of civil and human rights (to life, physical integrity, protection from and redress of various kinds of violence, movement, freedom of religious belief, and the like) has been enacted by the legal systems of practically all countries in the modern world. Today not many would argue, at least publicly, that these are not valid and actionable rights,[146] although in most of Latin America they are far from being fully implemented. The more complicated issue refers to human development, especially with respect to those who "die so slowly that none call it a murder" (Samuel Taylor Coleridge, quoted in Shue 1996: 58). Many contemporary theorists argue that these are unfortunate facts that may give raise to a moral claim for the provision of the needed capabilities. But these theorists deny that these facts ground positive rights, that is, actionable claims against the state and eventually society. Some of these arguments deny the validity of such claims; others point out the impossibility of achieving general agreement on what would be a proper set of such rights; others point out the factual impossibility of satisfying the corresponding needs, especially but not exclusively in poor countries; and still others point out that the deadweight costs of taxing the rich and eventually weakening their property rights would overcome, even for the very poor, the gains obtained by trying to attend to their needs.

Solely or in combination, these arguments have dominated the public agenda in the past two decades, both in rich and poor countries. Seen from the perspective of agency and its minimum enabling capabilities, however, I find it hard to deny that the achievement of these capabilities *is* a right. At this point we find ourselves back at the issue of democracy and its quality. We saw that the issue of what political rights, human development capabilities, and human and civil rights are inscribed and implemented as such rights, in what sequences, and with what trade-offs has been and will continue being the very stuff of democratic struggles. These are political processes that eventually lead to collective decisions enacted by the state and its legal system. History attests that no "full" package of these capabilities and rights has ever been simultaneously enacted, not to mention implemented. This fact shows that, as I already argued, it is inappropriate to ask for a priori specification of a minimal sufficient set of these rights and/or capabilities; it also shows that it is unfair to dismiss claims that do not purport to simultaneously achieve a "full package" of these goods. History also attests that the resources necessary for achieving *some* of these rights and capabilities were disputed and redefined through the conflictive and sometimes convoluted processes I sketched in sections 4 and 5.[147] Furthermore, the sequences of acquisition of some of these rights and capabilities, and their specific content and scope, have varied even among the originating countries.[148] In these cases, democratic politics under various kinds of circumstances and political alliances led to prioritizing some need-claims over others that were arguably no less basic than the former. These struggles were not deterred by the presumed injustice of only attending to some need-claims, or by predictions that assigning the necessary resources would provoke catastrophic economic consequences. In turn, gains in some of these rights enabled further struggles for other rights. These are the ways, frustrating at times and seldom linear, in which democratic politics work—but only when they work close to their best.

The great impulse for these processes has been the recurrent discovery and reinstatement, in various times and circumstances, of the moral import of democracy. This import never could have emerged from a conception of democracy as merely a set of procedures and institutions; rather, these procedures and institutions have mattered as one of the avenues—in the political realm—through which human beings may exercise and eventually develop their agency. Since classical Athens, albeit restricted to a segment of the population, up to contemporary times, when it has become inclusive, political citizenship has been based on the view that the respective individuals are actual or at least prospective agents. It is this view that lends to democracy its great normative import: Even if at times obfuscated or neglected, or dampened by appalling inequalities in the society in which it exists, the normative component of democracy always may be resurrected by appeal to the dignity and respect that the agent/citizen inherently deserves. It is for this reason that

> [N]o theory of democracy that failed to give the egalitarian idea a central place could possibly yield a faithful representation of the extraordinary grip of democracy in the modern political imagination. . . . We must keep in mind that historically a main goal of democratic movements has

been to seek redress in the political sphere for the effects of inequalities in the economy and society. (Beitz 1989: xi, xvi)[149]

For these potentialities to operate in Latin America, it will be crucial to increase the numbers and the organization of those who have capabilities for actually participating in politics, and, consequently, for broadening the public agenda so as to include their need-claims in it. In the process, what need-claims will be given priority will have to be decided according to the specific characteristics of each country, not only as a consequence of the existing objective needs but also of the relation of forces expressed, and mobilized, by various political alliances. Due to the extension and severity of the deprivations existing in most Latin American countries, for the foreseeable future the prioritization of some need-claims will entail the tragic postponement of other, also very important, rights and capabilities. Yet insofar as these processes are geared by a universalistic recognition of agency and its social, civil, and political rights, they will keep on the public agenda the need to continue struggling for the achievement of at last a decent social minimum for everyone.[150] If and as long as this happens, the quality of these democracies will concomitantly improve. For these purposes—and hopes—audits of the kind that has been carried out in Costa Rica should be helpful.

NOTES

This chapter benefited greatly from the discussion and written comments (the revised versions of which are printed in this volume) by participants in the Heredia workshop. Later on, I received further comments on this same text from Osvaldo Iazzetta, Gabriela Ippolito, Scott Mainwaring, and Jorge Vargas Cullell. To all of them my deep appreciation.

1. In their comments, Manuel Alcántara and Terry Lynn Karl criticize the omission of the impacts of globalization from my discussion. I believe this criticism is well taken. Yet methodologically I find it preferable to start by conceptualizing state/national units as the background against which the (differential, across issues and cases) impacts of globalization may be assessed. Still, as these commentators note, I do not undertake this further step in the present text.

2. As Juan Méndez notes in his comments, however, there are areas of problematic intersection between, especially, human rights and democracy. These are problems that deserve further discussion, to which I hope Méndez's comments and this chapter contribute.

3. Although some human rights organizations such as Amnesty International are reluctant to make this move, there is a distinct trend in the human rights movement to include social, economic, and cultural rights in their mandate.

4. In terms of human development, perhaps there is no more eloquent (albeit implicit) assertion of this universalism than the recent incorporation of the Gender-Related and Gender Empowerment data into the *Human Development Reports*. The obvious basis for this incorporation is the universalistic belief that women have no fewer rights than men and that the specific deprivations to which women are often subject merits special consideration and duties from the state and other social actors. Of course, this belief runs counter to views that are still deeply ingrained in not a few parts of the world.

5. I say "mainly" because, for example, cognitive impairment may be the consequence of malnutrition of the mother during gestation.

6. Here I am asserting that at the moment of vote counting, each vote should be computed as one (or, in the case of plural voting, in the same quantity as every other vote). In saying this I am glossing over the problem resulting from rules of vote aggregation in which votes cast in certain districts weigh more, in some cases significantly more, than in other districts (in relation to Latin America and the severe overrepresentation of some districts in some of these countries, see Snyder and Samuels 2001, and Calvo and Abal Medina 2001). At some point overrepresentation becomes so pronounced that any semblance of voting equality is eliminated; before this point, I believe it can be asserted that the lower the level of overrepresentation (that is, the more each vote counts as truly equal to all others), the better the quality of a given democratic election.

7. I use the term "originating countries" as a shorthand for designating the countries located in the northwestern quadrant of the world, plus, with some geographical license, Australia and New Zealand.

8. As with markets, few elections, if any, are completely fair or competitive (as the 2000 presidential election in the United States patently showed); see Elklit and Svensson 1997. This caveat points to the issue of the varying quality or degrees of democratization of the regime, which I discuss below.

9. For discussion of these and other definitions, see O'Donnell 2000.

10. This likelihood of endurance does not mean that after N rounds of such elections a democracy has "consolidated" (as argued, for example, in Huntington 1991), or that other aspects of the regime (as they are deemed to exist in the originating countries) are institutionalized or in the process of becoming so. For discussion of these matters, see O'Donnell 1996 (also published in O'Donnell 1999a).

11. Even if agents anticipate that elections at $t1$ will be fair, if they believe that there is a significant likelihood that elections at $t2$ will not be fair—by a regression explored in prisoner's dilemmas with fixed numbers of iterations—agents already will make these kinds of extra-electoral investments at $t1$.

12. This is, with slight changes, the definition offered in O'Donnell and Schmitter 1986: 73n1. For a useful discussion of this concept, see Mazzuca 1998 and 1999.

13. For apposite discussion of this matter, see Lechner 2000 and his comments in this volume. See also Berger and Luckman 1966.

14. In some countries these *egos* may be numerous, even though they are legally constrained to accept the wager. In a survey I conducted in the metropolitan area of São Paulo, Brazil (December 1991–January 1992, *n:* 800), an astounding 79% responded "No" to the question "Do Brazilians know how to vote?"; this rose to 84% among respondents with secondary education and higher (in the context it was clear to respondents that the question referred not to the mechanics of voting but to their evaluation of the choices other voters make among competing parties and candidates).

15. There is an obvious exception to this—when democracies emerge. In these cases there is a moment of choice. Rights and duties are established that, insofar as they are sanctioned by fairly elected constitution-making bodies or are ratified by fair referenda, may be construed as expressing majoritarian—and hence sufficient—agreement for the institutionalization of the democratic wager. After this moment, consecutive generations find themselves *ab initio* embraced and constituted in and by the legally defined relationships entailed by the democratic wager.

16. The reader has surely noticed that I have been mentioning both "rights" and "freedoms." The reason of this usage will become clear.

17. Of course, this is not the only reason why these rights are important. I return to this topic.

18. This is just one reason for this conundrum; I will discuss others.

19. In contrast, this issue has generated a large body of work among legal theorists. I will return to some aspects of this literature and its unfortunate split from most of political science and political sociology.

20. From a different but convergent angle, I have found useful the discussion of undecidability in Mouffe 1996 and 2000. On the other hand, for reasons that I hope will be clear, I disagree with Pablo da Silveira's argument that asserting this kind of undecidability necessarily entails subscribing to theories that are "purely culturalist" or "reduce rights to the logic of interest." On this matter, see also comments in this volume.

21. We will see that there is a double dimension to this. On the one hand, at an individual level, these are *rights* that are universalistically assigned; on the other hand, at a macro level, these are *freedoms* that characterize and co-constitute the social context in which these individuals are immersed.

22. For instance, Holmes and Sunstein (1999: 104) note that "What freedom of speech means for contemporary American jurisprudence is not what it meant fifty or one hundred years ago."

23. Among which, in addition, quite significant differences persist currently as to the scope of some of these rights.

24. In a similar context (concepts of equality), Amartya Sen puts it well: "If an underlying idea has an essential ambiguity, a precise formulation of that idea must try to *capture* the ambiguity rather than hide or eliminate it" (1993: 33–34, italics in the original).

25. I have also taken into account the useful "checklist for election assessment" furnished by Elklit and Svensson 1997.

26. I agree with the comments of Michael Coppedge that in the present and future excursi, the criteria proposed here are variables, about which we are interested in assessing the degree to which they are effective in each case. This, in turn, as Coppedge and Sebastián Mazzuca (see his comments) argue, is a necessary step for exploring the causal relationships that may exist among these analytically and empirically disaggregated factors. This clarification has seemed to me necessary because the original version of this text may have induced in these authors the mistaken view that we disagree on this matter.

27. The authors of the Costa Rican audit have done extremely careful and useful work in characterizing these and other items as *standards* and in explaining the rationale for this criterion. Here I can do no better than refer to Vargas Cullell's chapter in this volume.

28. I have taken this item from the comments of Terry Lynn Karl.

29. I have taken this clause from Coppedge's comments.

30. For example, can the executive unilaterally decide this matter, and in what policy areas?

31. For explication and discussion of these terms, see O'Donnell 1998a, 2002, and 2003.

32. In her comments María Hermínia Tavares de Almeida agrees with this point, asserting that "from the point of view of the quality of democracy, there is no way to decide, for example, between the Westminster model of fusion of powers and the model of separation of powers with checks and balances." In private communications, Coppedge has disagreed, stating that the more proportional (and, hence, antimajoritarian) an electoral system, the more democratic it is.

33. On this distinction, see the comments by Mazzuca; some of the topics he deals with in his comments go beyond the scope of my discussion here.

34. For a discussion of the various dimensions of publicness in democracy, see Iazzetta 2003.

35. In spite of frequent assertions to the contrary, not even in terms of universal male suffrage is the United States an exception to this. The early existence of this suffrage at the federal level was made purely nominal by the severe restrictions imposed on African Americans and Native Americans, especially in the South. Consequently, the achievement of inclusive political democracy in the United States must be dated to World War II or as late as the 1960s, in the aftermath of the civil rights movement.

36. On catastrophic predictions, see Hirschman 1991 and Rosanvallon 1992. As a British politician opposing the Reform Act of 1867 put it, "Because I am a liberal . . . I regard as one of the greatest dangers a proposal . . . to transfer power from the hands of property and intelligence, and to place it in the hands of men whose whole life is necessarily occupied in daily struggles for existence" (Robert Lowe, cited in Hirschman 1991: 94). See Goldstein 1983 for a discussion of violent resistance to extending political rights.

37. As Dahl says, "The burden of proof [of lack of agency] would always lie with a claim to an exception, and no exception would be admissible, either morally or legally,

in the absence of a very compelling showing" (1989: 108). Actually, this principle was first formulated, in terms similar to Dahl's, by John Stuart Mill (1962: 206 and passim).

38. Waldron comments that "The identification of someone as a right-bearer expresses a measure of confidence in that person's moral capabilities—in particular his capacity to think responsibly about the moral relation between his interests and the interests of others" (1999: 282).

39. The rediscovery of the Codes of Justinian in the eleventh century was particularly important to this process. As Berman notes, part of this importance was due to the fact that Roman law "had achieved a very high level of sophistication in the field of contracts" (1993: 245). From a different theoretical perspective, Anderson (1974) agrees, adding that Roman law conceptions of free disposition of land were also fundamental.

40. Rosanvallon comments that before the advent of liberalism, "This view of the autonomy of the will certainly appeared already juridically formulated in the civil law (*droit civil*)" (1992: 111, my translation). This, in turn, was part of broader changes in the conception of morality; as Schneewind notes, "During the 17th and 18th centuries established conceptions of morality as obedience came to be increasingly contested by emerging conceptions of morality as self-governance . . . centered on the belief that all normal individuals are equally able to live together in a morality of self-governance" (1998: 27).

41. "The result of contractual freedom, then, is in the first place the opening of the opportunity to use, by clever utilization of property ownership in the market, these resources without legal restraints as means for the achievement of power over others. The parties interested in power in the market thus are also interested in such a legal order . . . coercion is exercised to a considerable extent by the private owners of the means of production and acquisition, to whom the law guarantees their property. . . . In the labor market, it is left to the 'free' discretion of the parties to accept the conditions imposed by those who are economically stronger by virtue of the legal guarantee of their property." The author of these lines is Weber (1968: 730–31), not Marx.

42. In addition, political citizenship was extended after vigorous educational efforts were launched to make sure that these sectors would become "truly deserving citizens," that is, responsible agents. This had important democratizing effects in the long run, but for an account of the initial defensiveness of these efforts in France (which to my knowledge were not different from the other originating countries), see Rosanvallon 1992. In this respect it is significant the close attention that Condorcet, Locke, Rousseau, Adam Smith, and other towering members of the Enlightenment paid to education as a crucial medium for enabling agency in the political realm.

43. In relation to England, Marshall notes that by the 1830s "the civil rights attached to the status of freedom had already acquired sufficient substance to justify us in speaking of a general status of citizenship" (1964: 78). This also became true, at various times, in the other originating countries.

44. As Marshall notes, "The story of civil rights in their formative period is one of the gradual addition of new rights to a status that already existed and was held to

appertain to all adult members of the community" (1964: 18). These civil rights are, in his classic definition, "The rights necessary for individual freedom—liberty of person, freedom of speech, thought and faith, the right to own property and to conclude valid contracts, and right to justice" (1964: 10–11).

45. Jones puts it well: "Political authority is authority wielded over, and on behalf of, human individuals with rights" (1994: 88).

46. From now on, except when otherwise noted, "capabilities" refers to both the subjective ability to exercise practical reason by making reasonably autonomous and considered choices and the range of choice that the individual actually confronts; in addition to the works of Sen, for apposite discussion of this matter see Raz 1986.

47. As stated in Section 138 of the German Civil Code.

48. Furthermore, even before these relatively recent developments, this kind of legal system strongly implied—and even required—the presumption of agency for the validity of many legally grounded obligations. This can be seen in the evolution of criminal law away from establishing or allowing sanctions to collectivities and toward individual responsibility (see Lacey 2001). The same presumption also can be seen in relation to legislation referring to individuals not considered to be properly legal persons (such as minors) and their "re-presentation" by someone who may be thus legally construed.

49. According to Marshall, social rights include "from the right to a modicum of economic welfare and security to the right to a share to the full in the social heritage and to live the life of a civilized being according to the standard prevailing in the society" (1964: 72).

50. For example, the contemporary neoconservative offensive aims at eroding these partially equalizing measures. In most of contemporary Latin America, which has been shaken by severe economic crises and endowed with weak legal and welfare systems, the consequences of this offensive have been particularly devastating.

51. Weber (1968) dubbed these processes of "materialization" of the law, as they introduced nonuniversalistic criteria of substantive justice to formal-rational law. Recently, criticisms of the "legal pollution" (Teubner 1986 and Preuss 1986) produced by these developments have become widespread from both the right and left. This literature is not central to my present analysis. I note, however, that these criticisms seriously neglect the equalizing advances achieved in many respects by these developments. These criticisms should be tempered by the much more unfavorable situation of the poor and various discriminated sectors in countries, as in Latin America, where welfare policies and their consequent social rights were only partially adopted or implemented.

52. As Méndez notes in his comments, these should not be seen simply as aspirations but as demands for actionable rights.

53. As Gabriela Ippolito puts it in her comments, this assertion implies bringing a classic topic—the issue of the social conditions of democracy—back into central focus in the theory of democracy; as she asserts, "what is at issue in many of these countries is the very meaning of citizenship."

54. This issue was not ignored in the cradle of democracy. In his excellent study of Athenian democracy, Hansen (1991) argues that Athens became fully democratized only when it was decided that participants in the sessions of the assembly, the council, and other institutions would be paid the equivalent of a daily average wage. This decision entailed explicit recognition of the issue of capabilities I am discussing, as it was specifically aimed at facilitating the political participation of poor citizens. On his part, Aristotle (1968) recommended subsidizing the political participation of the poor in order to assure the effectiveness of their citizenship.

55. Of course, among the ratifiers are governments that blatantly ignore many of the rights involved. Yet, instead of using this fact for dismissing the significance of these treatises and covenants, I believe it should be seen as a tribute, even if a cynical one, paid to the moral force of the rights proclaimed in these international instruments.

56. For concurrent views about the legal system as a part of the state, see Bobbio 1989 and, of course, Weber 1968. In this section I present a rather cursory discussion of the state, which I am intending to complement by means of work presently in progress.

57. See especially Holmes and Sunstein 1999; Raz 1986; Sen 1984a, 1984b, 1985a, 1985b; and Skinner 1984.

58. Or, more or less equivalently (see O'Donnell 1999b), under a democratic rule of law. In my opinion, this kind of legal system, if effectively implemented, is "an intrinsic normative good." This phrase comes from the comments by Karl, although she means it critically, probably because she does not recognize that I am referring specifically to an *effective* and *democratic* kind of rule of law, not just any version of it.

59. This is what some German theorists have labeled the "indisponibility" of the legal system for the rulers; see especially Preuss 1996a, 1996b; Habermas 1996, 1988.

60. On this matter, from various but concurrent perspectives, see Fuller 1964; Garzón Valdés 1993; Habermas 1996; Hart 1961; and Kelsen 1967.

61. This useful concept has been proposed by Smulovitz and Peruzzotti 2000. See O'Donnell 2002 on the mutually supportive relationships between societal and horizontal accountability.

62. In all other political types somebody (a dictator, a vanguard party, a military *junta,* a theocracy, etc.) may unilaterally void or suspend whatever rights exist, including those that regulate their roles. There are, however, some hybrid cases. I refer to those where formally (as in Chile) or informally (as in Guatemala) the armed forces retain uncontrolled policy areas, as well as veto powers over some decisions by civilian authorities. The least that can be said about this matter is that it seriously hinders the democratic quality of the respective regimes.

63. *A contrario,* Méndez, O'Donnell, and Pinheiro 1999 conclusively shows that in Latin America this interlacing is repeatedly interrupted and the law consequently rendered ineffective; see also Brinks 2002, Domingo 1999, Domingo and Seider 2001, Garzón Valdés 1999, Hinton 2003, and Stanley 2003.

64. As Ippolito notes in her comments, the issue of foreigners, particularly the rights assigned to them and the treatment they receive from the state and from citizens,

should be considered an important issue in the assessment of the quality of a democracy. I recognize that the present text does not pay sufficient attention to this issue.

65. In line with this point, Ronald Dworkin asserts that "a particular demand of political morality . . . requires governments to speak with one voice, to act in a principled and coherent manner toward all its citizens, [and] to extend to everyone the substantive standards of justice or fairness it uses for some" (1986: 165).

66. The *Auditoría* (Proyecto Estado de la Nación 2001: 195, 200) has a thoughtful discussion of this matter; for sound empirical reasons, the authors decided to focus on various situations of *mistreatment* by state institutions. They further argue that "[T]he opposite of mistreatment of the citizen is not 'good treatment,' but democratic treatment which occurs, precisely, when the [state] institutions respect the rights and the dignity of the persons" (199).

67. Summarizing a series of studies in the United States, Tyler concurs: "To be treated with dignity and respect assures citizens that they are important and valued members of society, entitled to recognition of their status and rights. This [is a] recognition of one's inclusion in society" (2000: 990). On his part, Margalit (1996) sees this kind of treatment as the distinctive characteristic of a "decent society."

68. Even in situations where this inequality is sharpest (such as imprisonment), the moral duty of still respecting the agency of the subject remains. Nowadays this is usually also a legal duty, even if it is too often ignored.

69. In relation to social policies, Ippolito (in her comments) argues that "*how* the state gives what it gives" (italics in the original) is no less important than *what* the state gives.

70. For the concept of "problematic frontiers" between state and society, see Oszlak and O'Donnell 1984. Here I refer to situations where various kinds of mistreatment are frequent (if not systematic) and those who suffer it are dealing with issues (health, employment, issuance of documents, and the like) that are important for them. For the interesting and innovative method see Proyecto Estado de la Nación 2001: vol. 2.

71. Sen concurs: "Individual freedom is quintessentially a social product" (1999a: 31).

72. This point is made by, especially, Berlin 1969. Berlin's work has raised a series of interesting—and complicated—discussions about "value pluralism" (see, among others, Gray 2000 and Newey 1998), which I must sidestep here.

73. As Raz puts it: "A moral theory which recognizes the value of autonomy [that is, agency] inevitably upholds a pluralist view. It admits the value of a large number of greatly differing pursuits among which individuals are free to choose" (1986: 381) because "the routes open to be used in our lives are both incompatible and valuable" (1994: 119).

74. On the limitations of tolerance as a proper moral attitude toward agents and their rights, see Garzón Valdés 2001.

75. Of course, the extent to which this possibility is effected varies significantly from case to case; I discuss some of the relevant factors below.

76. Norbert Lechner's comments include a suggestive listing of "social capabilities that influence citizens' action." From a somewhat different but in this sense convergent

standpoint, Rawls argues that "These goods . . . are things citizens need as free and equal persons, and claims to these goods are counted as appropriate claims" (1993: 180).

77. Notice, too, that for this same reason such a context is congenial to the exercise of vertical societal accountability.

78. Alan Gewirth's "ethical rationalism" (1978) and the discussions it has generated (Regis 1984) are relevant to this point, but I cannot elaborate here.

79. In this and the next paragraph I am taking into account criticisms that Vargas Cullell made to a previous version of this chapter.

80. I have mentioned Raz's arguments in this respect; from various perspectives valuable concurrent arguments about the "social side" of rights may be found in Garzón Valdés 1993, Habermas 1996, and Waldron 1999.

81. I exclude from this classification El Salvador, Honduras, Nicaragua, and most Caribbean countries for the simple if not too satisfactory reason that I do not know enough about them. Furthermore, as the discussion at the workshop and several written comments make clear, this typology needs further refining and specification.

82. I owe the caveat concerning candidates of leftist parties to the comments of Manuel Alcántara.

83. These two countries score similarly to the democracies in the Northwest. In the 1990s the average support for democracy in these countries, elicited by a question similar to that in table 1, was 83% (Dalton 1999: 70, average calculated from data in table 3.5). I excluded Northern Ireland from this list—score of 65%—due to the peculiar circumstances of this region.

84. In their comments, Catherine Conaghan and Osvaldo Iazzetta usefully elaborate on these matters.

85. See O'Donnell 1993, where I draw a metaphorical map of "blue, green, and brown areas," in which the latter are where state legality is barely effective, if at all.

86. The reports of various human rights organizations repeatedly and abundantly document the permanent threat of violence to which these people are subjected. For Brazil see, among others, Dellasoppa, Bercovich, and Arriaga 1999, who document that the incidence of violent deaths in the poorest areas of the São Paulo metropolitan region is sixteen times higher than in the most affluent ones; for data on Argentina see, among others, CELS 1998. More generally, a study of several data sets on violent crime found in all of them a persistent and often strong positive correlation between violence and poverty and income inequality (Hsieh and Pugh 1993). The poor, of course, are the main victims of this violence.

87. This is another aspect that its narrow concentration on the national regime has led mainstream contemporary political science, with few exceptions, to ignore. This omission is empirically and theoretically costly; even approaches exclusively centered on the national regime would do well to consider the impacts of subnational authoritarian regimes on the workings of the former.

88. For a chapter in the sociology of knowledge, this assumption ignores no less than the experience of the United States, where for a long time the subnational regimes of the South were clearly authoritarian, even though they held (nonfair) elections.

89. As implied in the preceding note, neither of these sequences applies to the United States and the peculiar problems raised by slavery, but I will not deal with this exception here.

90. I should note that, basically for this reason, during the discussions of the workshop several participants questioned my inclusion of Chile in the same group as Costa Rica and Uruguay. I am unsure about this matter.

91. The extent and in relation to what cases of the originating countries this may be permissible is a moot question that I cannot discuss here.

92. This point is stressed by Karl in her comments.

93. Catherine Conaghan (in her comments) puts it well: "Policies promoting democratic development and economic development cannot and should not be segregated. . . . With good reason, people become skeptical about the authenticity of democracy when essential decisions affecting their quality of life are simply imposed by governments responding to the strictures of international financial institutions."

94. As Osvaldo Iazzetta discusses in his comments, this is the sad paradox of a cycle politically inclusive and socially exclusionary.

95. The tone of these assertions is tentative because important data-gathering efforts are pending in Latin America. It is important to collect and make compatible the large quantities of relevant data existing in various state, international, and private institutions.

96. In O'Donnell 1998b and 2001 I discuss some possible political coalitions related to this point.

97. See Scott 1985. The seminal argument for the positive uses of the law in the struggles of the popular sector is Thompson 1975.

98. Indeed, the *Human Development Reports* have been criticized in this respect, to my mind not without reason.

99. Among these rights are participation, freedom of physical movement, and due process or fair trial.

100. These capabilities, which Nussbaum also deems as rights, are to "life; bodily health; senses, imagination and thoughts; emotions; practical reason; affiliation; other species; play; and control over one's environment" (2000b: 78–80; 1997: 287–89) (some of these rights have their own subcategories). In addition, Nussbaum further distinguishes among basic, internal, and combined capabilities (2000b: 84, 85).

101. UNDP 2000a begins with a rather minimal list ("the three essential capabilities are for people to lead a long and healthy life, to be knowledgeable, and to have access to the resources needed for a decent standard of living" [17]). Throughout the report, however, a series of other capabilities and rights is added to the list (see, for example, 2, 8, 19, and 77).

102. As stated above, in the originating countries these rights were effected as civil ones long before they were "promoted" to the condition of political rights. I also noted that, quite obviously, these rights are exercised in manifold social locations, well beyond the regime.

103. Habermas puts it well: "Without basic rights that secure the private autonomy of citizens, there also would not be any medium for the legal institutionalization of

the conditions under which these citizens could make use of their public autonomy" (1999: 332).

104. This, I take it, is abundantly obvious, even by the definition of its subject matter, in the case of human rights. With respect to human development, even if less explicit, the same conception clearly can be detected in assertions such as "Human development . . . is a process of enhancing human capabilities—to expand choices and opportunities so that each person can lead a life of respect and value" (UNDP 2000a: 2, italics added).

105. I thought that in the version I presented to the workshop it was obvious that the above statement is intended to open, not foreclose, the way to the empirical exploration of the actual relationships of these and other dimensions. Some of the comments, however, have made me aware of the need to make this point more explicit.

106. Above I defined this minimal sufficient set as those rights that would be necessary and jointly sufficient for guaranteeing the existence and institutionalized persistence of a democratic regime. I also discussed various reasons that make it impossible to ever achieve generalized intersubjective agreement on a clear and firm definition of this set.

107. Specifically, Sen is discussing Robert Nozick's (1974) theory of justice. Consider, consistent with Sen's remarks, the roundabout ways (often involving views of a mythical, fully competitive market, the benefits of which would extend to everyone in due time) in which the present status quo is defended in contemporary Latin America.

108. I do not have space here to deal with this issue. For solid arguments against the anti-universalism of extreme cultural relativism, see especially Franck 2001; Garzón Valdés 1993; Nussbaum 2000b; Sen 1999a, 1999b, and 2000b; and Stepan 2000. See also Touraine 1997: "There is no multicultural society possible without universalistic principles that allow communication among socially and culturally different individuals and groups" (206, my translation).

109. I agree with the caution expressed by Karl (see her comments) to the effect that "a positive and self-reinforcing cycle, however hopeful and morally satisfying, cannot be taken for granted. This is especially true when the construction of the rule of law must be devoted to reshaping, redefining, and enhancing the interests of the broad majority of the population in highly unequal societies—and not just the status of corporations through the reform of commercial law or the protection of propertied interests through criminal law."

110. Concurrently, Dasgupta comments: "Much contemporary ethics assumes at the start of the inquiry that these [basic] needs have been met" (1993: 45). This assumption is explicit in the work of political philosophy which arguably has been the most influential in the last decades, at least in the Anglo-Saxon world. See Rawls 1971: 152, 542–43; his theory of justice is deemed to apply to countries where "only the less urgent material wants remain to be satisfied" [542]. For a restatement of this assumption see Rawls 2001.) In turn, albeit less explicitly, the same assumption is clearly entailed in the work of Habermas, probably the most influential contemporary continental European political philosopher (see, for example, Habermas 1999). The issue that remains is what can be said about countries, even ones that include a democratic regime, that do not meet this assumption.

111. This is what the Costa Rican audit calls "habilitación ciudadana mínima."

112. Holmes and Sunstein 1999; see also the comments of Conaghan, Iazzetta, and Tavares de Almeida.

113. Concerning this issue I have benefited from the comments by Laurence Whitehead. His emphasis on the socially defined character of rights, with which I agree, should dispel the view that mine is a version of "liberal individualism," as Karl fears in her comments. The fact that one of the analytical levels of a theory is centered on individuals does not make it necessarily "individualistic." Norbert Lechner's comments include apposite reflections on the inherent sociability of individual agency.

114. For an interesting analysis that stresses this aspect, see Ackerman 1980.

115. The fundamental work on these matters is Rueschemeyer, Stephens, and Stephens 1992. For Latin America and the labor movement, see Collier and Berins Collier 1991.

116. As Tavares de Almeida argues in her comments, even within Latin America there are significant variations in this matter, which would have to be taken into account when plotting possible sequences and trajectories. This important problem, which requires looking at each country individually, exceeds the possibilities of the present text.

117. This is the same situation we encountered in relation to political rights. For human development and human rights, however, the kinds of knowledge required are more varied and complicated—not only law and social science but also medical/biological and psychological knowledge for assessing, for example, the consequences of various material deprivations or types of violence.

118. For data and discussion of the situation of Latin America concerning this and related matters see Bartell and A. O'Donnell 2000. For discussion of these issues in general, see Dasgupta, who comments, "It is often said that even when a person owns no physical assets she owns one asset that is inalienable, namely *labour power* . . . [I] have revealed the important truth that this is false. . . . Conversion of potential into actual labour power can be realized if the person finds the means of making the conversion, not otherwise. Nutrition and health-care are the necessary means to this" (1993: 474).

119. Indeed, the international and national *Human Development Reports* are important steps in this direction, but to my knowledge even the data resulting from them still need to be put together and made compatible. Furthermore, the coverage of these data is still quite limited. On its part, I am impressed by the capacity of the World Bank to gather or (directly or indirectly) purchase various kinds of data; yet these data are not available in their original form for analysis by outside researchers (an important accountability issue?), and the view of development that guides their collection is quite different from the one articulated here and in the *Human Development Reports*.

120. Weale (1983) correctly insists on this point. On this basis, Weale proposes what may well be a useful rule of thumb: "The basic criterion of a social minimum . . . is that when it is satisfied persons should be able to meet the obligations that are conventionally expected of all persons in that society as producers, citizens, neighbors,

friends, and parents" (1983: 35). This in turn is based on "the principle that government should secure the conditions of equal autonomy for all persons subject to its jurisdiction" (42).

121. Some empirical studies are of considerable interest in this respect. In particular, Norman Frohlich and Joe Oppenheimer (1992) undertook a series of experiments to determine prevailing views of distributive justice. They asked their subjects (undergraduates in Canada, Poland, and the United States) to try to reach unanimous agreement as to what principle would generate "the most just distribution of income" in a society in which the subjects do not know in advance in what position they will be (Rawls's [1971] "veil of ignorance"). The principles were (1) "Maximize the floor (or lowest) income in the society"; (2) "Maximize the average income" (Harsanyi's [1975] principle of "maximum average utility"); (3) "Maximize the average income only after guaranteeing that the difference between the poorest and richest individuals . . . is no greater than a specified amount" (Rawls's [1971] "difference principle"); (4) "Maximize the average income only after a certain specified minimum income is guaranteed for everyone"; or (5) any other principle the subjects wished to formulate (Frohlich and Oppenheimer 1992: 35). The authors conducted a total of seventy-six relevant experiments; a remarkable 78% of these groups agreed on choosing criterion 4 without a ceiling; that is, establishing a guaranteed minimum for everyone and beyond it no restriction on how well-off some of them could be (ibid., 59). Notice that this is equivalent to choosing the basic rights and capabilities I have been discussing. Furthermore, Frohlich and Oppenheimer report that "democracy matter[ed]" in their experiments: the more open and extended discussions were during the experiments, the firmer and more stable the support for this principle was. See their study for further details. For a thoughtful argument in favor of this "floor" criterion, see Waldron 1999.

122. In his comments Whitehead rightly stresses that in Latin America whatever rights are conquered tend to be more easily reversed or cancelled than in the originating countries; as he graphically puts it, in the former "rights that seemed to be assured can abruptly evaporate."

123. I have not had space here to deal with important and complex issues of legal and cultural pluralism. Let me just note that, in contemporary times, democracies have dealt with these issues much more decently than authoritarian regimes. Of course, much remains to be done, and the intersection of the rule of law (even a democratic one) with communal legal systems (especially of indigenous communities) does not prevent the emergence of extremely complex and, at times, conflictive problems. Yet I take it that a rule of law of this kind should be able to deal with these matters in the universalistically decent and respectful ways that is demanded by its own premises.

124. I am using *elective affinity* in the sense originally used by Goethe, from whom Weber borrowed this metaphor: two or more components that do not cause each other but that exert strong and—to use a contemporary term—synergistic mutual influence.

125. I refer again to the comments by Méndez, who points to several problematic issues that will have to be dealt with if these convergences are to bear full fruit.

126. Remember that this consideration was made as early as Athens and that it drove the development of the welfare state in the originating countries.

127. This procedure is tantamount to the "precising" of a definition that Collier and Levitsky (1997) have usefully discussed.

128. Or the "map" of peaks, valleys, holes, and other geographical images that the Costa Rican audit (Proyecto Estado de la Nación 2001: 46 and passim) has imaginatively drawn with its data.

129. Thus, in spite of some misunderstandings that my original text has apparently provoked, I agree with the general bent of the comments by Alcántara, Mazzuca, Gerardo Munck, and Coppedge. For example, the latter argues that "we need not formulate any absolute right or list of absolute rights; we only need to know how much of each good corresponds to what degree of democracy." On the other hand, a major methodological issue that this chapter and the following comments leave pending is if it would be possible or convenient to reduce these vectors to some kind of index (see the comments by Munck and the literature cited therein).

130. By "democratic rules" I mean that the pertinent public institutions have proceeded in ways that correspond to the respective items in the preceding excursi.

131. For example, conservatives might assert that democracy is exclusively about the regime and that, even within it, increased participation would hamper the achievement of other values, such as political stability, the efficacy of economic policy, and others.

132. Another way to deal with this problem is to simply abstain from discussing these issues as relevant to a theory of politics and/or democracy. See, for example, the great care with which, in his various adjustments to his "theory of justice," Rawls has consistently argued that it does not apply to social institutions such as the ones I enumerate above (for a recent statement see Rawls 2001).

133. This point is usefully stressed in the comments of Conaghan and Lechner.

134. Even though, as noted, some may disagree as to the desirability of advancing in the democraticness of some of these items.

135. Indeed, the Costa Rican audit is an excellent example of how, with a good dose of imagination and effort, some of these difficulties may be overcome.

136. Furthermore, as I suggest above, there is every reason to foster cooperation in gathering, analyzing, and making compatible data among the respective institutions.

137. In making these recommendations and the ones that follow, I am closely following the criteria used by the Costa Rican audit (Proyecto Estado de la Nación 2001: 30–31), including its setting of standards for both the *Umbral Mínimo de Garantías Democráticas* and the *Umbral Superior de Calidad Democrática*. For more and valuable details I refer the reader to these two volumes as well as to the paper that their coauthors prepared for our workshop.

138. On adaptive (or endogenous) preferences see the seminal work of Elster (1985). Sen has emphasized this matter in several of his works as part of his critique of utilitarianism in its various versions and of Rawls's primary goods. In particular, Sen correctly warns against taking at face value the modest preferences that might be

expressed by severely deprived individuals. As he wryly comments, "The hopeless underdog loses the courage to desire a better deal and learns to take pleasure from small mercies. . . . The deprivations appear muffled and muted in the metric of utilities" (Sen 1984b: 512; see also Sen 1985a, and 1992).

139. These conceptual locations are exemplified by the standards used by the citizen audit and by the items I include in the excursi.

140. I should point out that this is my own reconstruction of the logic of the methodological steps adopted by the audit.

141. I say *per se* because the data, methodological experimentation, and revision of conceptual categories induced by the incorporation of internal views all constitute a very rich mine for fostering theoretical/academic research and advances.

142. Or, as I put in the "Decalogue," *un juego de espejos* (a "hall of mirrors") for this purpose (Proyecto Estado de la Nación 2001).

143. The efforts that the leaders of the Costa Rican audit are making in this direction are one of the many commendable aspects of this undertaking.

144. A good example of transpositional objectivity *avant la lettre* is the various methodologies and the combination of judgments by experts and well-informed citizens used in the audit.

145. This is a useful article for the interpretation of this and related aspects of Sen's work.

146. Although, disturbingly, in Latin America various studies and media reports show in several countries quite broad support for the arbitrary detention, torture, and even lynching of suspected criminals. Furthermore, demagogic politicians and mass media feed these feelings and the fear of social violence that underlies them.

147. Tilly has produced valuable works on this and related matters; see especially 1998, 1999a, and 1999b. Tilly concludes that "rights [are] historical products, outcomes of struggle" (1998: 5). For relevant references to Latin America, see Huber, Rueschemeyer, and Stephens 1997 and Huber and Stephens 1999; more generally in relation to the Latin American popular sector see Alvarez, Dagnino, and Escobar 1998 and Foweraker and Landman 1997.

148. A relevant example is the important differences in the welfare state and its policies exhibited among these countries.

149. Concurrently, Sartori comments that "What democracy *is* cannot be separated from what democracy *should be* . . . in a democracy the tension between facts and values reaches the highest point" (1967: 4; italics in the original), while Shapiro notes "[D]emocracy's historical association with opposition to unjust social arrangements" (1996: 6). In the same vein we see also Furet 1998 and Rosanvallon 1995.

150. In her comments, Tavares de Almeida draws an appropriate corollary: "The quality of democracy is not . . . an inquiry externally imposed by political scientists or philosophers. It is a question that springs from the very functioning of democratic systems. . . . it is a question that emerges from the comparison between democratic ideals and values with the reality of polyarchies."

BIBLIOGRAPHY

Ackerman, Bruce. 1980. *Social Justice in the Liberal State.* New Haven, Conn.: Yale University Press.

Alvarez, S., E. Dagnino, and E. Escobar, eds. 1998. *Cultures of Politics, Politics of Cultures: Re-Visioning Latin American Social Movements.* Boulder, Colo.: Westview Press.

Anderson, Perry. 1974. *Lineages of the Absolutist State.* London: NLB.

Aristotle. 1968. *The Politics.* Edited by Ernest Baker. Oxford: Oxford University Press.

Bartell, Ernest, C. S. C., and Alejandro O'Donnell, eds. 2000. *The Child in Latin America: Health, Development, and Rights.* Notre Dame, Ind.: University of Notre Dame Press.

Beetham, David, et al. 2002. *Democracy under Blair: A Democratic Audit in the United Kingdom.* London: Politico's Publishing.

Beitz, Charles R. 1989. *Political Equality: An Essay in Democratic Theory.* Princeton, N.J.: Princeton University Press.

Berger, Peter, and Thomas Luckman. 1966. *The Social Construction of Reality: A Treatise in the Sociology of Knowledge.* New York: Doubleday.

Berlin, Isaiah. 1969. *Four Essays on Liberty.* Oxford: Oxford University Press.

Berman, Harold J. 1993. *Law and Revolution: The Formation of the Western Legal Tradition.* Cambridge, Mass.: Harvard University Press.

Bobbio, Norberto. 1989. *Democracy and Dictatorship: The Nature and Limits of State Power.* Minneapolis: University of Minnesota Press.

Brinks, D. 2002. "Informal Institutions and the Rule of Law: The Judicial Response to State Killings in Buenos Aires and São Paulo in the 1990s." Paper presented at the Conference on Informal Institutions and Politics in the Developing World, Harvard University.

Calvo, Ernesto, and Juan Manuel Abal Medina, eds. 2001. *El Federalismo Electoral Argentino: Sobrerrepresentación, Reforma Política y Gobierno Dividido en la Argentina.* Buenos Aires: INAP/Eudeba.

Centro de Estudios Legales y Sociales (CELS). 1998. *La Inseguridad Policial: Violencia de las Fuerzas de Seguridad en la Argentina.* Buenos Aires: Eudeba.

Collier, David, and Ruth Berins Collier. 1991. *Shaping the Political Arena: Critical Junctures, the Labor Movement, and Regime Dynamics in Latin America.* Princeton, N.J.: Princeton University Press.

Collier, David, and Stephen Levitsky. 1997. "Democracy with Adjectives: Conceptual Innovation in Comparative Research." *World Politics* 49, no. 3: 430–51.

Dahl, Robert. 1989. *Democracy and Its Critics.* New Haven, Conn.: Yale University Press.

———. 1998. *On Democracy.* New Haven, Conn.: Yale University Press.

Dalton, Russell. 1999. "Political Support in Advanced Industrial Democracies." In *Critical Citizens: Global Support for Democratic Governance,* edited by Pippa Norris. Oxford: Oxford University Press, 56–77.

Dasgupta, Partha. 1993. *An Inquiry into Well-Being and Destitution.* Oxford: Clarendon Press.

Dellasoppa, Emilio, Alicia Bercovich, and Eduardo Arriaga. 1999. "Violência, Direitos Civis e Demografía no Brasil na Década de 80." *Revista Brasileira de Ciências Sociais* 14, no. 39: 155–76.

Domingo, Pilar. 1999. "Judicial Independence and Judicial Reform in Latin America." In *The Self-Restraining State: Power and Accountability in New Democracies,* edited by Andreas Schedler, Larry Diamond, and Mark Plattner. Boulder, Colo.: Lynne Rienner, 151–75.

Domingo, Pilar, and Rachel Seider, eds. 2001. *Rule of Law in Latin America: The International Promotion of Judicial Reform.* London: Institute of Latin American Studies.

Dworkin, Ronald. 1986. *Law's Empire.* Cambridge, Mass.: Harvard University Press.

Elklit, Jorgen, and Palle Svensson. 1997. "What Makes Elections Free and Fair?" *Journal of Democracy* 8, no. 3: 32–46.

Elster, Jon. 1985. *Sour Grapes: Studies in the Subversion of Rationality.* Cambridge and Paris: Cambridge University Press and Editions de la Maison des Sciences de l'Homme.

Fábre, Cécile. 1998. "Constitutionalising Social Rights." *Journal of Political Philosophy* 6, no. 3: 263–84.

Foweraker, J., and T. Landman. 1997. *Citizen Rights and Social Movements: A Comparative and Statistical Analysis.* New York: Oxford University Press.

Franck, Thomas. 2001. "Are Human Rights Universal?" *Foreign Affairs* 80, no. 1: 191–204.

Frohlich, Norman, and Joe Oppenheimer. 1992. *Choosing Justice: An Experimental Approach to Ethical Theory.* Berkeley: University of California Press.

Fuller, Lon. 1964. *The Morality of Law.* New Haven, Conn.: Yale University Press.

Furet, Francois. 1998. "Democracy and Utopia." *Journal of Democracy* 9, no. 1: 65–81.

Garretón, Manuel Antonio. 1987. *Reconstruir la Política: Transición y Consolidación Democrática en Chile.* Santiago: Editorial Andante.

Garzón Valdés, Ernesto. 1993. *Derecho, Etica y Política.* Madrid: Centro de Estudios Constitucionales.

———. 2001. "Prólogo." In *Liberalismo, Estado de Derecho y Minorías,* by Rodolfo Vázquez, 11–26.. México DF: Paidós.

Gewirth, Alan. 1978. *Reason and Morality.* Chicago: University of Chicago Press.

Goldstein, Robert. 1983. *Political Repression in Europe.* London: Croom Helm.

Gray, John. 2000. *Two Faces of Liberalism.* New York: Free Press.

Habermas, Jürgen. 1988. "Law as Medium and Law as Institution." In *Dilemmas of Law in the Welfare State,* edited by Gunther Teubner, 204–20. New York and Berlin: de Gruyter.

———. 1996. *Between Facts and Norms.* Cambridge, Mass.: MIT Press.

———. 1999. "Introduction." *Ratio Juris* 12, no. 4: 329–35.

Hamburger, Philip A. 1989. "The Development of the Nineteenth-Century Consensus Theory of Contract." *Law and History Review* 7, no. 2: 241–329.

Hamilton, Lawrence. 1999. "A Theory of True Interests in the Work of Amartya Sen." *Government and Opposition* 34, no. 4: 516–46.

Hansen, M. H. 1991. *The Athenian Democracy in the Age of Demosthenes.* Oxford: Oxford University Press.

Harsanyi, John. 1975. "Can the Maximum Principle Serve as the Basis of Morality? A Critique of John Rawls' Theory." *American Political Science Review* 69: 690–705.

Hart, Herbert L. A. 1961. *The Concept of Law.* Oxford: Clarendon Press.

Hinton, Mercedes. 2003. "Defaulting on Public Security: The Politics of Police and State Reform in Argentina and Brazil." Ph.D. diss., Faculty of Social and Political Sciences, University of Cambridge.

Hirschman, Albert O. 1991. *The Rhetoric of Reaction.* Cambridge, Mass.: Belknap Press of Harvard University Press.

Holmes, Stephen, and Cass Sunstein. 1999. *The Cost of Rights: Why Liberty Depends on Taxes.* New York: W.W. Norton.

Hsieh, Ching-Chi, and M. D. Pugh. 1993. "Poverty, Income Inequality, and Violent Crime: A Meta-Analysis of Recent Aggregate Data Studies." *Criminal Justice Review* 18, no. 2: 182–202.

Huber, Evelyne, Dietrich Rueschemeyer, and John D. Stephens. 1997. "The Paradoxes of Contemporary Democracy: Formal, Participatory, and Social Democracy." *Comparative Politics* 29, no. 3: 323–42.

Huber, Evelyne, and John D. Stephens. 1999. "The Bourgeoisie and Democracy: Historical and Comparative Perspectives." *Social Research* 66, no. 3.

Huntington, Samuel P. 1991. *The Third Wave: Democratization in the Late Twentieth Century.* Norman and London: University of Oklahoma Press.

Iazzetta, Osvaldo. 2003. "La Democracia y los Vaivenes de lo Público-Estatal." *Revista SAAP* 1, no. 2: 377–409.

Jones, Peter. 1994. *Rights.* New York: St. Martin's Press.

Kelsen, Hans. 1967. *Pure Theory of Law.* Berkeley: University of California Press.

Lacey, Nicola. 2001. "Responsibility and Modernity in Criminal Law." *Journal of Political Philosophy* 9, no. 3: 249–76.

Lane, Robert. 1988. "Procedural Goods in a Democracy: How One is Treated Versus What One Gets." *Social Justice Research* 2, no. 3: 177–92.

Lechner, Norbert. 2000. "Desafios de un Desarrollo Humano: Individualizacion y Capital Social." *Instituciones y Desarrollo* 7: 7–34.

Linz, Juan J., and Alfred Stepan. 1996. *Problems of Democratic Transition and Consolidation: Southern Europe, South America, and Post-Communist Europe.* Baltimore, Md.: Johns Hopkins University Press.

Margalit, Avishai. 1996. *The Decent Society.* Cambridge, Mass.: Harvard University Press.

Marshall, T. H. 1964. "Citizenship and Social Class." In *Class, Citizenship and Social Development,* edited by T. H. Marshall. Garden City, N.Y.: Doubleday.

Mazzuca, Sebastián. 1998. "Que es y que no es la democratizacion?" *Estudios Políticos,* no. 19: 73–122.

———. 1999. "Acesso al poder *versus* ejercicio del poder. Democracia y Patrimonialismo en América Latina." Berkeley: University of California at Berkeley, Department of Political Science, photocopy.

Méndez, Juan, Guillermo O'Donnell, and Paulo Sérgio Pinheiro, eds. 1999. *The Rule of Law and the Underprivileged in Latin America.* Notre Dame, Ind.: University of Notre Dame Press.

Mill, John Stuart. 1962. *On Liberty.* Glasgow: Collins/Fontana.

Mouffe, Chantal. 1996. "Democracy, Power, and the 'Political.'" In *Democracy and Difference: Contesting the Boundaries of the Political,* edited by Seyla Benhabib, 245–56. Princeton, N.J.: Princeton University Press.

———. 2000. *The Democratic Paradox.* London: Verso.

Netll, J. 1968. "The State as a Conceptual Variable." *World Politics* 20, no. 4: 559–92.

Newey, Glen. 1998. "Value-Pluralism in Contemporary Liberalism." *Dialogue,*439–552.

Nozick, Robert. 1974. *Anarchy, State, and Utopia.* New York: Basic Books.

Nussbaum, Martha. 1997. "Capabilities and Human Rights." *Fordham Law Review* 66, no. 2: 273–300.

———. 2000a. "Aristotle, Politics, and Human Capabilities: A Response to Antony, Arneson, Charlesworth, and Mulgan." *Ethics* 111: 102–40.

———. 2000b. *Women and Human Development: The Capabilities Approach.* Cambridge: Cambridge University Press.

O'Donnell, Guillermo. 1993. "On the State, Democratization and Some Conceptual Problems: A Latin American View with Glances at Some Postcommunist Countries." *World Development* 21, no. 8: 1345–69.

———. 1996. "Illusions about Consolidation." *Journal of Democracy* 7, no. 2: 34–51.

———. 1998a. "Horizontal Accountability and New Polyarchies." In *The Self-Restraining State: Power and Accountability in New Democracies,* edited by Andreas Schedler et al., 29–52. Boulder, Colo.: Lynne Rienner.

———. 1998b. "Poverty and Inequality in Latin America: Some Political Reflections." In *Poverty and Inequality in Latin America: Issues and New Challenges,* edited by Victor Tokman and Guillermo O'Donnell, 49–71. Notre Dame, Ind.: University of Notre Dame Press.

———. 1999a. *Counterpoints: Selected Essays on Authoritarianism and Democracy.* Notre Dame, Ind.: University of Notre Dame Press.

———. 1999b. "Polyarchies and the (Un)Rule of Law in Latin America." In *The Rule of Law and the Underprivileged in Latin America,* edited by Juan Méndez et al., 303–37. Notre Dame, Ind.: University of Notre Dame Press.

———. 2000. "Democracy, Law, and Comparative Politics." Working Paper no. 274. Notre Dame, Ind.: Kellogg Institute. Abridged version in *Studies in International Comparative Development* 36, no.1 (Spring 2001): 5–36.

———. 2001. "Reflections on Contemporary Latin American Democracies." *Journal of Latin American Studies* (Fall): 57–82.

———. 2002. "Notas sobre Varias 'Accountabilities' y sus Interrelaciones." In *Controlando la Politica: Ciudadanos y Medios en las Nuevas Democracias,* edited by Catalina Smulovitz and Enrique Peruzzotti, 87–102. Buenos Aires: Paidós.

———. 2003. "Horizontal Accountability: The Legal Institutionalization of Mistrust." In *Accountability, Governance and Political Institutions in Latin America,* edited by Scott Mainwaring and Christopher Welna, 48–77. (New York: Oxford University Press).

O'Donnell, Guillermo, and Philippe Schmitter. 1986. *Transitions from Authoritarian Rule: Tentative Conclusions about Uncertain Democracies.* Baltimore, Md.: Johns Hopkins University Press.

Oszlak, Oscar, and Guillermo O'Donnell. 1984. "Estado y Políticas Estatales en América Latina: Hacia una Estrategia de Investigación." In *Teoría de la Burocracia Estatal. Enfoques Críticos,* edited by Oscar Oszlak. Buenos Aires: Paidós.

Peruzzotti, Enrique, and Catalina Smulovitz, eds. 2002. *Controlando la Politica: Ciudadanos y Medios en las Nuevas Democracias.* Buenos Aires: Paidós.

Preuss, Ulrich. 1986. "The Concept of Rights and the Welfare State." In *Dilemmas of Law in the Welfare State,* edited by G. Teubner, 151–72. New York and Berlin: de Gruyter.

———. 1996a. "Two Challenges to European Citizenship." *Political Studies* 44, no. 3: 534–52.

———. 1996b. "The Political Meaning of Constitutionalism." In *Constitutionalism, Democracy, and Sovereignty: American and European Perspectives,* edited by Richard Bellamy, 11–27. Aldershot: Avebury.

Proyecto Estado de la Nación (coauthored by Jorge Vargas Cullell, Evelyn Villareal, and Miguel Gutiérrez Saxe). 2001. *Auditoría Ciudadana sobre la Calidad de la Democracia,* 2 vols. San José: Proyecto Estado de la Nación en Desarrollo Humano Sostenible.

Przeworski, Adam. 1988. "Democracy as a Contingent Outcome of Conflicts." In *Constitutionalism and Democracy,* edited by J. Elster and R. Slagstad, 59–80. Cambridge: Cambridge University Press.

———. 1991. *Democracy and the Market: Political and Economic Reforms in Eastern Europe and Latin America.* Cambridge: Cambridge University Press.

Przeworski, Adam, et al. 2000. *Democracy and Development: Political Institutions and Well-Being in the World, 1950–1990.* Cambridge: Cambridge University Press.

Rawls, John. 1971. *A Theory of Justice.* Cambridge, Mass.: Harvard University Press.

———. 1993. *Political Liberalism.* New York: Columbia University Press.

———. 2001. *Justice as Fairness: A Restatement.* Cambridge, Mass: Belknap Press of Harvard University Press.

Raz, Joseph. 1986. *The Morality of Freedom.* Oxford: Clarendon Press.

——— . 1994. *Ethics in the Public Domain: Essays in the Morality of Law and Politics.* Oxford: Clarendon Press.

Regis, Edward Jr., ed. 1984. *Gewirth's Ethical Rationalism: Critical Essays with a Reply by Alan Gewirth.* Chicago: University of Chicago Press.

Rosanvallon, Pierre. 1992. *Le Sacre du Citoyen: Histoire de Sufrage Universel en France.* Paris: Gallimard.

———. 1995. "The History of the Word 'Democracy' in France." *Journal of Democracy* 6, no. 4: 140–54.

Rueschemeyer, Dietrich, Evelyne Huber Stephens, and John D. Stephens. 1992. *Capitalist Development and Democracy.* Chicago: Chicago University Press.

Sartori, Giovanni. 1967. *Democratic Theory.* New York: Praeger Publishers.

Schneewind, J. B. 1998. *The Invention of Autonomy: A History of Modern Moral Philosophy.* Cambridge: Cambridge University Press.

Scott, James. 1985. *Weapons of the Weak: Everyday Forms of Peasant Resistance.* New Haven, Conn.: Yale University Press.

Sen, Amartya. 1984a. "Rights and Capabilities." In *Resources, Values and Development,* edited by Amartya Sen, 307–45. Cambridge, Mass.: Harvard University Press.

———. 1984b. "Goods and People." In *Resources, Values and Development,* edited by Amartya Sen. Cambridge, Mass.: Harvard University Press.

———. 1985a. "Rights as Goals (Austin Lecture)." In *Equality and Discrimination: Essays in Freedom and Justice,* edited by Stephen Guest and Alan Milne. Stuttgart: Franz Steiner Verlag.

———. 1985b. "Well-being, Agency, and Freedom: The Dewey Lectures 1984." *Journal of Philosophy,* 82, no. 4: 169–221.

———. 1992. *Inequality Reexamined.* Cambridge, Mass.: Harvard University Press.

———. 1993. "Positional Objectivity." *Philosophy and Public Affairs* 22, no. 2: 126–45.

———. 1995. "Rationality and Social Choice." *American Economic Review* 85, no. 1: 1–24.

———. 1999a. "Democracy as a Universal Value." *Journal of Democracy* 10, no. 3: 3–17.

———. 1999b. *Development as Freedom.* New York: Alfred A. Knopf.

———. 2000a. "A Decade of Human Development." *Journal of Human Development* 1, no. 1: 17–24.

———. 2000b. "East and West: The Reach of Reason." *New York Review of Books* 47, no. 12: 33–38.

Shapiro, Ian. 1996. *Democracy's Place.* Ithaca, N.Y.: Cornell University Press.

Shue, Henry. 1996. *Basic Rights: Subsistence, Affluence, and U.S. Foreign Policy.* Princeton, N.J.: Princeton University Press.

Skinner, Quentin. 1984. "The Idea of Negative Liberty: Philosophical and Historical Perspectives." In *Philosophy in History: Essays on the Historiography of Philosophy,* edited by Richard Rorty et al., 193–211. Cambridge: Cambridge University Press.

Smulovitz, Catalina, and Enrique Peruzzotti. 2000. "Social Accountability in Latin America." *Journal of Democracy* 11, no. 4: 147–58.

Snyder, Richard, and David Samuels. 2001. "Devaluing the Vote: Latin America." *Journal of Democracy* 12, no. 1: 146–59.

Stanley, Ruth. 2003. *Policing Argentina: Citizenship and Coercion.* Berlin: Habilitationsschrift, Freie Universität Berlin.

Stepan, Alfred. 2000. "Religion, Democracy, and the 'Twin Tolerations.'" *Journal of Democracy* 11, no. 4: 37–57.

Teubner, G., ed. 1986. *Dilemmas of Law in the Welfare State.* New York and Berlin: de Gruyter.

Thompson, E. P. 1975. *Whigs and Hunters: The Origins of the Black Act.* New York: Pantheon.

Tilly, Charles. 1985. "War Making and State Making as Organized Crime." In *Bringing the State Back In,* edited by Peter Evans et al., 169–91. Cambridge: Cambridge University Press.

———. 1990. *Coercion, Capital and European States.* Cambridge: Blackwell.

———. 1998. "Where Do Rights Come From?" In *Democracy, Revolution, and History,* edited by Theda Skocpol, 55–72. Ithaca, N.Y.: Cornell University Press.

———. 1999a. "Now Where?" In *State/Culture: State Formation after the Cultural Turn,* edited by George Steinmetz, 407–20. Ithaca, N.Y.: Cornell University Press.

———. 1999b. "Conclusion: Why Worry About Citizenship?" In *Extending Citizenship, Reconfiguring States,* edited by M. Hanagan and C. Tilly, 247–59. Lanham, Md.: Rowan and Littlefield.

Touraine, Alain. 1997. *Pourrons-nous Vivre Ensemble? Égaux et Différents.* Paris: Fayard.

Tyler, Tom. 1990. *Why People Obey the Law.* New Haven, Conn.: Yale University Press.

———. 2000. "Multiculturalism and the Willingness of Citizens to Defer to Law and Legal Authorities." *Law and Social Inquiry* 25, no. 4: 983–1020.

United Nations Development Program (UNDP). 2000a. *Human Development Report 2000: Human Rights and Human Development.* New York: Oxford University Press.

———. 2000b. *Poverty Report 2000: Overcoming Human Poverty.* New York: Oxford University Press.

Valenzuela, J. Samuel. 1992. "Democratic Consolidation in Post-Transitional Settings: Notion, Process, and Facilitating Conditions." In *Issues in Democratic Consolidation: The New South American Democracies in Comparative Perspective,* edited by Scott Mainwaring, Guillermo O'Donnell, and J. Samuel Valenzuela, 57–104. Notre Dame, Ind.: University of Notre Dame Press.

Vázquez, Rodolfo. 2001. *Liberalismo, Estado de Derecho y Minorías.* México DF: Paidós.

Waldron, Jeremy. 1999. *Law and Disagreement.* Oxford: Clarendon Press.

Weale, Albert. 1983. *Political Theory and Social Policy.* New York: St. Martin's Press.

Weber, Max. 1968. *Economy and Society.* 2 vols. Berkeley: University of California Press.

chapter 2

Democracy and the Quality of Democracy

Empirical Findings and Methodological and Theoretical Issues Drawn from the Citizen Audit of the Quality of Democracy in Costa Rica

JORGE VARGAS CULLELL

This chapter analyzes the complex links between democracy and issues surrounding the quality of democracy based on the experience and potential of the Citizen Audit of the Quality of Democracy in Costa Rica (hereafter referred to as the citizen audit). The audit is a tool for identifying (and acting upon) the problems of a democracy within an entire country or part of it. It contributes to this aim by assessing the current state of affairs, developing a system whereby democratic performance is observed and surveyed, and generating deliberation processes. This assessment leads to issues that are relevant to comparative democratic theory and methodology, but which have not received enough attention by scholars. The following discussion relies heavily on the lessons learned through the audit carried out in Costa Rica between

1998 and 2001, as well as on the partial update of its findings made by the 2001, 2002, and 2003 Costa Rican *Report on the State of the Nation in Human Development* and the 2003 *Second Central American Human Development Report* (PEN 2001c, 2002, and 2003; PNUD2003).

The empirical, methodological, and theoretical issues laid out below take as a starting point the citizen audit's two driving questions. On the one hand, in the absence of a theory regarding the quality of democracy, how can one make an empirical study of how democratic the political life of a democracy is (Dahl 1999, 1996; Linz 1997; Lijphart 1999; and see O'Donnell's chapter in this volume). This is the *democraticness question*. On the other hand, taking into account the widespread citizen discontent with regard to democratic performance, how can an assessment of political life become a tool for encouraging citizen participation in public affairs? This is the *civicness question*.

I will propose that, provided certain conditions are complied with, the citizen audit can be a springboard for exploring a new approach to democracy in which both its regime and, in particular, its nonregime dimensions are analyzed. I argue that research on dimensions of democracy that go beyond the political regime requires new data from that currently used in democratic studies. To this end, the audit used a variety of methods involving citizen participation at various stages of its implementation. These methods adapted previous international experiences in the evaluation and quality control of processes to the research of political issues. Finally, the citizen audit encourages new systems of citizen participation in the deliberation and evaluation of public affairs (societal accountability),[1] which clearly influence aspects of political life such as the agendas of political actors and the formulation of public policies.

In considering these matters, I make evident the difficulties involved in conducting an audit and the tentative and partial nature of the statements made here. The audit is, for the most part, an adventure through the (largely) unexplored terrain of democratic life beyond the regime. That is the reason why this chapter does not provide answers to all questions, although it does trace a basic map of relevant issues and proposes ideas to guide discussion on the quality of democracy. The need for new perspectives and methods, however, reminds us that largely unresearched topics such as the quality of democracy demand, in the words of C.W. Mills, exercises in "sociological imagination" (Mills 1959).

This chapter summarizes theoretical and methodological issues that have been discussed extensively in other works. I try not to repeat these arguments here, and I invite the reader to consult the sources directly.[2] I also deal with many issues discussed in Guillermo O'Donnell's chapter in this volume.

Where possible, I avoid reiterating points of view already mentioned by O'Donnell, to whom I am personally and intellectually indebted, in order to give an added value to my analysis.[3]

Finally, it is worth issuing a warning: The quality of a democracy is a wider issue than the citizen audit. The quality of a democracy may be studied using research methods other than an audit. I do not suggest that the audit is the best method, or that it is the only one. I aim to show, however, that an audit is an innovative tool that links participatory research and civic action and that, in given circumstances, this combination impacts the quality of a democracy and academic reflections regarding democracy.

The chapter is divided into six sections. Because little, if anything, is known about the audit, I begin by describing its main components and activities and the reasons for proceeding along these lines. Building upon this overview, the second section highlights the lessons learned and implications of the experience. I comment on issues such as the feasibility of a citizen audit, the strengths and weaknesses of the process of establishing standards with regard to the quality of democracy, the scope of citizen participation, and the assessment of the results. The third section presents some of the main findings of the Costa Rican audit. It is a selective presentation rather than a summary of the contents of the final report, and, thus, it aims to convey a sense of the wealth of data collected by the audit. The fourth section places the Costa Rican quality of democracy assessment within a larger regional context through a comparative glance at recent democratization processes in Central America. The fifth section analyzes both the findings and the method of the audit from a theoretical viewpoint. I conclude with some brief final thoughts.

1. The Basic Concept of the Citizen Audit

A citizen audit examines and assesses the political life and institutional performance of the democracy of an entire country or part of it (province, district, or municipality). It is (a) a system for monitoring and assessing the strengths and weaknesses of democratic life, with citizen participation in its different stages of implementation; (b) a new practice of political deliberation on public affairs; and (c) an exploration of people's day-to-day experience of living in a democracy using the notion of the quality of a democracy as a conceptual tool.

The audit is, at its most basic level, a deliberation (conversation or dialogue) between citizens concerning their democracy based on formal rules in order to arrive at a specific goal: to provide an informed assessment of the quality of their democracy. These formal rules provide people with access to general information and allow them to establish the conditions and criteria required for the assessment; the rules are also designed to facilitate dialogue and guarantee the utmost precision possible with regard to the meaning of the qualifications and the agreements and disagreements between these citizens.

The pillars of this initiative are two novel ideas: the quality of democracy and the citizen audit. The idea of the quality of democracy used in the audit comes from a document created for Costa Rica's State of the Nation Project and is based on a review of political science literature (Gutiérrez and Vargas Cullell 1998). For the purpose of the audit, the *quality of democracy* was defined as the extent to which political life and institutional performance in a country (or part of it) with a democratic regime coincides with the democratic aspirations of its citizens. This definition is largely an ad hoc working tool; its purpose was to facilitate the evaluation exercise—not to create a new theoretical concept or change the meaning of existing ones (Sartori 1991). From the beginning this idea was influenced by Guillermo O'Donnell's views on the problems and challenges of Latin American democracies and, in particular, by his insight into the fact that democracy may include dimensions beyond a political regime.

In contrast, the idea of the audit was adopted from the field of managerial science and, in particular, from its implementation by the International Standardization Organization (ISO) in relation to evaluating the quality of processes and the environment. In an audit the records and reports of an organization are examined by an outside entity or group "in order to ensure full accountability and to aid in . . . the fulfillment of assigned responsibilities" (General Accounting Office 1988; Reider 1994). An audit is not just an assessment. It involves a systematic examination, in the most exhaustive manner possible, of accounts (or records) to ensure accountability.

The First Pillar: The Idea of the Quality of Democracy

The definition of quality of democracy used in the audit and State of the Nation Project combines descriptive, normative, and evaluative components as a way to empirically assess the democraticness question. The descriptive components are the democratic regime,[4] citizenship, institutional performance, and political life. The normative component is the idea of democratic aspirations, and the evaluative component is the study of the extent to which aspirations and real practices coincide. These latter issues are built into the concept because studying the "quality" of something implies at least two things: a variable proportion of an attribute and a way of measuring that proportion. Quality is not a binary characteristic (for example, high or low quality), although for analytical purposes it may be divided into binary categories. Thus defined, quality of democracy is a low-level concept on the "abstraction ladder."[5]

From the onset, the quality of democracy was proposed as a multidimensional concept whereby the quality of each dimension of democracy can and should be assessed in terms of the "distance" between the actual practice of democracy and its normative horizon. In turn, this distance reflects the capacity of citizens to develop democratic practices for handling public affairs.[6] This ability can vary among dimensions. Moreover, in the citizen audit it was pointed out that the quality of democracy is not a general attribute of the whole democratic system but rather the accumulated effect of institutional performance and citizens' interactions on multiple fronts (Pérez-Liñán 1998).

It is worth looking more closely at the various components of the definition of the quality of democracy. The concept of a democratic regime is important because it establishes the minimum institutional framework needed for the study of the quality of a democracy. By definition, the latter deals with the greater or lesser extent to which citizens are able to make use of their civil and political rights and liberties. According to this definition, however, a political regime is not the subject of the study but rather a necessary condition of it. The subjects of a quality of democracy inquiry are the *political life* and the *institutional performance* that unfolds once a regime is in place. Political life should be understood as the political practices[7] established on a daily basis among citizens, their leaders and civil servants (who are also citizens), and others who are not citizens (for example, children and foreigners)[8] regarding the handling of public affairs both at the level of the regime and beyond it (Gutiérrez and Vargas Cullell 1998).[9] In turn, institutional performance is assessed in terms of normative democratic standards such as openness to public scrutiny, effectiveness of accountability, and the opportunities for citizen participation in determining policy priorities and policy implementation.

Democratic aspiration constitutes the central component of the quality of democracy idea because it provides the yardstick with which the assessment of the distance between the normative horizon and real practices can be undertaken. Aspirations are the standards used in the evaluation and can be defined as "the characteristics of democratic life that citizens consider desirable" (Gutiérrez and Vargas Cullell 1998). They also constitute a platform from which citizens can envisage a new democratic horizon and make efforts to steer their leaders, institutions, and fellow citizens in that direction.

The standards are not ideal types (utopias), and they do not conform to a set democratic model (Held 1996). In the real world citizens constantly negotiate disagreements, which may include, of course, their respective ideas of what a democracy is or should be. They must reach certain operative formal and informal agreements, however, in order to function collectively. These agreements may also address shared criteria of what is "right about" or "wrong with" their democracy. In this sense, according to Mouffe, despite the fact that confrontation is a condition of the existence of democracy, it could not survive without certain forms of consensus on basic principles (Mouffe 2000). In the context of the audit, the standards are intersubjective agreements that express the maximum common denominator within a group of social, political, and academic leaders in Costa Rica concerning certain democratic practices that are desired and viable in their present-day democracy. In this sense, they are realistic reflections on desired characteristics that citizens realize belong to the "domain of the possible."

The expression *democratic aspiration* underlines a second characteristic of the citizen audit's standards: In assessing the democratic quality of a country, the standards cannot oppose the basic characteristics of a democratic regime. Citizens can demand more from a democracy, but not less. For example, despite the fact that a large majority of citizens may declare themselves in favor of granting the president the power to close Congress, this could not be used as a standard for assessing the quality of democracy because it opposes a basic component of democracy.

The Costa Rican citizen audit assessed thirty-three high quality of democracy aspirations. The appendix presents these democratic aspirations in terms of O'Donnell's framework of analysis. Now I turn to an exploration of how the parameters of the aspirations were set.

The Second Pillar: The Idea of a Citizen Audit

The idea of auditing democracy is new to the field of political science (it appeared in the 1990s). The Costa Rican audit is an adaptation of audits carried out in other countries. There are important precursors in the political arena, such as the democratic audit carried out in the United Kingdom by Essex University and the Human Rights Centre, which developed a method of evaluation (Beetham 1994; Dunleavy and Margetts 1994; Livingstone and Morison 1995; Klug and Starmer et al. 1996; Beetham and Weir 1998; Baker 1999; and more recently, Beetham et al. 2002b), and some experiences in Latin America of groups of citizens exercising social accountability, which suggested it was important that democratic evaluation be guided by a strategy involving citizen consultation and participation (Smulovitz and Peruzzotti 2000; Peruzzotti and Smulovitz 2002; PEN 1999). More recently, the Institute for Democracy and Electoral Assistance (IDEA) applied the concept of a democracy audit to Peru (Ames et. al 2001) and other countries (Beetham et al. 2001, 2002a).

All audits consist of a series of inquiries, tests, and reports that, when compared to certain parameters of evaluation, allow for judgments based on the fulfillment of certain objectives or requirements. The inquiries are made through interviews, comments, and studies based on substantial evidence in order to provide the client (in the case of a citizen audit, the citizens) with an adequate understanding of the situation (Sheldon 1996). What the Costa Rican citizen audit contributes in relation to the experiences mentioned above is the methodology used to deal with these requirements, in particular, the social and technical process undertaken to evaluate the quality of democracy; efforts to make an impact on the deliberation of political affairs; and concern for generating issues for comparative theories on democracy.

By definition, an audit contrasts an actual situation with certain parameters with a view to examining to what extent these parameters are fulfilled in reality. In turn, a parameter must fulfill at least three requirements to be qualified as a standard.[10] First, it must be a documented agreement between several people, and its adoption must follow a process involving carefully registered activities open to public scrutiny. Second, the documented agreement must contain specifications or criteria that allow it to be used in an evaluation exercise. There is no protocol establishing the level of specification required for a standard (some have definitions one paragraph long, while others are extraordinarily detailed). Regardless of the amount of detail it contains, the parameter should be appropriate for the desired objective. The third requirement is that the parameter be used in a consistent manner, which implies a methodological design for gathering the information and for evaluating the findings.

Setting up the standards of a citizen audit is the result of a meticulous and controlled process of deliberation. The process is both inductive and deductive.[11] On the one hand, standards emerge from citizens' interpretation of what high quality of democracy means (inductive mode). On the other hand, at a minimum standards must be consistent with the requirements of a polyarchy. The standards are, in themselves, the audit's first practical product and constitute the starting point for the research and evaluation of the quality of democracy. An important fact should be taken into account, however: the standards are voluntary agreements that are not legally enforceable, and their purpose is evaluative.

In Costa Rica's citizen audit a civic forum was used as a substitute for the panel of experts required by the ISO for defining and validating the standards and assessing the results. As in the ISO, successive rounds of discussion were carried out until agreements on standards were reached. The civic forum, made up of forty-two academic, social, and political leaders, devised the thirty-three high quality of democracy standards that guided the research of the citizen audit.[12] These leaders reflected the country's diversity, and their presence provided guarantees for the different social and political power groups. This forum established the research mandate that the audit would address.

The research phase of the audit included a participatory strategy whereby a wide network of researchers and academic centers implemented different research tasks. The aim was to combine different sources of information and perspectives in a diverse and balanced manner. To this end, a range of methods for compiling people's views and experiences was applied (see below). A total of 4,800 people were consulted (a little over 2 per thousand of Costa Rica's citizens). In addition, hundreds of people collaborated in the research by facilitating access to administrative records at public institutions and private organizations.

The evaluation process consisted of ten panels of evaluators, composed of thirty-five individuals in total, who assessed the results of the audit's fieldwork based on an evaluation model developed for that purpose.[13] Each panel assessed a specific thematic area. Once the audit's *Final Report* was published a period of dissemination followed. This stage included activities in university and secondary school educational centers; press conferences, interviews, articles, and other media events; and sessions with civil society organizations, public institutions, and political parties.

The research strategy of an auditor consists of applying all the fact-compiling methods that he considers appropriate for obtaining the most thorough assessment. An appropriate image for this would be that of the auditor's duty to "go through all the drawers." The auditor's task consists of placing, gathering, verifying, and using the maximum number of pieces of information on which to base his assessment.

The purpose, style, methodology, and expected results of an audit can differ from those of academic research (see table 1). The audit assesses practices, but it does not necessarily identify causal links between things. It uses evaluation standards instead of research hypotheses, and its expected result is the improvement of the audited subject matter rather than the development of better scientific theories, although it may contribute to this (Lijphart 1971; Ragin 1987; Reider 1994; Ricchiute 1995; Valenzuela 1998).

The fieldwork of the citizen audit aimed at gathering the largest possible amount of information on the issues addressed by the quality of democracy standards. To this end, the Audit Coordinating Team (ACT) designed a research strategy open to different methods and perspectives. This strategy

Table 1 Differences Between an Audit and Academic Research

Criteria	Audit	Research
Purpose	Evaluate processes	Explain relations
Style	Comprehensive, nonselective	Selective
Participation by subject(s) of the inquiry	Required	Not required
Hypothesis	No	Yes
Expected outcome	Improvement of processes	Theory building
By-product(s)	Theory building?	Various

Source: Gutiérrez and Vargas Cullell 1998.

was based on five principles: (a) to encourage the most widespread social, academic, and institutional participation in the research process; (b) to promote multidisciplinary perspectives; (c) to treat the researching of each standard as an independent line of work; (d) to combine several research methods in the study of one issue; and, thus, (e) to apply methodological diversification as a principle of research compilation.[14] The citizen audit undertaken in Costa Rica used ten different research methods and involved a group of sixty-four researchers (see table 2).[15]

The evaluation model used in the audit contained a specification of the rules and criteria to be applied during the assessment of Costa Rica's democraticness (PEN 2000). Its aim was to ensure that these assessments were the result of the application of similar rules and procedures and that the same evaluation scale was applied throughout the audit and across the country. Assessments determined the difference between real democratic life and the high quality of democracy threshold.

Evaluation consisted of two processes: (a) the analytical disaggregation of standards (a move from general to specific), with a view to establishing clear criteria for assessing the results; and (b) a process of aggregating the evaluations of the expert evaluators in order to reach global judgments on each of the standards (that is, a move from specific to general). An additional step—which was not taken in Costa Rica—is that of adding the qualifications of the standards in order to arrive at a general score of the quality of democracy.[16]

The analytical disaggregation of the high quality of democracy standards involved the definition of variables, indicators, and conditions,[17] and it provided the evaluation criteria for the experts. In total there were 33 evaluation standards (one standard was dropped in the evaluation stage), 138 variables,

Table 2   Research Methods Used in Costa Rica's Citizen Audit, 1998–2001

Type of Research	Methods Used
Consultation	Surveys
	Focus groups
	Sentinel sites surveillance
	Juicio grupal ponderado
Anthropological	Ethnographic experiments (observations)
Interpretative	Specialized memos
	Theme research
	Legal analyses
Data compilation	Compilation of administrative records
	Literature review

Source: PEN 2001a.
Note: Detailed explanations of each method can be found in the appendix of chapter 1 in the audit's *Final Report* (available online at www.estadonacion.or.cr).

210 indicators, and 450 conditions or evaluation criteria (on average almost 2 evaluation criteria per indicator). Each of the research variables was transformed into an evaluation question. On the evaluation panels people answered and evaluated between 10 and 16 questions from one area of inquiry.[18]

In considering each question, the evaluators had to review information from various research methods. Each source offered data that could not necessarily be added or arranged a priori in order of importance. It was never assumed that one bit of information was more or less important than another. The panels were asked, for that very reason, to deliberate on the importance granted to each piece of information and to justify explicitly their arrangement of the information.[19] Evaluators scored the quality of democracy using a five-grade ordinal scale. Thereinafter, the ACT summed up scores according to some aggregation rules (see section 3 for further discussion of this aspect of the audit)

The work during the evaluation stage combined individual and collective tasks. Following an induction session, each person was given a dossier with duly classified information and an evaluation workbook. The first phase involved individual work, in which the evaluators graded the issues and wrote comments by themselves. This stage concluded when the evaluators returned the completed workbooks to the ACT. The ACT then processed the results of the evaluators' individual scores. It carefully checked the workbooks, consulted the evaluators when there were doubts, and presented the information on worksheets that summarized the results.

The next stage involved collective work. Each panel carried out meetings, which gave rise to detailed discussions on the quality of democracy in Costa Rica and to comments on the evaluation process being used. This stage was based on the scores and views expressed in the individual stage of the work and proved to be a crucial phase of the audit.

The panels did not have to reach unanimous assessments, although in many cases they did as a result of their deliberations or because, on reaching the collective stage, they realized that their evaluations of an indicator coincided. The panelists were expressly informed that they should not force a consensus or negotiate crossed qualifications (that is, accept an unfavorable qualification of one matter to obtain a favorable qualification from the rest of the group in another). In the *Final Report,* the cases in which the qualifications were divergent were meticulously recorded, and the motives and reasons for these disagreements were summarized.

Once the evaluation phase had concluded, the ACT prepared the preliminary version of the *Final Report.* Each panel was assigned a chapter, the preliminary versions of which were placed in a private section of the audit's Website. Private consultation with the panelists and members of the civic forum followed. Although everyone could comment on any chapter, the evaluators were asked to review the chapter that corresponded to their panel.

The nature of the audit resulted in the *Final Report* not being a conventional text in which an author establishes logical connections between paragraphs and makes conclusions. It is a "smidgen" of the most relevant pieces of information that the evaluation panels used to determine their scores and views. The text bombards the reader with information from administrative registers, legal arguments, and perceptions that helped shape the panels' scores and deliberations. At the same time, however, the report attempts to give the reader a wide margin for reaching her/his own conclusions. This style aims to reflect the audit's character as a process and product of collective conversation on the current state of democratic life, whose assessments not only need to be debated but also refuted by citizens.

2. Practical Aspects of Implementing a Citizen Audit

There is no manual for conducting a citizen audit of the quality of democracy. The procedure followed during the audit carried out in Costa Rica may serve as a guide, but it should not be mechanically applied anywhere or to all cases. Nonetheless, there are some lessons from the Costa Rican experience that highlight the importance of complying with certain requirements in order to not detract from the idea of a citizen audit.

Assessing the Feasibility of the Initiative

A citizen audit is a social and technical process highly dependent on its surroundings. Its implementation requires a careful assessment of the political, technical, and social conditions of these surroundings and the investment of time and effort to create the necessary conditions for making this initiative viable. Three types of conditions should be carefully reviewed. The first are the design restrictions, whose presence (or absence) influence the initial decision of beginning or flatly rejecting the initiative. The second type of conditions relates to the political feasibility of the mandate for undertaking the citizen audit—that is, the building up of a climate of legitimacy and support for the initiative on the part of the country's different social sectors Finally, the technical conditions guarantee the efficient implementation of the initiative.

There are several design restrictions that limit the feasibility of undertaking a citizen audit. First, the evaluation of the quality of democracy implies prior existence of a democratic regime—it makes no sense to assess the quality of something that does not exist. Therefore, it is necessary to verify that the country's regime reasonably fulfills polyarchical requirements;[20] in countries with reduced types of democracy—the so-called pseudo-democracies or semi-democracies—or those with authoritarian regimes, an audit should not be attempted. If an audit is undertaken, it should include a detailed analysis of the extent to which the polyarchical requirements are fulfilled in reality.[21]

Second, the extensive consultation with citizens regarding the research and assessment of the results and the detailed study of a significant number of issues imposes a limit on the size (with respect to territory and population) of the area in which a citizen audit may be applied in full. It is worth remembering that the first exercise was carried out in a small country (approximately thirty-two square miles) with a population of almost four million inhabitants, and yet the audit found marked subnational differences in the quality of democratic life.

In the larger countries in Latin America (for example, Mexico, Brazil, and Argentina) a nationwide citizen audit is not feasible. Subnational differences are too extreme. Data gathered on a nationwide level are so general that the audit would fail to probe in depth the state of democracy. We suggest that the exercise be limited to provinces (districts or states) and even to cities with local universities or academic centers, a variety of sources of information, and where studies and previous research on topics related to democracy have been undertaken.

Finally, a citizen audit requires a context with certain properties. The first of these is, naturally, that of political stability. In highly polarized situations (such as present-day Venezuela, for example) or armed conflicts (such as Colombia and Chiapas-Mexico), a citizen audit of the quality of democracy is not recommended. Risks for participants are high and the possibility of ensuring a degree of neutrality is very low. Furthermore, groups may use the audit as a weapon for attacking the opposition, thus detracting from one of its essential characteristics—its civic nature. On the other hand, even if the citizen audit is not as complex and ambitious as the Costa Rican initiative,[22] it still requires an infrastructure that includes research centers and local researchers as well as access to records of state and private institutions' policies and performance.

A climate of political legitimacy is vital for the audit, not only for its implementation but also for achieving the desired effects. It is important the people feel that they themselves gave rise to the audit, or at least that they approved and designed its implementation and that it will be a neutral and useful exercise. This is why setting up a civic forum is of such pivotal importance. This forum may be a preexisting entity or one that is convened ad hoc for the audit. In any case, the forum must be a pluralistic and independent entity. In the Costa Rican experience the forum's operational rules were established from the outset, in particular, the rules for resolving discrepancies.

The citizen audit should not be an exercise imposed by third parties in order to rank a country but rather a tool for societal self-criticism and improvement. An audit imposed on a country is highly likely to be regarded as an external and unsolicited criticism. This is one of the ways the audit differs from other assessments from such institutions as Freedom House or the U.S. State Department.

A key factor is the acceptance, on the part of those who make up the civic forum, of a basic rule: that a consensus be reached on the standards established for high democratic quality. Deliberation ensures that these parameters are the shared aspirations of all. This rule of consensus may be interpreted in two ways, which are not mutually exclusive. The first interpretation, which was applied in the Costa Rican case, is that for a standard to be audited the forum must be unanimous. Therefore, research is not carried in those areas where the participants disagree. If that line is adopted, once all other resources have been exhausted in order to reach a consensus, and if the panel considers the unresolved issue fundamental, the members themselves should probe the use of other mechanisms such as the qualified vote, arbitration, the intervention of experts, and other activities involving further deliberation and dialogue. The second interpretation—also valid—is that standards not unanimously decided upon may be audited. In terms of these issues, although consensus has not been reached regarding the formulation of the standard or democratic aspiration, it has been reached with respect to the importance of including the topic in the evaluation. The audit compiles information about these issues and generates deliberation on the results, but this will not necessarily lead to an assessment.

Finally, we turn to the technical conditions that must be taken into consideration before an audit is undertaken. Although a great number of people participate in the citizen audit, the basic operational core consists of a small group of people—the Audit Coordinating Team.[23] An essential feature of an audit is that the civic forum and the public in general consider the ACT an impartial, trustworthy, and objective entity. Its independence in the face of the government and other social groups is fundamental in this assessment: the audit cannot be controlled by any social or political actor.

Though a nongovernmental initiative, the audit is not antigovernment. It cannot be implemented without governmental participation. Collaboration by public authorities directly impinges on the audit's success. Among other reasons, some members of the civic forum may be public authorities, invited to participate on a personal basis due to their prestige and public recognition. Furthermore, the administrative records of public institutions are a basic source of information.

Just as the audit demands transparency, the ACT must guarantee its openness to public scrutiny. The organization, methods, research networks, and even administrative details must form part of a written record open to consultation by any interested party. Many unforeseen decisions will be made along the way, and it is important that they be registered and stated clearly. This contributes to the transparency of the process and constitutes valuable input for other audits.

Setting up Standards of Democratic Quality

Although there is a temptation to make rapid progress by using predefined standards to save time and money, we do not recommend this. Deliberation is crucial to the audit's feasibility and for maximizing its civic potential. An assessment that employs standards people do not recognize as legitimate is an easy target for criticism.

Due to the fact that the standards used in the Costa Rican audit were the result of a process of deliberation, they presented certain difficulties that are worth noting. First, the thirty-three standards are not exhaustive. The forum did not include some aspects relevant to democratic life because its members were not able to reach an agreement on those issues.[24] These exclusions may present difficulties for the comparison of the results with future audits. In the future the civic forum may decide to include new standards and reject others. The procedures for governing these decisions are pending, although in principle obstacles to the easy adoption or rejection of standards should be created in order to work with a stable core of democratic aspirations.

Second, not all democratic aspirations were able to be set down with the level of precision required by a standard. In some cases the members of the forum opted for a language of "compromise" that gave rise to complications when it had to be broken down into variables, indicators, and conditions of evaluation. For example, the ACT dropped one of the standards because the topics it addressed had been covered by others.

Third, the number of aspirations (or issues) to be evaluated in an audit should be reduced. Though the audit's scope may narrow, the exercise gains in depth and simplicity. On the one hand, dealing with fewer issues allows the allocation of more resources in the investigation of each one; on the other hand, the number of the research methods applied during the fieldwork stage may also decrease. Finally, new procedures for identifying and elaborating the standards must be developed. If the identification and selection of standards is determined entirely by the issues citizens themselves are able to define, several risks arise. Some of the key problems of democracy may not be mentioned by the people because they lack the conceptual ability to define them, and others may be flatly rejected because the forum does not reach an agreement. In this respect, a combined method is recommended. For instance, a group of scholars may offer their expert opinion and then a panel of citizens employing participative consultation methods works on this proposal.

The ACT asked the members of the Costa Rican civic forum to reach agreements as a means to assess *their* democracy. People were not asked to define a concept of the quality of democracy. Hence, the task entrusted to the forum was not to establish standards that could be valid for a wider region, for example, Latin America.[25] Convenience (for the purpose of achieving legitimacy) and relevance (in establishing a system of deliberation and follow-up on democratic life in Costa Rica) underpin this way of framing the civic forum's task. A more fundamental reason justifies it, however; there are no appropriately defined concepts grounded on comparative democratic theories regarding the quality of a democracy. There are—and there will continue to be—conceptual problems to deal with before "jumping ahead" to establishing a link between comparative theories on the quality of democracy and the standards of a citizen audit.

While this does not mean the audit lacks comparative potential, it calls for cautiously assessing this potential. The democratic aspirations of a country's citizens may be different from those of citizens of another country. It is worth pointing out, however, that both the differences and similarities of these aspirations are relevant to comparative research (Valenzuela 1998). They are relevant in this case because they refer to the way citizens in different countries interpret and experience democracy, which is an extremely important issue. O'Donnell points out that:

> the audit is a product that may be exported, but not "llave en mano." The audit respects the characteristics of each national case. One can think on this issue as if encompassing three different parts. One would be a hard comparative nucleus shared by all cases. Another would gather specifications of each case. A third part, "in between" the previous two, would consist of data that the respective national teams, guided by the team's general coordinator, should attempt to make comparable, but without reaching the point where specifications that are considered important are ignored or neglected. (O'Donnell 2001b)

The main problem arises when one wishes to compare the "qualities" of two or more democracies, particularly if one includes in the assessment the nonregime dimensions of democracy. Apart from Lijphart (1999) and Altman and Pérez-Liñán (2002), this has not been attempted. Lijphart's concept of the quality of democracy and its indicators are incipient;[26] Altman and Pérez-Liñán narrow the quality of democracy comparison to regime variables. In spite of the conceptual and measurement problems involved, I think that the democraticness question is a relevant theoretical and political question: Swedish, Costa Rican, or Indian citizens do have widely different democratic experiences. Unfortunately, this topic is largely *terra incognita*.

The Scope of Citizen Participation

The scope of citizen participation in the auditing exercise must be specified in order to ward off images of a mass-based intervention in the undertaking of this initiative. With respect to the range of citizen participation, the audit cannot compete, nor does it attempt to do so, with democratic mechanisms such as elections or referenda or with public policies aimed explicitly at promoting people's intervention in the planning, execution, or evaluation of public programs.

Participatory mechanisms vary depending on the audit's stage of implementation. In general they are more open during the compilation of information, for which the audit requires the cooperation of thousands of people willing to provide information: citizens consulted during surveys and observation exercises; research centers willing to participate in the audit; civil servants who provide access to their institution's administrative records; and media directors and those of other private companies who provide the researchers with access to their offices and databases. On the other hand, participatory mechanisms tend to narrow down at the point in the process when standards are established and results evaluated. Herein the audit uses more closed mechanisms such as selective panels with leaders.

This participatory strategy involves risks. There is always the danger that someone (important) will be left out. A jealous critic may rightly argue that the audit does not reflect the will of the "citizens" because no mass consultation took place. In our experience, this criticism is inevitable because the audit cannot encompass citizen participation on a mass scale.[27] The audit's only defense is that, on the one hand, the leaders who participate constitute an "umbrella" that guarantees political neutrality and, on the other hand, all the audit's activities are open to public scrutiny.

Evaluation Difficulties

During the course of the audit's evaluation process, the panels became aware of problems regarding some evaluation indicators and conditions. The fact that the evaluation model was defined when the implementation process had already begun created some problems regarding the consistency of evaluation indicators and conditions. Given the fact that this was the first citizen audit to be implemented, at the beginning there was no clear idea of the methodological and technical complexity of a participative evaluation. The main lesson learned is that future audits should specify the evaluation model at the onset, together with the design of the fieldwork. In addition, determination of the evaluation standards involved defining a large number of indicators and evaluation criteria in a short period of time due to pressing time limits. This prevented the proper verification of the consistency and reliability of the indicators and conditions. On two panels—civic culture and public opinion—the evaluators were particularly critical of this problem.

The care taken in setting up the panels with a balance of people from diverse social sectors and politicians was an attempt to minimize bias in favor of one particular line of thinking. In any situation involving the judgments and opinions of various people, however, different people may reach different conclusions, even after having studied the same information. This risk could not be avoided in the audit, even (and perhaps especially) if all the country's inhabitants participated in the evaluation. Thus, the evaluating panels' assessments are intersubjective agreements (or disagreements), not objective and irreversible evaluations on Costa Rican democracy.

In spite of these problems, the evaluation panels' assessments constituted a new form of public deliberation. Based on extensive information, the panels probed beyond the prejudices and common places of inquiry. Citizens from diverse social and political backgrounds engaged in critical and respectful debates.

Implications and Potential

The findings and assessments of the citizen audit shed light, using inductive methods, on nonregime dimensions of democracy, which are nonetheless important arenas for the exercising of citizens' rights and democratic governance. These dimensions are relevant to the question of the democraticness of politics—how democratic a democracy is—a topic theoretically relevant to comparative politics research but not addressed by concepts such as polyarchy, democratic consolidation, or governability.

As we shall see in section 5 below, the quality of democracy calls for (re)examining the links between democracy (as a perspective), polyarchy (in terms of the democratic regime), and democratization beyond polyarchy. It does not brush aside existing concepts. The proposal to research the democraticness question using the concept of quality of democracy seeks to avoid, first of all, conferring meanings on existing concepts that are not appropriate and, secondly, not recognizing their importance (Sartori 1991). These concepts do address important questions, albeit different from those surrounding the quality of a democracy (see table 3).

A practical outcome of the study of democracy beyond the political regime is the uncovering of information that enables studying democratic performance in new dimensions. In two areas in particular, the audit contributed to the gathering of information previously unavailable to citizens. The first was the interaction of citizens and institutions, where preliminary research detected serious dissatisfaction on the part of citizens. This led to reflection upon how institutions' treatment of citizens could be proposed as a democratic problem—"micro-political" situations in which people form part of a (day-to-day) power relationship with civil servants or political representatives. In turn, this gave rise to the concept of "citizen maltreatment"—situations in which a person's rights (and even his/her dignity) are seriously affected by state

Table 3 Insights Suggested by the Citizen Audit Regarding Some Concepts and Issues in Comparative Political Studies

Concept	Question	Ideas Suggested by Audit's Findings[a]
Polyarchy	Are there dimensions of democracy beyond the regime?	Polyarchy is a core dimension of democracy (but not the only one). A regime may be one subject of quality of democracy assessments.
Governance	Do high-quality democracies have sound governance?	At the local level, high quality of democracy is associated with more citizen participation, accountability, and public trust.
Regime transition	Does the end of a regime transition ensure a high-quality democracy?	The end of transition does not ensure the emergence of high-quality democracy in all dimensions.
Social equity and economic growth	Are social equity and economic growth dimensions/requirements/enabling conditions for a high-quality democracy?	At the local level, areas of poor social development are associated with lower quality of democracy in local government.
Civic culture	Is the civic culture a dimension/requirement/enabling condition for a high-quality democracy?	No information available.
Democratic consolidation	Is a consolidated democracy a high-quality democracy?	A "consolidated" democracy is not necessarily a high-quality democracy.[b] The quality of democracy varies along different dimensions of an existing democracy.

Source: Based on an original table in Gutiérrez and Vargas Cullell 1998.
[a]Includes findings in the *Second Central American Human Development Report* and Costa Rica's seventh and eighth *Report on the State of the Nation* (PNUD 2003; PEN 2001c, 2002).
[b]This idea was formulated originally by Linz and Stepan (1996: 5); see also Linz (1997).

institutions.[28] This concept was used to analyze the claims filed by people to the ombudsman, the Constitutional Chamber of the Supreme Court, and service controllers within public institutions and to implement ethnographical observation of different state institutions.

Proposing that citizens do not, "on average," experience democracy led to the exploration of subnational differences and ways of measuring them, the second area in which new information was gathered. The audit carried out research on the democratic quality of local governments, which allowed for good and bad practices to be identified and for an approximation of the "brown" areas of democratic life proposed by O'Donnell (1993).

However, the audit did not develop a system of indicators with proven consistency, validity, and precision stemming from a theoretically anchored concept of the quality of democracy. This requires a conceptual and methodological preparation that exceeded the audit's objectives and that, in fact, were nonexistent when the audit began. The audit takes place at a step before the development of a theory, at the exploratory stage, which consists of identifying issues, searching for relevant information, and encouraging social deliberation for assessing how democracy works. The concrete outcome of this cautious strategy was a wide range of opinions and much information, which provided valuable guides for initiating, now, a move toward conceptual and methodological systematization.

In pointing out the challenges, strengths, and weaknesses of an audit, we see that it is an instrument in the hands of citizens, their social and political organizations, and public authorities with the goals of making them better informed and, especially, of strengthening their democracy and its institutions. The information used in a citizen audit to monitor and evaluate political life broadens the capacity of social, political, and institutional actors to make timely "political readings" and develop wide-ranging policies of alliance in favor of strengthening their democracy.

From a wider perspective, the citizen audit can be a tool for generating a "critical mass" of civic action with a view to maintaining democratic achievements and expanding them to new areas of political life. In addition, by extending democratic thought and indicators beyond the consideration of democracy as a political regime, the audit contributes to systematizing and linking visions of democracy "from below," from the citizens' perspective.

The civic potential of the citizen audit in Costa Rica can be illustrated by its impacts. The audit helped to place new topics on the country's political agenda, such as public servants' treatment of citizens. For example, in 2001 the government proposed a bill to reform the administrative structure of public management that included a chapter on citizens' rights. According to then vice president Ms. M. Odio (who was a member of the audit's civic forum), this chapter is based on research that deals with how public servants treat citizens. Furthermore, since 2001 the Civil Service Department has included the issue of maltreatment of citizens in the training process of civil servants. Finally, this subject has been used by the country's trade union organizations in their proposals regarding state reform. In the same manner, the trade unions included the audit's findings regarding the limitations on trade union organization in the private sector in their negotiations with the government and entrepreneurial and international organizations.

The very idea of a citizen audit was taken up by political parties. In the presidential elections of 2002, two of the three most important political parties included this idea as part of their electoral platforms. One of them also placed the issue of how citizens are treated by the state on its platform. The issue was brought to the fore once again during Costa Rica's first elections for mayors, held in December 2002.

From the day it was presented, the audit's *Final Report* has had a high profile in the media. This is complemented by the demands of public institutions, universities, and social organizations to discuss the results of the audit. Activities have been (and continue to be) carried out in conjunction with political parties, business chambers, and trade unions; civil servants from the Judicial Power, Congress, the Supreme Elections Tribunal, and local governments; and secondary education centers and universities.

The audit also opened new research topics. The seventh, eight, and ninth *Report on the State of the Nation in Human Development in Costa Rica* (PEN 2001c, 2002, 2003) updated data, indicators, and issues used in the audit, in particular those related to the administration of justice and citizen participation in public policies. I have already mentioned that the audit also proved relevant for sections of the United Nations Development Program's (UNDP) *Second Central American Report in Human Development* (PNUD 2003).

3.   Findings of the Citizen Audit

Taking Citizens' Definitions of Democracy Seriously

For the majority of Costa Ricans, democracy is a broad idea in which elements necessary for free and periodic elections of a government extend beyond the level of the regime. Without rejecting the fact that, at its core, democracy[29] is a regime, the audit reported as follows:

By daily experiencing [democracy, Costa Ricans] have pushed the limits of citizens' imagination and demands towards new territories. For them democracy is, today, a more comprehensive idea that includes:

- A system for electing government that, in addition to being based on free, fair, contested and reiterated elections and on the protection of civil and political rights, develops forms of political representation responsive to citizens' interests.
- A method of organizing state institutions and how they relate to the citizenry with regard to the elaboration, implementation and evaluation of public policies.[30]
- A way of coexistence between people capable of ensuring a minimum of social and individual opportunities and capabilities in order that people may exercise their rights as citizens.

This broad notion of democracy . . . is not a precise concept; however . . . it addresses crucial matters for evaluating the democracy's performance and perspectives. If democracy for these citizens is a broad notion, then the issue of the quality of democracy will also necessarily be so. When one speaks of the quality of a democracy, one surveys the extent to which actual practices coincide with (or are far removed from) citizens' expectations with regard to what a democracy is or how it should work.

The practical discovery of the fact that the democratic idea extends beyond the maternal womb of "regime politics" lends unsuspected impetus to the issue of the quality of democracy. In the struggle to extend the exercising of their rights as citizens to new activities, people generate new demands on democracy. The State needs to do more than ensure free, fair, and hard-fought elections. Citizens also need it to function [in ways that enable them to have a say in public management issues]. How civil society organizations conduct their affairs and how political representatives and civil servants are accountable become important issues.

Extending the democratic notion to new affairs creates all kinds of negotiation, friction and conflict as to what it is possible, desirable or reasonable to ask of the democratic idea. This is unexplored territory in which there is no pre-existing social or political agreement as to what democracy is and should be, as there might have been when this understanding was essentially limited to choosing a government by means of free and fair elections and a certain level of protection of civil and political rights. However, this is no excuse for passing the buck. At the end of the day, the course of democracy will depend on the ability of citizens to steer these explorations in the right direction. (PEN 2001a: 40–41)

A careful examination of the responses to the audit's national survey[31] (coupled with focus groups) found that when citizens were questioned in depth about their understanding of what high quality of democracy means, seven out of ten people included issues exceeding the procedural definition of democracy. Roughly, five different understandings of what constitutes a high-quality democracy were identified:

29.8% of total respondents defined democracy in basically procedural terms. These individuals think that democracy means free and fair elections and protection of civil and political liberties. Consequently, an assessment of the quality of a democracy should limit itself to examining the regime's performance.

20.7% of respondents chose an expanded understanding of political democracy, including in their definition (and expectations) of democracy issues such as better representation, more opportunities to participate in public policies, and improved citizen control over the government.

8.2% of respondents defined democracy in behavioral terms. Within the framework of the regime, they included in their understanding of democracy a better political leadership. For them, a democracy includes an ethical dimension in which the existence of honest politicians capable of steering a clear course for the country is critical.

10.2% of respondents included issues such as economic progress and some degree of social equalization as constitutive elements of democracy. According to this view, democracy is substantive as well as procedural.

31.2% of respondents had a hybrid understanding of what democracy means. That is, they mixed elements from all of the above definitions. Better political leaders, expanded democratic rules, protection of civil and/or political liberties, and/or economic and social results form part of their high quality of democracy threshold (PEN 2001a: 43–45).

One may dismiss citizens' understandings of democracy by claiming that these are uninformed opinions (true); that they do not correspond to well-grounded theoretical propositions (true); or that people are simply wrong (not necessarily true). Even if segments of the citizenry conflate democracy with other issues, however, one at least has to ask oneself whether seasoned citizens such as the Costa Ricans should have a say in the definition of their democracy. Given that these inquiries were part of a citizen audit, we took these findings seriously, and they became one of the cornerstones of the assessment of the country's quality of its democracy. Issues beyond the boundaries of the regime but consistent with fundamental democratic principles, such as participation in public policy, legal equality, or accountability, were framed as the "non-regime dimensions of democracy" and included in the audit assessment.

It is worth noting that the broad notion of democracy utilized in the audit's assessment marks an important departure from its original proposal, in which quality of democracy was set as a normative horizon beyond polyarchy (the regime). In turn, polyarchy was posited as a "minimum" core of regime institutions. In other words, quality of democracy was paired next to poly-archy as the "other"—a concept encompassing political issues related to gover-nance and citizen mobilization of rights not related to regime institutions and politics (see figure 1). The audit's *Final Report* outlines a new understanding of how the concepts of polyarchy, democracy, and quality of democracy relate. As we shall see in sections 4 and 5 below, polyarchy is one of the components of a broader notion of democracy, so that rather than just covering the nonpoly-archical dimensions of democracy, quality of democracy refers to all of its dimensions. Thus, it becomes a cross-sectional perspective whereby one can assess the democraticness of all dimensions of democracy (see figure 2).

Highlights of the Audit's Findings

In contrast to Freedom House's and other international institutions' mea-surements of democracy, in which Costa Rica always scores at the top with almost no variations over time (Freedom House 2004), the citizen audit's *Final Report* traces a map of democratic life in Costa Rica of greater depth and preci-sion.[32] In the introductory paragraph of the *Final Report,* Costa Rica's rugged terrain is used as a metaphor to sum up the reply to the question, What is the

Figure 1   Citizen Audit Original Methodological Framework Polyarchy/
Quality of Democracy

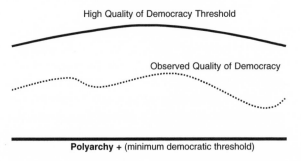

Figure 2   Citizen Audit Final Report Methodological Framework Quality of
Democracy as a cross section perspective

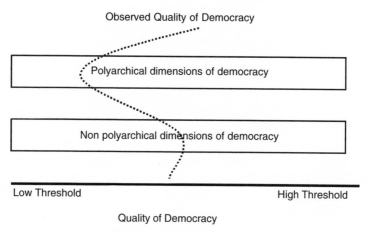

quality of Costa Rica's democracy? The metaphor is intended to drive home
two ideas: first, that the image of peaks, ravines, and valleys reflects the multidimensional character of a democracy; and second, that the strengths and
weaknesses of Costa Rica's democracy are not evenly distributed among different dimensions.

> The quality of [Costa Rican] democracy at the beginning of the XXI cen-
> tury is like the country's terrain: full of peaks, valleys and ravines, fertile
> land, areas of risk, areas in dispute and other, practically unexplored,
> territory, all above sea-level. Alongside critical boundaries of low quality
> democracy (the "ravines"), that breed discontent among citizens, such as
> the abusive treatment people have to endure in their dealings with pub-
> lic institutions, are extensive areas (the "valleys") that, to continue with
> the territory metaphor, are not necessarily green pastures, but rather,
> intermediate areas where democratic performance shows a mixture of
> achievements and weaknesses. This is the case, for example, with how
> justice is administered—showing the effective protection of constitu-
> tional rights alongside considerable problems in providing timely and
> equal justice for all. However, democratic coexistence also shows
> strengths (the "peaks"), areas with a satisfactory performance, although
> perhaps hidden behind the haze of the public's discontent. This is true,
> for example, of the respect of political leaders and candidates for public

posts, for the rights of their opponents and, in general, for the rule of law during electoral processes. The quality of the Costa Rican democracy reveals a fertile and productive land with, however, patterns of activity and use that have produced risks and particularly vulnerable areas. . . . The areas of low quality democracy—those in which impunity, authoritarian practices, patronage, or obstacles to exercising citizen liberties prevail—are like human settlements on precarious land: an invitation to avoidable tragedies. These areas of risk are, according to this report, not yet extensive enough to place the entire democracy in a position of extreme vulnerability but considerable enough to cause, first of all, visible damage to certain parts of the democratic edification and, if the situation is not remedied, eventually shake the foundations of its permanence. (PEN 2001a: 39)

The main strengths of the Costa Rican democracy lie in its political regime.[33] The audit documented the respect for democratic rules during election campaigns and the public's ample access to information for assessing party platforms. A review of the electoral information from 1990 through 1998 showed no accusation, whether in the courts or the mass media, on the part of a candidate regarding threats to physical or material integrity or her/his dignity (PEN 2001b: 190–94). The audit documented only one claim of electoral irregularities in presidential, legislative, and/or local elections during the 1986–1998 period (another claim arose in the 2002 elections, after the report was issued [PEN 2002]).[34] The growing participation of women in positions of popular representation, a result of the 1996 Reform of the Electoral Code, was hailed as a democratic strength. At the time of the audit, some of the code's requirements had still not been fulfilled (PEN 2001b: 85–87), but in 2002 women accounted for 33% of Congress—the highest proportion in Latin America. Progress in the representation of women in local governments has been remarkably fast (see table 4).

According to the *Final Report,* constitutional protection of civil rights is effective, and democratic norms are applied with respect to the passing of laws and administrative rules and regulations. The Supreme Court of Justice's Constitutional Chamber—created in 1989—exercises effective judicial review over the legislature's and executive's powers. It has declared scores of laws, decrees, and administrative regulations unconstitutional. This behavior marks a remarkable departure from the prevailing situation prior to 1989, when both the legislative and, especially, the executive power frequently issued laws or decrees that arbitrarily interpreted the Constitution—in practice exerting a benign neglect of it. The result has been an "opening of the gates" to consti-

Table 4   Evolution of Political Representation of Woman in Costa Rica: 1994, 1998, and 2002 Elections

Women Political Representatives	1994	1998	2002
Congresswomen (%)	—	11 (19.3)	20 (33.3)
Local governments (% of counties)			
Women make up 55% or more of municipal council	1.2	7.4	30.9
Women make up 40%–55% of municipal council	6.2	34.6	60.5
Women make up 40% municipal council	92.6	58.0	8.6

Sources: PEN 2002, based on Alfaro 2002 and PEN 2001c.

tutional issues. While less than 200 cases related to constitutional matters were presented to the Supreme Court from 1938 to 1989 (the year the Constitutional Chamber was founded), over 63,000 were presented from 1990 to 1999 (PEN 2001b: 72). In 2001 the rate of claims to the Constitutional Chamber per 100,000 inhabitants was 306.2, twenty times that registered in neighboring countries.[35] In spite of the workload, the chamber's effectiveness as well as citizens' chances to obtain a favorable decision have remained steady over time (see table 5).

Vast differences regarding democratic quality exist in dimensions of democracy beyond the regime. The performance of the judicial system is, at best, a mixed blessing. On the positive side, the audit found that citizens have wide access to the courts, that the judiciary has political and administrative independence, and that there is a vigorous normative and institutional development toward protecting people's rights. In a country with a population of four million, approximately 800,000 new cases were presented before the justice administration system in 2000 (almost 1 million were presented in 2002). Even if traffic violations and *incompetencias* are not taken into account, the net figure—roughly 50% of total new cases—sharply increases from 392, 213 in 1999 to 459, 665 in 2002 (see table 6). On the negative side, the overstretched legal system is unable to provide efficient services. On average, a Costa Rican judge receives roughly 700 new cases per year, and a public defender receives one new case per day (PEN 2003). With regard to efficiency, over 35% of agrarian, labor, and civil cases took two years or more to reach a judgment. In 2001 this figure surpassed 40%. With respect to labor issues—an important aspect of the defense of workers' rights—tribunals passed judgments on less

Table 5   Performance of the Costa Rican Constitutional Chamber, 1991–2001

Criteria of Performance Assessment	1991–1995	1996–2000	2001
Habeas corpus			
Average annual new cases	880	1,307	1,442
Sentences cases/total new cases (%)	101	100	100
Cases accepted/cases rejected ad portas (%)	66	56	40
Recursos de amparo			
Average annual new cases	3,988	7,260	10,740
Sentences cases/total new cases (%)	95	98	95
Cases accepted/cases rejected ad portas (%)	45	103	105
Inconstitutionality actions			
Average annual new cases	372	358	338
Sentences cases/total new cases (%)	102	105	102
Cases accepted/cases rejected ad portas (%)	23	24	19

Source: PEN 2002, 2001b, based on Anuarios de Estadísticas Judiciales del Poder Judicial (1991 thru 2000) and Informe de la Sala Constitucional (2001).

than 40% of the cases they received each year during the period 1993–98 (PEN 2001b: 64–76). The audit also identified difficulties encountered by ethnic minorities in the defense of their rights and in cases involving discrimination (PEN 2001b: 77–83).

Concerning the transparency and accountability of public affairs, the audit found that the legal system has not fully adjusted to the Inter-American Convention against Corruption, even though the country ratified it. Several crimes have not yet been typified, notably, inside information and international bribery (PNUD 2003). Of almost 100,000 cases received each year by the Prosecution (the entity that exercises action in all criminal cases), only 5 out of every 1,000 are complaints involving corruption allegations against public officers (PEN 2001b: 88–101). Of this small contingent, less than 10% are heard in court (PEN 2002). In contrast with most criminal matters, only a minority of those found guilty of public corruption crimes serve time in prison (see table 6).

The citizen audit identified several areas of low quality of democracy. First, evidence of impediments to the exercising of trade union organization in the private sector was found despite the fact that Costa Rica has ratified the agreements with the International Labour Organization (ILO). In 2001 there were only 33 operating trade unions in Costa Rica's private sector with worker-enterprise relations (excluding nonfunctioning trade unions and wrongly

Table 6 Performance of Costa Rica's Judicial System, 1999–2001

Indicator	1999	2000	2001	2002
New cases entered in judicial system (net)[a]	726,757 (392,213)	798,198 (406,897)	933,614 (443,341)	995,822 (459,665)
New cases per judge[b]	707	700	726	706
New cases per public defender	262	355	not available	not available
New cases entered into the prosecutor's office[c]	92,238	94,525	101,582	105,751
New cases related to public corruption[d]	538 (6 per thousand)	608 (6 per thousand)	544 (5 per thousand)	524 (5 per thousand)
Corruption cases completed by the prosecutor[e]	not available	144	not available	118
Cases sent to court % of those found guilty in corruption cases that were given conditional freedom	not available 71	11 57	16 not available	11 40
% of those found guilty in other criminal cases that were given conditional freedom	34	29	not available	34
% of criminal trials lasting more than 18 months	59 (total cases = 4,301)	48 (total cases = 3,886)	46 (total cases = 4,644)	52 (total cases = 5,256)

Sources: Audit *Final Report* (available online at www.estadonacion.or.cr); seventh and eighth *Report on the State of the Nation* (PEN 2001c and 2002).

[a] Net = total cases minus traffic cases and *incompetencias*.

[b] 2002 figures includes 438 judges assigned to local courts plus a task force of 50 additional judges. Due to methodological changes, the time series for 1999–2001 presented in the eighth and ninth *Report on the State of the Nation* varies. The table shows the figures of the latter report.

[c] Total new cases, including *incompetencias*.

[d] Includes embezzlement, misuse of public funds, and prevarication. Does not include abuse of authority.

[e] Total cases reported as closed by the prosecutor's office.

included organizations), and these had memberships below 2.5% of the work-force (PEN 2001b: 310, 323–26). Excluding the traditional banana plantation labor unions—formed in the 1930s and 1940s—there were 23 trade unions in the nonagricultural private sector in 1997, an extremely low figure (see table 7). Employers argue that this figure stems from workers' low confidence in trade unions (PEN 2001b: 48). Protection of workers' right to organize by the Labor Ministry is weak, however, and trade unions have consistently complained to the ILO concerning violation of this right. Of the 76 cases filed by trade unions regarding persecution of workers by employers during 1997–99, only 3 (4%) were ruled in favor of workers (PEN 2002: table 5.1). In addition, the judiciary attends to labor cases at a particularly slow pace. In 1998 only 25.4% of labor cases were ruled on within a year, and the judiciary took more than two years to hand down sentences in 36.8% of them (PEN 2001b: 325). A 2002 update of the judiciary's performance shows little if any change. In any given year the total number of cases ruled on by the judiciary was less than 40% of the new cases filed (PEN 2003).

Second, the audit managed to find evidence of extensive abusive treatment of citizens on the part of state institutions—situations in which the rights or dignity of individuals were affected during the course of dealings with a public office. While maltreatment has been analyzed as a public management issue, the audit found that it has a democratic dimension as well. In dealing with public institutions, people mobilize their constitutionally and legally enacted rights. This does not mean, from a democratic perspective, that citizens should obtain whatever they deem fit from their public institutions. It does mean, however, that public servants, even when not conceding to a petition, have a duty to respect the law and the rights and dignity of citizens. Interaction between a citizen and a public servant may be construed as a micro–power relation that in a democracy has an interesting bent: the weaker party—the citizen—has rights that cannot be forfeited or ignored by the more powerful party—the public servant. From an individual viewpoint, the outcome of these dealings may be of little if any consequence to a democracy in general. But the fact of the matter is that every day millions of these dealings are carried out. From this constellation of interactions, patterns of relationship between citizens and the state emerge. If the pattern is of widespread violation of the rights and/or dignity of many citizens, then we have the democratic problem of a state showing little or no respect for citizens' legal and political rights—precisely the topic the audit addressed.

The audit identified two types of maltreatment: "soft" and "hard." The former involves situations in which citizens endure inconveniences that can loosely be construed as violation of their legal right to receive full and timely

Table 7 Trade Unions in Costa Rica's Private Sector

Number of trade unions in the private sector according to the Labor Ministry Registry (February 1997)	190
Number of nonsalaried workers trade unions (peasants, informal workers)	−120
Gross number of salaried workers trade unions in the private sector	70
Number of public servants trade unions wrongly included in the registry	−4
Number of domestic workers trade unions (Domestic Workers Association)[a]	−1
Net number of registered salaried workers trade unions in the private sector	65
Number of nonfunctioning trade unions (formal existence only)	−24
Total number of operating salaried workers trade unions in the private sector	41
Number of trade unions in institutions owned by other worker organizations (i.e., Teachers Insurance Society)	−5
Number of trade unions in privatized public firms (i.e., a national airline)	−3
Net number of operating salaried workers trade unions in the private sector	33
Number of banana plantation trade unions (traditional labor organizations, dating from pre-industrialization era, before 1950)	−10
Number of operating salaried workers trade unions in non–banana sector private firms	23

Source: Adapted from PEN 2001b: 310.
[a]Domestic workers to do not belong to the private sector (firms) because they work at households.

public services. Hard maltreatment involves outright violations of citizens' rights and/or dignity that are considered crimes according to Costa Rican laws (for example, bribes, discrimination, or abusive treatment). The survey showed that soft maltreatment is much more extensive than hard but that, unfortunately, the latter does occur quite often. Depending upon the specific issue, between 15% and 30% of people reported having experienced hard maltreatment. For instance, one out of every six people had been requested a bribe for presenting their case before a state institution, and almost one in four said they had been discriminated against, due to their condition, by a public official (PEN 2001b: 208–22). As table 8 shows, people of middle and higher incomes tend to report maltreatment more often than lower-income people, but even among the lower-income segment the incidence of maltreatment is quite frequent.

Table 8   Mistreatment by Public Servants as Perceived/Experienced by Costa Rican Citizens, 1999

Nature of the Mistreatment	*Experienced by total citizens (%)*	*Experienced by low-income citizens (%)*	*Experienced by middle-income citizens (%)*	*Experienced by high-income citizens (%)*
Soft maltreatment				
Long queues	84.2	77.2	87.8	90.9
Red tape (unnecessary procedures)	50.8	34.4	57.9	70.6
Incomplete information	59.2	43.8	65.7	78.0
Hard to find information	44.1	35.3	49.6	50.1
Unnecessary waiting periods	64.9	50.8	70.0	84.5
Hard maltreatment				
Discrimination	27.9	25.3	29.2	30.7
Asked for a bribe	15.6	9.8	15.8	29.3
Abuse	39.8	30.4	42.8	54.1
Did not receive requested information	34.7	27.5	38.9	40.6

Source: PEN 2001b: 209.
Note: n = 1,618.

A study of the claims filed at the Office of the Ombudsman showed that most maltreatment cases stem from outright misconduct by public officials. The review of the legal and administrative framework concluded that despite the progress recorded in the last decade, there remain considerable weaknesses in protecting people from institutional abuse. Some entities set up to deal with this issue, such as the Service Comptrollers (*Contralorias de Servicio*), lack independence in the face of institutional leaders; others, such as the Office of the Ombudsman, which has a legal framework that guarantees its independence and defines specific jurisdiction in this matter, do not have the means to monitor compliance to its rulings (PEN 2001b, 2002).

A third area of low quality of democracy identified by the audit was the weakness of Congress's political control over the executive and the low quality of much of the legislation it approves. In terms of political control, investigative commissions are a prime example of Congress's weakness. These commissions study any matter that Congress deems important. During 1990–98, Congress created seventy-seven commissions. Those dealing with removing immunity from senior public officials (half of them) fulfilled their mandate on the whole; in contrast, the majority of those investigating the use of public resources did not fulfill their mandate because they either did not produce a report or it was only a partial and untimely one. In the few cases in which reports were produced, they were created almost entirely along party lines (PEN 2001b: 377–80). In 2002 the eighth *Report on the State of the Nation*, updating a problem discussed in the audit, reported that in the previous year 69.6% of the time Congress forfeited exerting political control during the time allotted to that purpose (they called off these sessions 112 out of 161 times) (PEN 2002).

Concerning the low quality of the legislation approved by Congress, a detailed review of laws passed by the Costa Rican Legislative Assembly in1998 and 2002 (following the audit's insight) found that while most of them dealt with recognizing new rights, deepening the recognition of others, and defining new obligations of the state, less than half of this legislation included any economic provisions. In other words, the institutional and fiscal framework of rights seems to lag far behind the legal recognition of them (see table 9).

A study of selected municipalities found significant differences in the quality of democracy in local governments (see table 10). While some governments have opened themselves up to participation, held themselves accountable to communities, and won public trust, others are fraught with authoritarianism, lack of transparency, outright corruption, and low public esteem (PEN 2001b:250–64). Local governments are one of the most denounced institutions at the Office of the Ombudsman, and they make scarce

Table 9 Legislation Approved by Costa Rica's Congress, 1998 and 2002

Type of Law	Assigns new economic resources # (%)		Reassigns existing economic resources # (%)		No economic provisions # (%)		Total Laws	
	1998	2002	1998	2002	1998	2002	1998	2002
Deepens recognition of already enacted rights[a]	2 (14.3)	1 (25.0)	5 (35.7)	1 (25.0)	7 (50.0)	2 (50.0)	14	4
Grants new rights[b]	3 (42.9)	1 (33.3)	0	1 (33.3)	4 (57.1)	1 (33.3)	7	3
Sets new state obligations[c]	5 (33.3)	6 (24.0)	1 (6.7)	4 (16.0)	9 (60.0)	15 (60.0)	15	25
Neutral legislation[d]	0	1 (5.0)	0	6 (30.0)	10 (100.0)	13 (65.0)	10	20
Total[e]	10 (21.7)	9 (17.3)	6 (13.0)	12 (23.1)	30 (65.2)	31 (59.6)	46	52

Note: The total number of laws in 1998 does not include nine laws that either were not available at the time of the analysis or to which the analysis did not apply. In 2002 thirteen laws were excluded from the analysis due to the same conditions.

Source: PEN 2003.

[a] The law text explicitly states that it rewrites, develops, and/or enables rights already enacted by previous laws.

[b] The law text explicitly states that it creates a new right.

[c] The law text does not enact new rights, but it explicitly states a new and specifically framed obligation for a public institution regarding the needs and/or rights of the population.

[d] The law text does not enact rights or state new public obligations.

[e] The percentages for 1998 neutral legislation adds up to 99.9 because of rounding.

use of direct democracy mechanisms included in the 1998 Municipal Code (PEN 2002,2001b,2001a: 251). The audit found evidence of links between the economic and social development of a county and the incidence of patronage. In counties with low levels of social development—as measured by the Social Development Index[36]—approximately one in three people received clientelistic offers, while the rate was half that or less in areas with higher levels of development (PEN 2001b: 246–47).[37]

The citizen audit identified controversial issues about which the available information triggered intense and unsettled discussions. One case in point is the legal framework that regulates the freedom of the press. In Costa Rica individuals must prove the veracity of an accusation, media directors have objective responsibility over what is published or broadcasted, and, until 2002, journalists could be accused of contempt. Journalists argued that by virtue of these regulations they censor information on a daily basis (and exert self-censorship), but other evaluators indicated that this legislation is required to protect people's honor. The fact that this matter creates conflict within Costa

Table 10   Differences in Local Governments' Quality of Democracy

Indicator	Mean of 7 municipalities	Best municipality	Worst municipality
Citizen participation in municipal board sessions (%, n=3,273)	7.1	9.2	4.4
Citizen participation in activities promoted by municipality (%, n=3,274)	9.9	26.4	4.3
Respondents that believe in their municipal officials' honesty (%, n=2,190)	42.0	63.4	17.9
Focus groups with local leaders that believe in their municipal officials honesty (%)[a]	47.9	87.1	17.3
Citizens that received clientelistic offerings in 1998 election (%, n=3,017)	20.3	10.8	30.8

Source: PEN 2001b.
Notes: Best and worst municipalities are the same across indicators.
[a]In each county, a selected group of local leaders were asked to participate in a focus group session. Attendance varied between 7 and 12 people per group.

Rican society was later ratified. Of the eight legal reforms presented before Congress at the end of 2001 (after the *Final Report* was presented), only one—that of contempt—was approved. The scrutiny, on the part of the collective media, of public affairs and journalists' protection against media owners and directors were equally controversial issues. Cases of retaliation were reported on the part of state institutions (basically using cuts in advertising as weapons) as well as threats to journalists; there were also cases of journalists losing their jobs or having to end an investigation as a result of pressure from media owners or directors (PEN 2001b: 419–24).

The audit identified problematic areas where, despite the lack of information, worrisome evidence was gathered. Among these areas are private financing of political parties and the prevalence of nondemocratic practices in civil society organizations that claim social and/or political representation. Legislation establishes minimum controls (basically, a voluntary register) concerning private financing of parties. In 1998 political parties declared that private contributions amounted to less than 10% of their electoral expenses—a situation that does not tally with the expense of advertising and other campaign activities undertaken (PEN 2001b: 184–89, 285–97). One investigation into civil society organizations revealed the lack of protection of their members' rights and the lack of development of accountability mechanisms on the part of leaders (PEN 2001b: 319–33).

The *Final Report* contains general and specific public policy recommendations aimed at influencing the agendas of different political and institutional actors (see PEN 2000a). The general recommendations were the following:

> Simultaneously improve the mechanisms of political representation and citizen participation. The audit suggested a combination of measures[38] and took issue with theses opposing "participative democracy" with "representative democracy."

> Include a democratic perspective in reform policies for public institutions. The audit noted that most debates and policies concerning institutional change have focused on the state's economic functions and setting up new incentives for private investment. Without ignoring the importance of economic issues, the audit suggested the need of a political perspective. In particular, it recommended the development of systems for evaluating the process and impact of public policies[39] and specific mechanisms for detecting and sanctioning corrupt practices in public offices.

> Implement a gradual and selective decentralization of public institutions. Given the differences in the democratic quality of local governments, the

audit proposed that the transfer of resources and capabilities from the central government to the municipalities should be subjected to the fulfillment of minimum standards of local democratic management by municipal governments (PEN 2001a: 65–67).

Seventeen practical ideas for improving the quality of the Costa Rican democracy are discussed in the *Final Report*. These ideas do not amount to a strategic agenda, and they certainly will not cure all of the problems identified by the audit. Rather, they are topics that, if addressed, could help to improve democratic performance in certain areas. Some tasks involve new legislation but would require comprehensive institutional reforms; others are matters of institutional responsibility, and others concern citizens. These practical ideas include upgrade audit controls over public and private political financing; strengthen the protection of democratic rights within political parties; institute effective legal recognition and protection of the right of access to public information; shift the burden of proof in matters related to public officials' and political representatives' personal wealth; modify the mechanism for electing magistrates for the Supreme Elections Tribunal; guarantee the exercise of freedom of workers to form trade unions in the private sector; and separate legal and administrative tasks currently concentrated in the Supreme Court in order to create internal checks and balances within the judicial system. Finally, the audit calls for strengthening the commitment to eradicate extreme social inequalities (second- and third-degree malnutrition, extreme poverty, and illiteracy among children)[40] (PEN 2001a: 67–69).

Some Comparisons with Neighboring New Democracies

Costa Rica is one of the oldest—and certainly the most stable—democracies in Latin America. Nonetheless, the audit uncovered data suggesting low-quality performance in certain dimensions of this veritable democracy. Given the fact that the country is surrounded by a score of new democracies that emerged in the 1990s, one important step is to place Costa Rica's spotted liabilities, especially those in the nonpolyarchical dimensions of democracy, within a larger Central American perspective. As it will be shown, this comparison underscores the importance of more thorough and detailed assessments of the *real* democracies emerging in Latin America. Information and analysis are drawn from the *Second Central American Human Development Report* (PNUD 2003), which updated and expanded some of the audit's indicators and analysis.[41]

In Central America regime democratization has not been accompanied by similar progress in the development of the norms and institutions of an *Estado democrático de derecho*. Institutions are weak and lack necessary resources and capabilities to ensure adequate protection of citizens' rights. Meager budgets are an indicator of this feebleness. In spite of the fact that a demilitarization process has taken place in Central American countries, in some of them military expenditures greatly exceed the combined expenditures by basic democratic institutions such as the judiciary, the National Comptroller—the most important horizontal accountability institution—and public funding of electoral campaigns (see table 11).[42] This is the case in Guatemala and Honduras, where military expenditures are twice that of the above-mentioned institutions. In addition, Costa Rica's per capita expenditures in democratic institutions are—with the exception of El Salvador—three or more times those in the rest of the region. Certainly, these findings do not heal Costa Rica's problems; rather, they suggest the extent of the quality of democracy problems faced by the Central American democracies.

Table 11 Central America: Per Capita Expenditures of Key Institutions in Central American Democracies

Country	Military (2000)[a]	Public funding to parties (c. 2000)[b]	Judiciary (2001)[c]	National Comptroller (2001)[d]
Costa Rica	NA	2.9	22.4	4.0
El Salvador	14.8	1.2	16.6	2.1
Guatemala	15.1	0.1	5.9	1.0
Honduras	9.7[e]	0.2	4.4	0.8
Nicaragua	4.9	2.1	5.3	0.9
Panama	NA	2.1	10.5	No data available

Note: Per capita expenditures are in U.S. dollars.
[a] Source: PNUD 2003, based on Stockholm International Peace Research Institute (SIPRI) 2001.
[b] Estimated country population for the year 2000, although the election year does not coincide. Source: PNUD 2003 based on Casas 2002.
[c] Source: PNUD 2003, based on Departamento de Planificación del Poder Judicial (Costa Rica); Ministerio de Hacienda y Crédito Público respectivo (El Salvador and Nicaragua); Organismo Judicial, 2002 (Guatemala); Oficina de Presupuesto, Corte Suprema de Justicia (Hondurus); Contraloría General de la República (Panama).
[d] Source: PNUD 2003, based on Contraloría General de la República (Costa Rica); Corte de Cuentas (El Salvador); Contraloría General de Cuentas (Guatemala); Tribunal Superior de Cuentas (Hondurus); Contraloría General de la República (Nicaragua and Panama).
[e] Data from 1999.

Weak public defense systems are a second indicator of the meager develop-ment of the judiciary, a key component of an *Estado democrático de derecho*. In societies where the majority of the population lacks resources to hire lawyers—roughly 50% of the regional population is poor according to official estimates—public defense systems are pivotal to the protection of the right to due process. El Salvador and Costa Rica have robust public defense systems. In these coun-tries the proportion of inhabitants per defense lawyer is the lowest in the region (less than 30,000). The other side of the coin is Nicaragua, where there is one defense lawyer for every 400,000 people. Only fourteen lawyers work for Nicaragua's *Defensoría Pública*. Panama also has a poorly developed public defense system, but it still fares much better than Nicaragua (see table 12).

Access to public defenders, as measured by a combination of indicators, varies remarkably across Central America. In 2001, in addition to having the

Table 12   Citizens' Right to Justice in Central America, 2001–2002

Country	Lawyers in the public defense system[a]	Inhabitants per public defense lawyer	Cases per public defense lawyer	Prisoners awaiting sentence (%)[c]	Prison overcrowding (%)[e]
Costa Rica	178	22,052	355.0	25.5	110[f]
El Salvador	331	19,326	315.7	49.8	167
Guatemala	301	38,826	82.5	60.9	113
Honduras	202	32,950	160.7	76.0	157
Nicaragua	14	371,993	529.1[b]	30.8[d]	104[g]
Panama	42	72,859	No data available	57.6	137[h]

Sources: PNUD 2003, based on Solana 2003; Carranza 2002; El Salvador public defense system data comes from www.pgr.gov.sv.
[a] 2001 data for Guatemala, Nicaragua, Panama, and Costa Rica; 2002 data for El Salvador and Honduras.
[b] The figure for Nicaragua is overestimated. The available data for the number of cases attended to by the public defense system covers the period from August 1999 thru May 2002. If one assumes that new cases distribute evenly throughout this period, then the 2001 estimate would be close to 186.
[c] Most recent data for Nicaragua and Guatemala is from 1999.
[d] Does not include individuals detained on police premises. Data as of June 30, 1999.
[e] Most recent data for Guatemala is from 1999; for Honduras, 2001.
[f] Includes individuals imprisoned in penitentiary centers. Data as of June 30, 2002.
[g] Does not include individuals detained on police premises. Data as of October 31, 1999.
[h] Data as of April 2002.

lowest proportion of inhabitants per lawyer, the Costa Rican and El Salvadoran public defense systems had the heaviest workloads (on average, almost one new case per day). In those countries with proportionally fewer lawyers, the workload was two to four times less.[43] This not only means that public defense systems are less developed but also less open to people—in spite of the fact that Guatemala, Honduras, and Nicaragua have the highest poverty levels in the region. Finally, in El Salvador and Costa Rica the public defense systems attend to most matters serviced by the judiciary (criminal, civil, labor, and family cases). In contrast, in Guatemala and Honduras the public defense system is responsible for criminal matters only.

People waiting for trial or serving sentences face harsh conditions. In fact, in Guatemala, Honduras, and Panama the majority of the imprisoned population has not received a trial; the figure is roughly one half in El Salvador (49.8%). Honduras is the worst case: three out of four people in prisons are waiting for a court ruling. As expected, Costa Rica is the best case; one of four inmates are awaiting trial[44]—a figure still higher than that in the United States. Overcrowding of prisons—an indicator of how the system protects the rights of inmates—is a severe problem (see table 12). El Salvador is the worst case, where overcrowding is almost 67%, followed closely by Honduras (57%). In Nicaragua and Costa Rica overcrowding is less severe, although this does not mean that inmates have decent living conditions. On April 6, 2003, the *New York Times* reported an incident in Honduras's main penitentiary center in which scores of prisoners were assassinated.

A citizen's right to petition and the obligation by elected representatives and public officials to account for their actions—a basic feature of an *Estado democrático de derecho*—are not constitutionally enacted in most Central American countries (see table 13). Even if their constitutions state that public officials are subject to the law, no accountability mandate can be found in El Salvador, Guatemala, Honduras, and Panama. Only in Costa Rica and Nicaragua does the constitution explicitly set out accountability as a duty. In Nicaragua the constitution expands this mandate to matters related to public officials' patrimony. In Costa Rica Congress approved the constitutional accountability mandate in 2001, but the law compiling the uneven and scattered collection of norms, parameters, and procedures regarding public administration accountability is still pending. Panama is a curious case: the constitution states that public officials have the obligation to answer "respectfully addressed" petitions.

Given this shaky constitutional and legal framework, laws enacting and protecting citizens' right to access public information are basically absent in the region. With the exception of Panama, no laws normalize issues such as

Table 13 Constitutional Accountability Mandate, Habeas Data, and Access to Information Laws in Central America, 2002

Country	Constitutional accountability mandate	Hábeas data	Access to information law
Costa Rica	Yes (article 11)	No	No
El Salvador	No	No	No
Guatemala	No	No	No
Honduras	No	No	No
Nicaragua	Yes (articles 130–31)	No	No
Panama	No	No	Ley 6, Acceso a la Información Pública

Source: PNUD 2003.

the extent of state secrecy (*secreto de Estado*), the rights and duties of citizens and public officials with regard to releasing public information, the creation of agencies where citizens can file claims when access to information is denied, and punishment of officials who hold back information (see table 13). Some of these issues are partially addressed by existing laws not specifically designed for this purpose and/or by court rulings. In general, access to information depends on the will of public officials. A related matter is the *habeas data*—the action a person can file to access his or her information in public databases or to protect its confidentiality. No Central American country recognizes the *habeas data,* though some legislatures are currently examining bills.

Horizontal accountability is poorly developed in the new democracies of Central America. In all countries a National Comptroller has supervised public expenditures since the mid-twentieth century (with the exception of Nicaragua, where the Comptroller was not created until the 1990s). In most of Central America these institutions have small budgets and a narrow scope of authority: they exert ex post facto controls but do not have enforcement powers. As table 14 shows, however, this is not the case across Central America. Panama and Costa Rica have strong National Comptrollers, both in terms of their budgets and legal powers. In Panama the Comptroller centralizes public information, and in Costa Rica it approves two-thirds of public expenditures without congressional intervention. In contrast, Honduras and Nicaragua have small National Comptrollers (their budgets are roughly three times less those of Panama and Costa Rica) and narrow legal powers—no ex ante controls and weak enforcement faculties. El Salvador is closer to the Panamanian

Table 14   National Comptrollers' Budgets and Scope of Control in Central American Democracies

Average 1998–2001 annual budget	Expanded scope of controls[a]	Narrow scope of controls[b]
More than U.S. $10 million	Costa Rica Panama	El Salvador
U.S. $5–10 million		Guatemala
Less than U.S. $5 million		Honduras Nicaragua

Source: PNUD 2003.
[a] Expanded scope of controls means that the institution has the ability to exert both ex ante and ex post facto controls over public expenditures and approve budgets requested by institutions.
[b] Narrow scope of controls means that the institution has the ability to exert ex ante controls over public expenditures.

and Costa Rican situations while Guatemala resembles Nicaragua and Honduras.

To compound problems, Comptrollers face serious restrictions of their legal and operational independence. Even though its independence is legally enacted throughout the region, some governments maintain control over the Comptroller through thinly disguised manipulation of high-ranking officials' nominations and/or through a recent legal development: the creation of a collegiate Board of Comptrollers. This has allowed parties to cut deals in Congress with respect to "representation" quotas for the National Comptroller's Board. Nicaragua, under President Alemán, is a prime example of the Comptrollers' lack of independence. Alemán fired the comptroller—with whom he was openly fighting—jailed him, and then succeeded in forcing Congress to pass a law creating the Comptroller's Board.

Data on selected dimensions of an *Estado democrático de derecho* suggest that most Central America countries face severe problems concerning the recognition and protection of citizens' rights and the ability of citizens to hold elected representatives and public officials accountable for their actions. Even within a procedural concept of democracy, these are severe shortcomings that negatively affect the performance of a regime. For example, the judiciary's lack of political and economic independence concurs with the lack of independence of electoral boards—the entities in charge of organizing free and fair elections and administering electoral justice—from political parties. In some Central American countries the executive and the main parties colonize both the Supreme Court and the electoral board (PNUD 2003). No wonder that most of these countries rank in the "partially free" segment of the *Freedom House Index* (Freedom House 2004).

The poor development of *Estados democráticos de derecho* in Central America underscores an often forgotten fact: the regimes are embedded in the state's institutional structure (see section 5). On the other hand, it reminds us that the lack of horizontal accountability and legal protection of citizens' rights are democratic problems in their own right, even if they involve institutions beyond the regime—something that flies in the face of many political analysts. Weak *Estados democráticos de derecho* prove unable to exert effective controls over the executive. One consequence of this unfortunate situation is that executives, although democratically elected, govern with utter disregard of the law. In Nicaragua, Alemán and his cronies were able to take advantage of the state—and international cooperation as well—and take a firm grip over the judiciary, Congress, and the Comptroller. Due to practically nonexistent institutional restrictions, a democratically elected president amassed economic and political power to such an extent that democratic governance was deeply impoverished and electoral guarantees curtailed (through restrictive electoral reforms and outrageous rulings by a rubber stamp electoral board). Another consequence is that effective protection of citizens' rights, a basic polyarchical condition, is not by any means guaranteed. In the last four years scores of Guatemalan judges, prosecutors, and journalists have been threatened and are currently in exile; homicide rates in El Salvador, Guatemala, and, to a lesser extent, Honduras are among the highest in Latin America; in Guatemala, according to the Misión de las Naciones Unidas para Guatemala (MINUGUA), an average of one hundred *linchamientos* occurred in 1998–2002 (PNUD 2003).

The unfortunate fact that working democratic regimes may coexist with weak *Estados democráticos de derecho* may not come as a surprise. Creation of robust and working *Estados de democráticos de derecho* may take a long time and demand steady political and financial commitments. The complexity of the task is far greater than periodically organizing free and fair elections. At stake is the effective demolition of the authoritarian organization of the state and building up institutions that recognize, promote, and protect citizens' rights and their ability to exert control over their government—in other words, building up the nonregime foundations of democracy. Yet, in spite of its pivotal importance to democratic performance and, eventually, to its endurance, we know little about democratic life beyond the political regime and how it impacts the regime's performance. This lack of knowledge is, naturally, appalling. If significant unevenness in the quality of democracy was found in a mature democracy such as Costa Rica's, differences deepen when examining newer democracies (as the above cursory examination of Central America suggests). Consequently, those who study politics miss out on crucial information for understanding Latin American political systems, in particular, the connections between regimes and other polity dimensions where a robust democratization impulse may prove key to regime survival.

Most importantly, this situation has political implications worth pointing out here. The absence of knowledge of democratic life beyond the regime restricts the ability of citizens to exercise control over their government and to participate in an informed way in the deliberation and management of matters of public interest. It constitutes the milieu for exerting power beyond the citizens' reach—power with impunity. Assuming, not unrealistically, that it is appropriate for governments to be more respectful of people's rights, there is an urgent need for tools that facilitate citizen action aimed at dismantling the social and institutional legacy of authoritarianism. Without appropriate information, citizens lack direction for acting, and a basic instrument for efficient action is to shed light on the reality of democratic life beyond the regime. In order to remove the legacies of authoritarianism, citizens must play a more central and less passive role with regard to their own democracies. Devising methods, such as a citizen audit, that contribute both to uncovering new information and engaging citizens in public affairs may also help this endeavor.

4. Revisiting Costa Rica's Democratization Process

Costa Rica has been rightly characterized as an early Latin American democratizer (Booth 1995, 1998; Lehouq 1995, 1998; Mahoney 2001; Peeler 1991, 1985; PEN 2001a; Yashar 1997). While there is some dispute as to when Costa Rica became a polyarchy, it is widely accepted that by the 1950s basic regime institutions were already in place and functioning effectively. In addition, recent research by Lehouq and Molina highlight the fractious democratic institution building that took place in the late nineteenth century and first half of the twentieth century (Lehouq 1998; Lehouq and Molina 1999).

The audit's findings do not dispute the early timing of Costa Rica's democratization process or its conflictive nature (conveniently overlooked by current Costa Rican mythology that posits democracy as the crown of an almost genetically driven peaceful development). The audit does not argue against what, in Pierre Vilar's words, may be called the long historical process through which democracy finally took root. (As a matter of fact, the long duration of the democratic transition makes the Costa Rican experience closer to the U.S., English, or French cases than to the rather speedy transitions of the Spanish or Portuguese, which are the focus of most of the literature concerning Latin American democratic transitions.) By bringing new democratic dimensions into the analysis, however, the audit does present a more nuanced picture of Costa Rica's democratization. In a nutshell, regime building was part and parcel of a larger state-building process and struggles to expand citizens' rights in which the strengthening of the institutional recognition and protection of political, civil, and social rights was pivotal.

In the ninety years or so that the transition lasted, a sea change can be traced both at the level of the institutions related to the access to power (the electoral system) as well as at the level of the institutions ensuring that elected governments respect citizens' rights and other laws. In the early twentieth century, at the same time that the executive directly controlled and manipulated the electoral system (Lehouq and Molina 1999; J. Salazar 1981; O. Salazar 1997), the judiciary was subordinated to Congress; appointments at all levels were made by the legislature and resources were meager, even by standards of that time (Segura 1990; Román 1995). By the 1960s a fully independent and transparent electoral system, ruled by an autonomous electoral board, was functioning, and the judiciary had become an independent branch of the state—not only because it was decreed in the 1949 constitution but also because a 1957 law backed up legal autonomy with financial autonomy (Peralto 1962; Jiménez 1974; C. J. Gutiérrez 1983; PEN 2001a; Jurado 2001). The 1949 constitution also created an independent National Comptroller, the first legal and administrative accountability mechanism within the Costa Rican state, in charge of reviewing the legality of public financial management.

In addition to institutional changes, regime democratization was accompanied by an increasing recognition and protection of social rights (Acuña 1993; Pérez 1997). In fact, the struggle for social rights became one of the leitmotifs of Costa Rican politics in the first half of the twentieth century. Struggles for social rights intermingled with the struggles for more effective political inclusion (such as the struggles of banana plantation workers and urban artisans in the 1930s and 1940s) and expansion of rights (such as voting rights for women) (Aguilar 1989). Although the main social reforms were enacted in the 1940s—a labor code, social security, public health and housing—since the beginning of the twentieth century the Costa Rican state has implemented what one can today recognize as an incipient social policy. In the first decades of the twentieth century, state expenditures in public education rose while military expenditures decreased (Muñoz 1990; Román 1995; Vargas 1999). Public health and sanitation legislation and policies can be traced back as far as the 1920s. Indeed, the social reforms of the 1940s did not reach the larger population until the 1960s and 1970s (Garnier 1990; Rosenberg 1980; Rovira 1982). At the beginning the reforms had a limited coverage, targeting basically the urban middle class and some workers. What is worth highlighting, however, is that heavy, sustained, and expanded investments in social issues went hand in hand with the institutional building process of an *Estado democrático de derecho* and a polyarchy.

As table 15 summarizes, building regime institutions was not a first stage in Costa Rica's democratic transition. The transition was not a neatly patterned sequence of events where the regime transformed first and the rest of the democratic "kit" later. From the beginning, regime institutions were backed up by sustained institution-building efforts related to the strengthening of the *Estado de derecho* and the effective recognition of a (limited albeit significant) set of social rights.

The insight that democratization is a process in which regime and non-regime dimensions interact may have some policy consequences for contemporary Latin American polities. For once, unilateral focus on regime institutions may be a flawed strategy. I think that this unilateralism takes to an extreme a conceptual distinction and separation between a regime and an *Estado de derecho* (which is analytically important) without sufficiently acknowledging the extent to which both of them are interrelated. Even worse, the conceptual separation is turned into a policy assumption whereby first, an *Estado democrático de derecho* will be a sort of after-effect of the setting up and beginning functionings of a polyarchical regime; and second, the absence of an *Estado democrático de derecho* is inimical to a polyarchy. Both assumptions need to be thoroughly debated. I think that a closer look at how the most stable and successful democracy in Latin America came into being has helped unearth the usually invisible nonregime dimensions of democratization.[45]

5. Theoretical Afterthoughts

The effort by the Costa Rican citizen audit to closely examine the democraticness of an existing democracy using new methods and data may be placed in the context of the larger Latin American democratization experience. Indeed, one has to acknowledge that never before in Latin American history has there been such an extended period of democracy as there is now (Mainwaring 1999). Almost all the countries in the region enjoy democratic regimes that have, up until now, managed to survive outbreaks of recurrent economic, social, and political crises (Przeworski et al. 1997). The democratization of Latin America, however, is undergoing serious difficulties. There are

Table 15   Key Features of Costa Rica's Democratization

Dimensions of Democracy	Authoritarian republic (independence–end of 19th century)	Transition Period			Democracy, polyarchy, & an Estado democrático de derecho (1975–present)
		Stage 1: Liberalization (end of 19th century–1917)	Stage 2: Inclusion (1919–1948)	Stage 3: Institutional foundations	
Citizen inclusion[a]	Extremely restricted	Restricted	Restricted	Quasi-universal	Universal
Elections	Elections are one mode for accessing power	Key to accessing power / Executive control / Selective exclusion / Electoral fraud	Key to accessing power / Executive control / Selective exclusion / Electoral fraud	Key to accessing power / Independent electoral board / Selective exclusion / No electoral fraud	Key to accessing power / Independent electoral board / No exclusion / No electoral fraud
Rights and freedoms	No institutional protection / No tolerance	No institutional protection / Variable intolerance	No institutional protection / Variable intolerance	Weak institutional protection / Targeted intolerance	Strong institutional protection / Tolerance
Judiciary	Weak and controlled	Weak and controlled	Weak and semi-independent	Independent	Strong and independent
Control over public actions	No controls	No controls	No controls	Few but strong controls	Diversified and strong controls
Recognition of social rights	No legal recognition. Almost nonexistent social expenditures	Legal recognition of the right of universal primary education. Rising educational expenditures	Legal recognition of workers' rights. Restricted recognition of social security and housing.	Legal recognition of a set of social rights. Universalization of social security and public health. Rising social expenditures.	

Source: Modification of table 2.1 in PEN 2001a.
[a] Extremely restricted: less than 10% of the population of 18 years of age is enfranchised as citizens. Restricted: enfranchisement extended to less than 50% of the population of 18 years of age (women excluded). Quasi-universal: communists were disenfranchised but the rest of the population over 18 years of age had citizen rights.

growing signs of political instability in several countries (Venezuela, Ecuador, Peru); in others delegative attempts have emerged (Peru), and all of them show widespread discontent and impatience on the part of citizens with the way in which public affairs are conducted (Latinobarómetro 2002). If these political problems remain unchanged, a grave situation may arise: Latin America's democratizing process could end up being an interlude within its age-old authoritarian tradition. The democratic transitions of the last third of the twentieth century can be reversed.

In part, political instability and citizen malaise may stem from failed promises (or overoptimistic expectations). The democratization of the continent per se has not generated the development many people thought it would.[46] Latin American democracies have not been any more effective in generating greater economic growth than the preceding authoritarian governments. In the past decade, growth has been intermittent and, with few exceptions, sluggish. In addition, social inequality has worsened during the continent's democratization (CEPAL 2002). Nonetheless, a great deal of the current political problems that many Latin American democracies face may have a political genus rooted in their political institutions.

When compared with European and North American democracies, the Latin American democracies show deep-rooted authoritarian intrusions with regard to the organization of the state and its interaction with citizens. Although many of them are, in general terms, full-fledged polyarchies (Dahl 1971, 1989), the development of democratic rule of law (*Estado de derecho*) is incipient; thus, protection of citizens' rights and mechanisms of horizontal accountability are weak, even though they exist on a formal level (O'Donnell 2002). Consequently, those who exercise power do not confront an institutional framework that effectively ensures their abiding by the law. The weak nature of the mechanisms of horizontal accountability means that citizens lack efficient means for demanding that those in power account for their actions; that the opportunities for participating in public decisions are rare and, when they do exist, are not very significant; and that citizens lack the means for defending themselves from (and repairing) the damage done by the violation of their rights.

On the other hand, these are democracies that, in contrast to their European and North American counterparts, have developed in societies with extreme social inequalities and where the poor, rather than a minority, often constitute the majority of citizens. Although democracies throughout history have always coexisted alongside social inequality, there are extreme social inequalities that prevent people from exercising their status as citizens (Gutiérrez and Vargas Cullell 1998).[47] Unfortunately, a significant number of citizens in Latin America are affected by these extreme inequalities. In short, Latin American democracies are polyarchies that coexist alongside nonreformed states—whose organization corresponds to authoritarian legacies—and societies with pervasive and extreme social inequalities in which a significant number of citizens suffer the consequences of social exclusion.

A first glance at the existing democracies in Latin America leads us to conclude easily that they are "a long way off" from the condition of those of Europe and North America. Certainly, a comparison with more advanced democratic horizons is not inappropriate as it allows us, among other things, to adapt experiences and imagine new ways of deepening democracy in the region. This is, however, perhaps the least relevant conclusion. The coexistence of democratic regimes and states whose organization has been maintained in almost pristine condition since authoritarian eras highlights the importance of something that conventional theories have cast aside: Political regimes are embedded into state structures.

Political regimes are not free-floating entities. Counting votes requires an institutional framework that ensures free and fair elections. It also requires institutions where grievances—for example, fraud, intimidation, or violation of rights—can be presented and dealt with.[48] Norms and institutions are needed to ensure that, once in office, democratically elected governments will continue to respect polyarchy's core requirements. These institutions go beyond electoral systems and involve some aspects of the complex network of norms and entities we have come to know as *Estado democrático de derecho* (O'Donnell 2001a, 1999, 1998, 1997)—at least those that make free and fair elections possible and protect political rights. In sum, procedural democracy cannot exist without certain state structures in place. Rather than an external factor affecting democracy, as O'Donnell argues, I think that some dimensions of the state organization are democratic dimensions in their own right.

I think it is a mistake to conflate polyarchy with a political regime. This amounts to a one-dimensional understanding of the concept. Polyarchy is a multidimensional concept that has other built-in components. In the first place, a minimum degree of institutionalization or an *Estado de derecho* is required, as stated above, so that enacted democratic norms do not become a facade for authoritarian regimes. At the same time, democratic institutions must make their presence felt at the subnational level; if not, local ringleaders and *caudillos* steal the ballot and curtail political liberties. O'Donnell underscores the importance of what he calls "subnational" regimes to the study of Latin American democratization. In turn, universal enfranchisement requires minimum political equality assurances such as universal citizen identification. Without identification people cannot exercise their right to vote, and their dealings as legal persons as well as their minimum enabling capabilities (meaning that citizens are not malnourished and/or illiterate and, if facing legal problems, justice is delivered in a language in which they are proficient). Figure 3 illustrates the point I am trying to make, although it does not preclude the possibility that there are other dimensions of democracy.[49]

In addition, the Latin American experience vividly reminds us of a basic fact of life: democracy does not surface sporadically during electoral processes. By itself a regime cannot ensure that those elected democratically will govern democratically. In the contemporary European and North American experiences this is a moot issue given the robust political and legal institutions in place—the judiciary and the horizontal and vertical accountability mechanisms. Even if a ruler wants to circumvent the law, there are institutional restrictions at work that curtail his or her attempts to do so. Citizens do have a gamut of opportunities to make their voices heard—and their input matters. Maybe these factors help to obscure the political regime's embeddedness in state structures. When analyzing democratic regimes many scholars take for granted the existence of these structures or, at most, take them as "external" facilitating conditions.

Figure 3   Multidimensionality and Thresholds of Polyarchy and Democracy: An Illustration

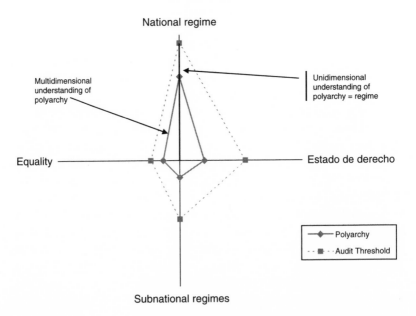

This is a mistake, however. It is true that, as the Latin American democratization process shows, democratic regimes can emerge even among the unfavorable and hostile conditions that follow from authoritarian legacies—basically, no horizontal accountability structures and no independent and working judiciary open to citizens' complaints. But, as it also shows, regimes are deeply affected by these legacies and do exhibit extensive areas of low quality of democracy.

At this stage, one precision is in order: The point being made here is *not* that the whole of the state is a democratic dimension. I am *not* saying that all dimensions of a state pertain to the democratic realm. The state is a complex set of institutions with different origins and purposes that perform widely different functions (see O'Donnell's chapter in this book). Some dimensions of the state are attributes of any state, democratic and authoritarian—for example, the claim to monopolize the means of force or the attempt to set up an order over a given territory (to gloss over Max Weber's definition of a state). Some institutions have developed in the past few centuries to regulate and protect markets—notably, the judiciary and central banks (Ferguson 2001). Others deal with exaction of resources to fund public works (taxation systems); technical and administrative issues (procurement standards) far removed from democracy issues; and the provision of goods and services to attend to what a society deems are legitimate "social needs" (public education, public health care, emergency relief). In this sense, the state can be viewed as an arena where competing—and often conflicting—modes of organizing social, economic, and political life coexist and materialize in institutions, which in turn frame and process conflicting demands.

What I am trying to say is that some state institutions and structures, although they exceed the sphere of the political regime, do belong to the realm of democracy. On a cursory note, one can identify at least three conditions without which I do not think a democracy can exist[50]—conditions that, as a matter of fact, lie beyond the regime: (a) a judiciary whose institutional organization and resources enable it to minimally uphold the rule of law and protect citizens' rights; (b) functioning horizontal accountability mechanisms that are checks on the government's decisions and are capable of holding the government accountable to the law; and (c) a steady and constant separation (and interrelation) of power between the branches of the state. In my view, these conditions are, so to speak, democratic chromosomes within the state structures that need to be in place for democracy—even procedural democracy—to exist.

Advanced democracies have developed their *Estados democráticos de derecho* far beyond what a polyarchy requires. They have pushed regime institutions beyond the procedural minimum—for example, by creating direct democracy mechanisms to revoke mandates and to propose or reject policies. Others have expanded democracy in terms of political equality, through, for example, consociational agreements and the recognition and protection of the multicultural and multinational nature of their states. Subnational regimes have democratized by means of expanded participatory opportunities in local governments. In other words, currently broader and richer applications of democracy have expanded the thresholds of democracy along different dimensions, a fact that some theories of democracy do not acknowledge. Judging from this expanded threshold of democracy, some of the Latin American democracies may grossly miss the mark—though I am not sure if there has ever been a democracy that fully met all democratic standards.[51] As shown in figure 3, new and broader thresholds of democracy exist today.

In sum, conflating polyarchy with democracy hides the importance of the "democratic chromosome" within the state. In truth, polyarchy lies at the core of democracy; yet it is not a contradiction in terms to stress that polyarchy is so deeply woven into certain state structures that they cannot live independently. A broader concept of democracy may increase understanding of democracy's other vital nonregime dimensions. Procedural theories of democracy assume that the rule of law and certain state institutional arrangements are, at most, conditions that facilitate democracy.[52] My point is that this separation is misleading, which brings us precisely to the issue of the quality of democracy—both of the regime and of the democratic dimensions beyond it. In any given dimension of democratization, quality of democracy refers to the distance between actual democratization and a threshold or level of constitutionally and legally enacted democratic rights. For polyarchy, this threshold has been clearly spelled out—not without hesitation and conflicts—since Dahl's (1971) seminal work. The fact that, as O'Donnell argues, Dahl's threshold left out fundamental issues and that, unfortunately, we still do not have an agreement as to what specifically the threshold should be for these dimensions underscores the urgency of further research on the democraticness question.

There is a political dimension of this discussion. The (almost unilateral) focus on regime performance has prescriptive consequences. If regime is what matters, then the prescription is to achieve democracy first (meaning on the level of the regime), and the rest will come later in an almost natural way. The Latin American experience, however, underscores that democracy is not confined to the political regime *and* that progress in nonregime dimensions of democracy may prove vital to the political regime's improvement and performance.

6. Final Considerations

The findings of the citizen audit on the quality of democracy first implemented in Costa Rica, and its updates in Costa Rica and Central America, suggest that the democratization of political regimes does not necessarily lead to improvement in the quality of democracy. This improvement requires, among other factors, a firm jump start by citizens interested in materializing the fundamental promise of a democracy: that in a democracy the sovereignty of power resides in its citizens.[53]

The political argument underlying the audit could be briefly expressed as follows: Once the period of transition leads to the emergence of democratic regimes, the new challenge in Latin America is to craft high-quality democracies. The assumption is that the poor quality of many Latin American democracies makes them vulnerable to political setbacks or the protraction of hybrid systems with authoritarian intrusions.

The new horizons of high quality of democracy—and this is the normative hope of the citizen audit—can be forged by consultations with citizens. The experience of living in a democracy allows them to discover that citizenship means more than just going to vote every so often. Individuals generate and negotiate collective expectations to evaluate and guide their day-to-day dealings with public institutions and with others—endeavoring to legally enshrine new rights and ways of exercising them.

The Costa Rican citizen audit took advantage of the fact that the majority of its citizens are not willing, for now, to put an end to their adventure with democracy. Certainly, their discovery that democracy can be applied to other areas creates expectations and demands that, somewhat chaotically, help shape new democratic horizons. This poses challenges to our theoretical and practical imaginations in order to access topics that comparative democratic theories, focused on the study of political regimes, have not tackled in depth. The audit calls theorists to pay more attention to a more encompassing collection of topics. In doing so, new (and old) issues are brought to light that may lead us to rethink the very concept of democracy.

Tracing the map of the strengths and weaknesses of a democracy—its good and bad practices—is a powerful tool in the hands of citizens. In-depth knowledge of the areas in which political practices coincide with democratic aspirations remind people of the often forgotten progress that has been made. Identifying those areas in which patronage practices, authoritarianism, and lack of public scrutiny and accountability predominate helps, in turn, to introduce new issues for public deliberation.

The challenge of improving the quality of democracy may bring together diverse social and political actors. A citizen audit may be conceived as a bridge between civil society, government, and citizens in general because all of them have a legitimate role in its endorsement. Governments may require support for generating new areas of convergence with society in order to resolve, by democratic means, the precarious legitimacy many of them enjoy. For example, if new policies for addressing poverty are promoted, how does the government create monitoring and evaluation systems that reinforce public scrutiny, citizen participation, and the protection of the population's rights? If decentralization is advocated, how do policy makers help to improve the democratic quality of local governments? If, as a result of a transition, new electoral systems are created, how does it ensure these will not set high barriers to citizen participation? If reforms to upgrade the judiciary are to be implemented, how does it improve the systems for public scrutiny of its performance?

Civil society organizations may require, among other things, support for creating new opportunities for citizen participation in public affairs and mechanisms for demanding accountability from their political representatives. In the same manner, the members of the civil society organizations themselves may find in the question of democratic quality a means for promoting democracy within their own organizations. The media may be interested in promoting extensive debate on press legislation and the protection of journalists. Finally, citizens possess tools for enhanced protection of their rights and timely information to assess their institutions' performance.

APPENDIX: High Quality of Democracy Standards of Costa Rica's Citizen Audit[54]

With regard to an effective rule of law:

Citizens and noncitizens have open access to equal, fair, and timely justice delivered by an independent judiciary.

Citizens and noncitizens have open access to diverse, nondiscriminatory, and effective means to protect their human, civil, and political rights.

Public institutions exert effective protection of women and people who belong to minority ethnic groups.

Citizens have open access to effective means to prevent and sanction public corruption.

The judiciary and National Comptroller impose, after due process, expeditious sanctions against elected representatives, political appointees, and civil servants who transgress the law.

With regard to democratic public policy decision making:

In principle no issue of public interest is excluded from the reach of democratic norms.

Congress and the executive engage in a working relationship regarding policy making that does not compromise their respective constitutional powers.

Congress abides by democratic norms.

With regard to the electoral system:

Citizens that run for public office do not confront social and/or cultural prejudices.

All citizens have open access to credible and timely information to evaluate candidates and their electoral platforms.

New and/or minority parties exert their political representation without confronting discriminatory barriers.

During the electoral competition political leaders respect the rule of law and the civil and political rights of their opponents.

With regard to public institutions' treatment of the public:

Citizens and noncitizens have open access to public services that abide by legal, fair, accountable, and well-known norms and procedures.

Public servants do not treat citizens and/or noncitizens in ways considered humiliating by the population.

Public institutions select their employees according to technical rules and procedures subject to public scrutiny.

Noncitizens can obtain legal residence and/or citizenship through legal, fair, accountable, and well-known norms and procedures.

With regard to local governments:

Local governments govern democratically.

With regard to political parties' internal affairs:

Political parties conduct internal affairs through democratic norms and procedures.

Political parties' funding is legal and open to public scrutiny.

With regard to civil society:

Citizens and noncitizens exert their right to organize freely through the creation of diverse and active civil society organizations.

Civil society organizations that claim political and/or social representation apply democratic norms and their internal affairs are open to public scrutiny.

Relationships between civil society organizations and public institutions are open to public scrutiny.

With regard to citizen participation in public policy making:

Citizens and noncitizens have open and effective means of participation in policy decision making and implementation.

Citizens and noncitizens make use of the available opportunities to participate in policy decision making and implementation.

Citizens and noncitizens actively hold elected representatives, political appointees, and civil servants accountable for their actions.

With regard to public opinion:

Citizens have working knowledge of their rights and duties and the procedures through which they can exert them.

Citizens and noncitizens freely and timely express their opinions of public issues of concern to them.

A diverse media exerts a comprehensive and responsible scrutiny over public affairs.

The media is an open and independent forum for a pluralist public opinion.

With regard to the civic culture:

Citizens are able to identify with and feel part of a larger democratic and civic political community.

Citizens show strong belief in democracy as a value and as a means to achieve social well-being.

Citizens and noncitizens show tolerance in their dealings with other people.

NOTES

1. This concept was coined by Peruzzotti and Smulovitz to denote the initiatives that, from outside the apparatus of the state, citizens undertake in matters concerning (a type of vertical) accountability (Smulovitz and Peruzzotti 2000; Perozzotti and Smulovitz 2002).

2. The works compiled during the course of the audit and that serve as the basis for the present text are the following (English titles):

"The Citizen Audit of the Quality of Democracy: A Proposal for Its Implementation in Costa Rica" (September 1998, Gutiérrez and Vargas Cullell, 1998)

"Model of Evaluation of the Citizen Audit of the Quality of Democracy" (March 2000, PEN 2000)

"Fieldwork Strategy of the Citizen Audit of the Quality of Democracy" (January 1999, PEN 1999)

"Prologue to the Report: Citizen Audit of the Quality of Democracy" (June 2001, in PEN 2001a)

Final Report: Citizen Audit on the Quality of Democracy, appendix to chapter 1 (June 2001, in PEN 2001a)

These documents are available online at www.estadonacion.or.cr.

3. From the moment the idea of a citizen audit was conceived we received theoretical and practical suggestions from Guillermo O'Donnell on a wide variety of issues. This is reflected in the constant references to his work throughout the text. Some of his comments on the citizen audit can be found in the "Decalogue" (O'Donnell 2001b).

4. *Democratic regime* is understood, essentially, as that which Dahl describes as "polyarchy" (1971, 1989, 1999) and Sartori (1987) as "democracy." For the definition of *political regime,* see O'Donnell and Schmitter (1994) and O'Donnell's chapter in this book.

5. The low level of the concept is determined by the nature of the question that the idea of the quality of democracy attempts to answer: How democratic is the political life of a democracy? The question implies the existence of a democracy (and a prior definition in this respect), the definition of criteria for evaluating its democraticness, and methods and techniques for measuring the democratic quality.

6. According to the *Diccionario de la Real Academia,* the second meaning of the word *capacity* is "aptitude, talent, quality that enables someone to exercise something well" (Real Academia Española 1992: 396). That is the meaning used here. We are aware of the intense debate on the nature and scope of what is "public" and, by extension, public

affairs. This topic has been addressed in particular by feminists and radical democrats, who have criticized the purely legal definitions of what is public. This debate is far from being resolved and, for the purpose of the quality of democracy, does not need to be.

7. A political practice is an action whereby a person exercises constitutionally and legally established civil and political rights and obligations.

8. Noncitizens are included because a democracy is obliged to respect the human rights of the people who live in or are passing through the country.

9. The boundaries between the public and private spheres are difficult to set. Whatever these limitations may be, topics recognized by a variety of actors as of interest to all of them collectively do need to be included in the public sphere.

10. The International Standardization Oganization (ISO) defines a *standard* as "a documented agreement that contains technical specifications or other specific criteria for consistent use as rules, guides or definitions or characteristics," that allow for it to be decided whether something is appropriate for the purpose for which it was intended (see www.iso.com).

11. The process was not free of tension, which is inevitable because citizens' opinions and aspirations concerning a high-quality democracy differ. Instead of assuming that differences can be eliminated through dialogue, the methodological design of the citizen audit was aimed at creating the means for people to be able to handle both consensus and disagreements.

12. The process for establishing standards of high quality of democracy adhered to the following measures:

> Exploratory research for detecting problems regarding democratic coexistence that are relevant to citizens was carried out. In the Costa Rican experience, this research coupled focus group sessions with a public opinion survey. The exploratory research identified 135 problems that people felt deeply about in relation to Costa Rica's democratic life, thus mapping citizens' discontent and aspirations.

> Subsequently, an exhaustive literature review was carried out on available bibliographical and statistical material concerning the issues identified during the exploratory research. This review included revising comparative theories of democracy (Gutiérrez and Vargas Cullell 1998), systematizing the issues and indicators used by the international measurements for democracy (Altman 1998), and a statistical reprocessing of the results of the exploratory research by applying factorial analysis for determining the issues underlying the concerns voiced by citizens (Pérez Liñán 1998). During this phase, consultations with Latin American academics were very significant.

> The Audit Coordinating Team (ACT) issued a first version of democratic standards using the above input. A very important analytical operation during this step was to ensure that this list was consistent with the basic requirements for qualifying a political regime as a democracy.

> The civic forum was set up. This involved the meticulous task of political persuasion based on the explanation of the nature of the citizen audit, the scope of the

participation requested, the forum's operational rules, and the type of responsibilities assumed by each person.

The members of the forum began a stage of individual work. The audit's technical team gave a questionnaire to each member containing a preliminary list of possible democratic standards. They were asked to provide a systematic reaction to each proposal: their views on the relevance of each standard, how clearly it was expressed, and corrections and additions they deemed important.

The ACT processed the information in the questionnaires. This allowed the team to determine the agreements and disagreements, to qualify these disagreements, and to reformulate the standards.

At the same time focus group sessions with ordinary citizens were carried out. This step emerged from adapting the notion of group control, which is characteristic of an experimental design, to the conditions of the citizen audit. The ACT monitored the reactions to the standards, registered observations, and analyzed the extent to which these reactions corresponded to those of the civic forum. In Costa Rica's case, the opinions of each group coincided to a large extent.

The ACT implemented a second specification of the high quality of democracy standards. This document was given to the civic forum, together with a report of the results of the first consultation and the focus group sessions. The document included a first breakdown of the standards' main components.

The civic forum's first plenary session was carried out. During this session the forum debated each of the standard proposals in turn, made changes, and established a body of standards that were adopted by consensus and used as assessment parameters. The issues that were not agreed upon were rejected.

Lastly, the ACT drew up the final standards, based on the agreements made at the civic forum's plenary session. This document was sent to its members for them to check that their observations had been included and, if they found changes that did not adequately reflect their agreements, to make any final comments. The standards were only made official following the fulfillment of this stage.

13. See the document "Evaluation Model" (www.estadonacion.or.cr) and the methodological appendix to chapter 1 of the *Final Report* (PEN 2001a).

14. See the document "Field Strategy for the Citizen Audit on the Quality of Democracy" (www.estadonacion.or.cr) and the methodological appendix to chapter 1 of the *Final Report* (PEN 2001a).

15. The technical details of each method can be found in the methodological appendix to chapter 1 of the *Final Report* (PEN 2001a).

16. This would require creating an index with several qualifications. These qualifications imply decisions on the hierarchy and associations between standards without a theory to back them up. On the problems of inclusion, refer to Munck and Verkuilen 2002.

17. An example of an evaluation indicator and conditions can be seen in table 1A.7 of the *Final Report* (PEN 2001a: 88).

18. At this point the differences abound between audits for companies or institutions and the citizen audit. The first difference is based on the fact that companies hire external auditing firms. The citizen audit is a tool in the hands of citizens and calls for their participation at different stages of implementation. The second difference is that in addition to strengthening accountability, the audit aims to contribute to the engagement of citizens in public life. Although the traditional concept of an audit does not include this aspect, no better one was found to express the nature of evaluating the quality of democracy.

19. The decision not to rank a priori the pieces of information generated some debate, not only due to the understandable differences of opinion but also because, in some cases, different methods supplied information that did not necessarily correspond, and, at times,was frankly contradictory. These discussions extended over the period specified for the evaluation. Discussions on the merits of different information bits and pieces, however,provided the audit with valuable input. The agreements and disagreements gave way to more rational consideration and paved the way for in-depth discussions on the substantive issues the panels had to evaluate.

20. Reasonable fulfillment means that although the regime does not fully comply with all of the conditions, none of the ones it fails to comply with are important enough to disqualify the regime as a polyarchy.

21. In Costa Rica's experience, the conditions set out by Dahl (1971) were broken down into variables and indicators, which became the threshold or minimum level of democratic rights. Once the evidence was gathered, each condition was assessed using a scale of three categories: full compliance, partial compliance, or failure to comply.

22. As it was the first initiative of its kind, Costa Rica's audit dealt with a very broad range of issues and aimed to have a nationwide scope. Both these things are not properties of an audit per se but were the result of contingent decisions. Citizen audits on specific dimensions of democracy are also an option.

23. In Costa Rica's case, the State of the Nation Project. This project was created in 1994 as a joint venture of the Council of Public Universities of Costa Rica (CONARE), the Defensoría de los Habitantes (Ombudsman), and the United Nations Development Program (UNDP). Its main goal was to publish the annual *Costa Rica's Country Report on Sustainable Human Development*. In addition, the project has been responsible for preparing and publishing the first and second Central American Human Development Reports (PNUD2003). In 2003 the State of the Nation initiative became a permanent program, fully funded by the Costa Rican counterparts. Currently, the National Comptroller forms part of the venture, while UNDP no longer participates.

24. For example, the forum did not include standards for assessing the democratic quality of the electoral system, which would require examining aspects such as the disproportional nature of the system and the performance of the Supreme Election Tribunal (the entity in charge of organizing, supervising, and certifying the results of the elections).

25. This is one way in which the citizen audit differs from the democracy audit developed by Beetham (1994) and his colleagues in Great Britain and then applied to other countries (Beetham et al. 2001, 2002a). The latter identified two basic dimensions of democracy, and the evaluation standards were defined deductively.

26. In the 1999 edition of *Patterns of Democracy,* Lijphart includes a chapter on the quality of democracy. From a conceptual point of view, however, his elaboration is poor; he quotes a slogan taken from former president George Bush's 1988 electoral campaign to define the quality of democracy ("a kinder, gentler democracy"). His indicators are, above all, macro (country) indicators of social outcomes (Lijphart 1999). Linz has referred to the theme of the quality of democracy but, apart from underlining its importance, has not effected a conceptual and methodological proposal in this respect (Linz 1997).

27. Nor do we believe it is necessary to do so. Social scientists work with samples, and when using qualitative methods they make it clear that the results are not representative. The citizen audit was particularly punctilious in this respect.

28. We are again indebted to Guillermo O'Donnell for visualizing the topic of citizen abuse as relevant to democratic coexistence.

29. The audit's broad concept of democracy summarizes the results of the inquiries that were made in this respect during the time the initiative was prepared and implemented. For further details see PEN 2001a: chap. 1 and appendix.

30. This method of organization is based on recognizing people's dignity, protecting civil and political rights, and promoting opportunities for citizens to exercise their rights to participate in public affairs and to demand and attain accountability from their political representatives and other civil servants

31. The survey sample consisted of 1,618 persons, with level of confidence at 95% and a margin of error of 2.4%. The audit's survey sample was larger than the usual public opinon surveys in order to allow comparisons at the regional level.

32. From 1980 through 1993 Costa Rica scored 1 on Freedom House's 7-point scale; from 1994 to 2004 it scored 1.5 (Freedom House 2004).

33. This section is a selective review of some of the citizen audit's findings. Its aim is to provide an idea of the nature of the results, in order that the reader may grasp their usefulness. I am not attempting a summary of the results. The conclusions and data are available in PEN 2001b.

34. In 1998 a party whose candidate for Congress lost by a margin of fifty-five votes asked for a recount (PEN 2001c). In 2002 another party that was narrowly defeated in an electoral district asked for a recount (PEN 2002b).

35. In 2001 the rate of claims to the Constitutional Tribunal per 100,000 inhabitants was 15.6 in El Salvador, 13.3 in Guatemala, 15.4 in Honduras, and 17.1 in Nicaragua (PNUD 2003).

36. The Social Development Index (*Indice de Desarrollo Social,* IDS) was developed in 1984 by the Planning and Economic Policy Ministry. Following the 2000 census, the ministry updated the index's calculations at county and subcounty levels. The IDS ranks counties by taking into account nine education, health, and electricity consumption variables (MIDEPLAN 2001).

37. On average, politicians fulfilled their promises of clientelistic offerings one out of ten times. Delivery was lower in the poorest areas (where offerings were more frequent).

38. For example, revoking congresspeople's mandates, logroll voting in Congress, and plebiscites and referenda.

39. The State of the Nation Project implemented a system to monitor the quality of the delivery of programs belonging to the Social Development and Family Allowances Fund.

40. In Costa Rica extreme poverty affected roughly 7% of households during 1990–99. Moderate and severe malnutrition affected 4.8% of preschool children (PEN 2001a).

41. As stated in note 23, the same entity that implemented the citizen audit was charged with the responsibility of preparing the first and second Central American Human Development Reports.

42. One can argue that military expenditures may be several times larger than the expenditures of the judiciary, comptroller, and electoral campaigns in many if not all of the advanced European and North American democracies. The indicator must be placed in proper context, however. In the advanced democracies, the judiciary is composed of a network of strong institutions, which is definitely not the case in the new Central American democracies. For example, annual per capita expenditure of the judiciary totals less than six dollars in Guatemala, Honduras, and Nicaragua (see table 11). Given the extremely scarce public resources, allotting more resources to the military than to building up basic democratic institutions is a political decision with dire consequences.

43. These indicators do not measure qualitative issues such as the nature and complexity of the job the public defense lawyers in different countries do (whether they assist defendants in all stages of the trial, whether they visit inmates, whether they look after all cases or only criminal cases, etc).

44. Figures may vary according to the source. A 1999 UNDP report on criminal justice in Central America reported that in Honduran prisons, 87% of inmates were waiting for a court ruling and only 13% had been sentenced. That same year research by U.S. consultants put the figure of prisoners waiting for a ruling at 90%. In El Salvador the *Dirección General de Centros Penales* figures acknowledge that prisoners awaiting court rulings remain a steady 55% of the prison population, while the *Procuraduría para la Defensa de los Derechos Humanos* reports that, as of July 2001, the real figure was close to 70% (PNUD 2003: 328n21).

45. I have used the concepts of *Estado de derecho* and *Estado democrático de derecho* in the same paragraph. This is not a *lapsus linguae*. In an *Estado de derecho* justice is administered according to some sort of codified rules that are universally applied to all the people the law states. These rules need not abide by democratic principles. In fact, they may discriminate among different social, economic, or political segments of the population and may not recognize equal rights to all. Thus, not all *Estados de derecho* are *Estados democráticos de derecho*. As O'Donnell

stresses, in the latter rights are enacted and upheld, and the ruler is subject to the law. An *Estado democrático de derecho* is deeply intertwined with a democractic regime and cannot function without it (see O'Donnell's chapter in this book).

A variety of *Estados no democráticos de derecho* may exist side by side with authoritarian and/or totalitarian regimes. What distinguishes an *Estado de derecho* as a genre (democratic or not democratic) from other modes of delivering justice (for example, justice idiosyncratically administered by the ruler) is the existence of codified rules.

When I refer to *Estado de derecho,* I am speaking in general terms about the relation of any *Estado de derecho* and the regime—not only of democratic ones. I use *Estado democrático de derecho* when speaking of polyarchical regimes.

46. The theory of modernization claimed that economic development would lead to democracy (Lipset 1981)—in other words, that democracies are not to be expected in underdeveloped countries. Recent experience in Latin America (Coppedge 2000) shows that despite claims to the contrary, neither one or the other is necessarily true. Nor is it true that "democracy feeds, cures and educates," as pronounced by former Argentinian president Raúl Alfonsín. Recent literature on the links between democracy and development is more circumspect. It recognizes the profound differences in how democracies are conducted. In effect, some but not all spearhead the democratic experience and constitute solid platforms for development. In general, democracies promote economic growth at least as efficiently (although no more so) as authoritarian regimes, but democracies are more resistant to economic and social crises (Cheibub and Przeworski 1997; Przeworski and Limongi 1997; Przeworski 2000). Some democracies, however, have been pinpointed as being actually or potentially unstable political systems that are encountering serious difficulties in attempts to promote development.

It is true that literature on development warns that while countries with greater institutional development experience increased economic growth (World Bank 1997; Hildebrand and Grindle 1997), this institutional development often occurs in non-democratic political systems (such as that of the so-called Asian Tigers). Successful development policies include mechanisms for people's participation in their design, implementation, and evaluation, which allows incentives to be adapted to local needs (Ostrom et al. 1993). These are matters that, although theoretically viable in a democracy, are not necessarily present in all of them. We know that when citizens have means of control over public management, it reduces corrupt practices, patrimonialism, and the illicit pursuit of unlawful revenues, but this requires the development of mechanisms of horizontal accountability, which are incipient in the majority of Latin American countries. The spread of market economies involves the development of legislation that protects the investor and the consumer, and this, in turn, requires preparing people to act as such (World Bank 1997; Naim 1994, 1993) and implies the existence of effective rule of law. These are notoriously underdeveloped in Latin America (O'Donnell 2002; Becker 1999).

47. Picture the following situation: Country X has an average life expectancy of 67. Approximately 15% of its population (one in six people), however, lives less than 40 years, mainly because of precarious living conditions. In terms of citizenship, social inequalities prevent this group of people from exercising their rights at all for at least 27 years (as they are dead), which is more than 50% of the time span an average citizen could expect to exercise their rights. A second example can clarify the barriers that extreme social inequality creates for exercising citizenship: Third-degree malnutrition (severe malnutrition) in children affects human beings' ability to reason because it affects their cerebral development. This situation contradicts the principle of autonomy on which democracy rests: that each individual is the best judge of her/his own interests (Dahl 1989; see also O'Donnell's chapter in this book).

48. If institutions for dealing with these issues do not exist or are extremely weak, then the regime is downgraded. A case in point, as noted in section 1, was Nicaragua during President Alemán's government (1996–2001).

49. I could argue that the principle of autonomy (Dahl 1989), which lays the foundation of the status of citizenship, implies certain degrees of social equalization among those the law defines as citizens (Marshall 1950; Sen 1999; O'Donnell 2001a).

50. I wonder if, with our present state of knowledge, one can come up with such a list of additional requisites of democracy. I posit these items as a way to entice discussion. In this line of argumentation I am following, once again, O'Donnell's lead (2001a). Nonetheless, I take the argument a bit further.

51. Democracies differ in the extent to which they expand along these dimensions. For example, some democracies push along the dimension of subnational regimes further than others.

52. A methodological offspring of this position is the claim that one gains analytical depth by keeping different things separate. Thus, conflating democracy with a political regime allows one to study the causal links between democracy and, say, the *Estado democrático de derecho*. As a general statement, keeping different things separate makes sense except when they introduce artificial and/or arbitrary distinctions. My point is that both the regime and the *Estado democrático de derecho* are dimensions of a broader concept of democracy.

53. The idea of a fundamental democratic promise is taken from O'Donnell 1998.

54. As approved by the Audit Steering Committee in June 1998 (in this English version some editing was done to clarify meaning).

BIBLIOGRAPHY

Acuña, V. 1993. *Conflicto y reforma en Costa Rica (1940–1949)*. San José: Editorial Universidad Estatal a Distancia.

Aguilar, M. 1989. *Los derechos civiles en Costa Rica, 1940–1980: Historia de un proceso democrático*. San José: Instituto Costarricense de Estudios Sociales.

Alfaro, R. 2002. "Estudio sobre la administración de la justicia en Costa Rica." Paper prepared for the Segundo Informe sobre Desarrollo Humano en Centroamérica y Panamá. San José: PNUD.

Altman, D. 1998. "Revisión de los indicadores utilizados para medir la democracia." Paper prepared for the State of the Nation Project.

Altman, D., and A. Pérez-Liñán. 2002. "Assessing the Quality of Democracy: Freedom, Competitiveness, and Participation in 18 Latin American Countries." *Democratization* 9, no. 2: 85–100.

Ames, R., E. Bernales, S. López, and R. Roncagliolo. 2001. *Situación de la Democracia en el Perú (2000–2001).* Lima: Idea Internacional, Pontificia Universidad Católica del Perú.

Baker, B. 1999. "The Quality of Democracy in the Developing World: Why and How Should It Be Measured?" Paper presented at the 27th ECPR Joint Session of Workshops, 26–31 March, Mannheim.

Becker, D. 1999. "Latin America: Beyond 'Democratic Consolidation.' " *Journal of Democracy* 10, no. 2.

Beetham, D. 1994. "Key Principles and Indices for a Democratic Audit." In *Defining and Measuring Democracy.* London: Sage.

Beetham, D., and S. Weir. 1998. *Political Power and Democratic Control in Britain.* London: Routledge.

Beetham, D. et al. 2001. *International IDEA Handbook on Democracy Assessment.* New York: Kluwer Law International.

———. 2002a. *The State of Democracy: Democratic Assessments in Eight Nations.* Boston: Kluwer Law International.

———. 2002b. *Democracy under Blair: A Democratic Audit of the United Kingdom.* London: Politico Human Rights Centre, University of Essex.

Booth, J. 1995. "Elites and Democracy in Central America." In *Elections and Democracy in Central America,* edited by M. Seligson and J. Booth. Chapel Hill: University of North Carolina Press.

———. 1998. *Costa Rica: Quest for Democracy.* Boulder, Colo: Westview Press.

Carranza, E. 2002. *Sobrépoblación pénitenciaria como obstáculo a la vigencia de la normative de Naciones Unidas en América Latina y el Caribe.* San José: ILANUD.

Casas, K. 2002. *Sistemas de financiamiento político en Centroamérica.* Paper prepared for the Segundo Informe sobre Desarrollo Humano en Centroamérica y Panamá. San José: PNUD.

CEPAL. 2002. *Panorama económico y social de América Latina.* Available online at www.eclac.un.org.

Cheibub, J. A., and A. Przeworski. 1997. "Government Spending and Economic Growth under Democracy and Dictatorship." In *Understanding Democracy,* edited by Albert Breton et al., 107–24. New York: Cambridge University Press.

Coppedge, M. 2000. "Modernización y umbrales de democracia: Evidencias de un camino y un proceso comunes." In *Democracia: Discusiones y nuevas aproximaciones,* edited by Ernesto López and Scott Mainwaring, 103–35. Buenos Aires: Universidad Nacional de Quilmes.

Dahl, R. 1971. *Polyarchy.* New Haven, Conn: Yale University Press (Spanish translation, *La poliarquía: Participación y oposición,* Buenos Aires: Rei, 1989).

———. 1989. *Democracy and Its Critics.* New Haven, Conn.: Yale University Press (Spanish translation, *La democracia y sus críticos,* Barcelona: Paidós, 1993).

———. 1996. *The Future of Democratic Theory.* Madrid: Instituto Juan March.

———. 1999. *On Democracy.* New Haven, Conn.: Yale University Press (Spanish translation, *La democracia: Una guía para los ciudadanos,* Buenos Aires: Taurus, 1999).

Dunleavy, P., and H. Margetts. 1994. "The Experiential Approach to Auditing Democracy." In *Defining and Measuring Democracy,* edited by D. Beetham, 155–81. Londen: Sage.

Ferguson, Niall. 2001. *Poder y dinero.* Madrid: Taurus.

Freedom House. 2004. *Country Ratings.* Available at www.freedomhouse.org/ratings/allscore04.htm.

Garnier, L. 1990. "Gasto Público y desarrollo social en Costa Rica." In *Cuadernos de política económica.* Heredia: Universidad Nacional.

General Accounting Office. 1988. *The Yellow Book.* Washington, D.C.: GAO.

Gutiérrez, C. J. 1983. "Síntesis del proceso constitucional." In *Derecho constitucional costarricense,* edited by C. J. Gutiérrez. San José: Editorial Juricentro.

Gutiérrez, M., and J. Vargas Cullell. 1998. *La Auditoría ciudadana de la calidad de la democracia: Propuesta para su ejecución.* San José: Proyecto Estado de la Nación (PEN).

Held, D. 1996. *Models of Democracy.* Stanford, Calif.: Stanford University Press.

Hildebrand, M. E., and M. S. Grindle. 1997. "Building Sustainable Capacity in the Public Sector: What Can Be Done?" In *Getting Good Government: Capacity Building in the Public Sectors of Developing Countries,* edited by M. S. Grindle, 31–61. Cambridge, Mass.: Harvard University Press.

Jiménez, M. A. 1974. *Desarrollo constitucional de Costa Rica.* San José: Editorial Costa Rica.

Jurado, J. 2001. *El valor de la Constitución y el desarrollo constitucional costarricense.* San José: Revista de Historia, Universidad de Costa Rica.

Klug, F., and K. Starmer et al. 1996. *The Three Pillars of Liberty: Political Rights and Freedoms in the United Kingdom.* London: Routledge.

Latinobarómetro. 2002. *Informe de prensa 2002.* Available at www.Latinobarometro.org/and2001/prensa2002.pdf.

Lehouq, F. 1995. "La dinámica político institucional y la construcción de un régimen democrático: Costa Rica en perspectiva latinoamericana." In *Identidades nacionales y Estado moderno en Centroamérica,* edited by A. Taracena and B. Piel. San José: Editorial Universidad de Costa Rica.

———. 1998. *Instituciones democráticas y conflictos políticos en Costa Rica.* Heredia: Editorial Universidad Nacional Autónoma.

Lehouq, F., and I. Molina. 1999. *Urnas de lo inesperado*. San José: Editorial Universidad de Costa Rica.

Lijphart, A. 1971. "Comparative Politics and the Comparative Method." *American Political Science Review* 65, no. 3.

———. 1999. *Patterns of Democracy*. New Haven, Conn.: Yale University Press.

Linz, J. J. 1997. "Some Thoughts on the Victory and Future of Democracy." In *Democracy's Victory and Crisis,* edited by A. Hadenius, 404–26. Cambridge: Cambridge University Press.

Linz, J. J., and A. Stepan. 1996. *Problems of Democratic Transitions and Consolidation*. Baltimore, Md.: Johns Hopkins University Press.

Lipset, S. M. 1981. *Political Man: The Social Bases of Politics*. Baltimore, Md.: Johns Hopkins University Press.

Livingstone, S., and J. Morison. 1995. *An Audit of Democracy in Northern Ireland*. Belfast: Fortnight Educational Trust.

Mahoney, J. 2001. *The Legacies of Liberalism*. Baltimore, Md.: Johns Hopkins University Press.

Mainwaring, S. 1999. "The Surprising Resilience of Elected Governments." *Journal of Democracy* 10, no. 3: 101–14.

Marshall, T. H. 1950. *Citizenship and Social Class*. Cambridge: Cambridge University Press.

Mills, C. W. 1959. *The Sociological Imagination*. New York: Oxford University Press.

Ministerio de Planificación Nacional y Política Económica (MIDEPLAN). 2001. *Indice de Desarrollo Social*. San José: Serie de Estudios Especiales.

Mouffe, C. 2000. *The Democratic Paradox*. London: Verso.

Munck, G., and J. Verkuilen. 2002. "Measuring Alternative Data Sets." *Comparative Political Studies* 35, no. 1: 5–34.

Muñoz, M. 1990. *El Estado y la abolilción del Ejército*. San José: Editorial Porvenir.

Naim, N. 1993. *Paper Tigers and Minotaurs: The Politics of Venezuela's Economic Reforms*. Washington, D.C.: Carnegie Endowment for International Peace.

———. 1994. *Latin America's Journey to the Market: From Macroeconomic Shocks to Institutional Therapy*. San Francisco: ICS Press.

O'Donnell, G. 1993. "Acerca del Estado, la democratización y algunos problemas conceptuales. Una perspectiva latinoamericana con referencias a países poscomunistas." *Desarrollo Económico* 33, no. 130: 163–84.

———. 1997. "¿Democracia Delegativa?" In *Contrapuntos: Ensayos Escogidos Sobre Autoritarismo y Democratización,* 287–304. Buenos Aires: Paidós.

———. 1998. "Accountability Horizontal." *Agora* 4, no. 8: 5–34.

———. 1999. "Polyarchies and the (Un)Rule of Law in Latin America." In *The Rule of Law and the Underprivileged in Latin America,* edited by Juan Mendez et al., 303–37. Notre Dame, Ind.: University of Notre Dame Press.

———. 2001a. "Accountability Horizontal: La Institucionalización Legal de la Desconfianza Política." *PostData* 7: 11–34.

————. 2001b. "Lo que la Auditoría es y no es." In *Auditoría Ciudadana sobre la calidad de la democracia: Tomo 1,* Proyecto Estado de la Nación, 35–36. San José: Editorama.

————. 2002. "Las poliarquías y la (in)efectividad de la ley en América latina." In *La (In)Efectividad de la Ley y la Exclusión en América Latina,* edited by J. E. Méndez et al., 305–36. Buenos Aires: Paidós.

O'Donnell, G., and P. C. Schmitter. 1994. *Transiciones desde un Gobierno Autoritario.* Volume 4 of *Conclusiones Tentativas sobre las Democracias Inciertas.* Barcelona: Paidós.

Ostrom, E. et. al. 1993. *Institutional Incentives and Sustainable Development: Infrastructure Policies in Perspective.* Boulder, Colo.: Westview Press.

Peeler, J. A. 1985. *Latin American Democracies: Colombia, Costa Rica, Venezuela.* Chapel Hill, University of North Carolina Press.

————. 1991. "Elite Settlements and Democratic Consolidation." In *Elites and Democratic Consolidation in Latin America and Southeastern Europe,* edited by J. Highley and R. Gunther. New York: Cambridge University Press.

Peralta, H. 1962. *Las constituciones de Costa Rica.* Madrid: Instituto de Estudios Políticos.

Pérez, H. 1997. *Historia de Costa Rica 1940–1980: Una síntesis interpretativa.* San José: Editorial Universidad Estatal a Distancia.

Pérez-Liñán, A. 1998. "Assessing the Quality of Democracy in Costa Rica: The Citizens' Perspective." Document prepared for the State of the Nation Project.

Peruzzotti, E., and C. Smulovitz, eds. 2002. *Controlando la política: Ciudadanos y Medios en las nuevas democracias latinoamericanas.* Buenos Aires: Temas.

Programa de Naciones Unidas para el Desarrollo (PNUD). 2003. *Segundo Informe sobre el desarrollo humano en Centroamerica y Panama.* San José: Editorama.

Proyecto Estado de la Nación (PEN). 1999. *Estrategia de trabajo de campo de la Auditoría ciudadana sobre la calidad de la democracia.* San José: PEN.

————. 2000. *Modelo de evaluación de la Auditoría ciudadana sobre la calidad de la democracia.* San José: PEN.

————. 2001a. *Auditoría ciudadana sobre la calidad de la democracia: Tomo 1.* San José: Editorama. (also available online at www.estadonacion.or.cr)

————. 2001b. *Auditoría ciudadana sobre la calidad de la democracia: Tomo 2.* San José: Editorama. (also available online at www.estadonacion.or.cr)

————. 2001c. *Informe sobre el Estado de la Nación,* vol. 7. San José: Editorama.

————. 2002. *Informe sobre el Estado de la Nación,* vol. 8. San José: Editorama.

————. 2003. *Informe sobre el Estado de la Nación,* vol. 9. San José: Editorama.

Przeworski, A., et al. 2000. *Democracy and Development: Political Institutions and Well-Being in the World, 1950–1990.* Cambridge: Cambridge University Press.

Przeworski, A., and F. Limongi. 1997. "Democracy and Development." In *Democracy's Victory and Crisis,* edited by A. Hadenius, 163–94. Cambridge: Cambridge University Press.

Przeworski, A. et al. 1997. "What Makes Democracies Endure?" In *Consolidating Third Wave Democracies,* edited by L. Diamond, M. Plattner, Y. Chu, and H. Tien, 1:295–311. Baltimore, Md.: Johns Hopkins University Press.

Ragin, C. 1987. *The Comparative Method: Moving Beyond Qualitative and Quantitative Strategies.* Berkeley: University of California Press.

Real Academia Española. 1992. *Diccionario de la Lengua Española.* Madrid: Real Academia Española.

Reider, H. 1994. *The Complete Guide to Operational Auditing.* New York: John Wiley and Sons.

Ricchiute, D. 1995. *Auditing and Assurance Services.* Cincinnati: South-Western College Publishing.

Román, A. C. 1995. *Las finanzas públicas de Costa Rica: metodología y fuentes (1870–1948).* San José: Centro de Investigaciones Históricas de la Universidad de Costa Rica.

Rosenberg, M. 1980. *Las luchas por el seguro social en Costa Rica.* San José: Editorial Costa Rica.

Rovira, J. 1982. *Estado y política económica en Costa Rica, 1948–1970.* San José: Editorial Porvenir.

Salazar, J. 1981. *Política y reforma en Costa Rica, 1914–1958.* San José: Editorial Porvenir.

Salazar, O. 1997. *El apogeo de la república Liberal en Costa Rica.* San José: Editorial Universidad de Costa Rica.

Sartori, G. 1987. *The Theory of Democracy Revisited.* Chatham, N.J.: Chatham House Publishers.

———. 1991. "Comparing and Miscomparing." *Journal of Theoretical Politics* 3, no. 3: 243–57.

Segura, J. 1990. *La clase política y el poder judicial en Costa Rica.* San José: Editorial Universidad Estatal a Distancia.

Sen, A. 1999. *Development as Freedom.* New York: Alfred A. Knopf (Spanish translation, *Desarrollo y Libertad,* Buenos Aires: Planeta, 2000).

Sheldon, D. R. 1996. *Achieving Accountability in Business and Government.* Westport, Conn.: Quorum Books.

Smulovitz, C., and E. Peruzzotti. 2000. "Social Accountability in Latin America." *Journal of Democracy* 11, no. 4: 147–58.

Solana, E. 2003. "Estudio sobre administración de justicia de los países centroamericanos de acuerdo con varios indicadores." Document prepared for the Segundo Informe sobre Desarrollo Humano en Centroamérica y Panamá. San José: PNUD.

Valenzuela, J. S. 1998. "Macro Comparisons without the Pitfalls: A Protocol for Comparative Research." In *Politics, Society, and Democracy: Latin America,* edited by S. Mainwaring and J. S. Valenzuela. Boulder, Colo.: Westview Press.

Vargas, C. 1999. "Historia política, militar y jurídica de Costa Rica entre 1870 y 1914."
     In *Costa Rica, desde las sociedades auctóctonas hasta 1914,* edited by A. M. Botey. San
     José: Editorial Universidad de Costa Rica.
World Bank. 1997. *World Development Report.* New York: Oxford University Press.
Yashar, D. 1997. *Demanding Democracy.* Stanford, Calif.: Stanford University Press.

part II

Comments by Workshop Participants

About the Comments

The following comments are the workshop participants' reactions to the preceding chapters by O'Donnell and Vargas Cullell. They provide new perspectives on the themes proposed for discussion and, as a group, offer an approximation of the exchange of ideas that took place during the February 2002 workshop in Heredia, Costa Rica, on the "Quality of Democracy and Human Development in Latin America."

The following section includes comments by well-known Latin Americanists who, from various disciplinary approaches and national perspectives, enrich the debate opened by the first two chapters. While these comments share a common thematic axis and raise similar concerns, they choose different points of entry that result in greater emphasis and concentration on certain aspects, depending on the case. As a result, we have organized the comments into three groups.

The first group includes authors who were most interested in reflecting on the contributions and implications contained in the proposal to broaden the concept of democracy. These essays also examine the accomplishments of the citizen audit in Costa Rica. In her comments, Gabriela Ippolito reexamines ideas about paradigm shifts originally introduced by Kuhn. She presents the broader approach to democracy as a spearhead for a new paradigm that can respond better to the anomalies that current approaches have been unable to explain. For Laurence Whitehead, the value of the two main chapters lies in their search for a new theoretical framework to integrate topics and areas of analysis that have developed as independent specializations. Likewise, he ponders the citizen audit's usefulness as a tool for channeling exchanges between governors and the governed, as well as its potential for uniting normative and empirical research. Terry Lynn Karl appreciates in general terms the effort to go beyond minimalist concepts of democracy, human rights, and development that currently predominate. Nevertheless, she argues against the existence of a "virtuous cycle" between democracy, human development, and human rights created by the existence of a rule of law. Juan Méndez offers a perspective that emphasizes the juridical dimension of the debate and highlights the importance of the existence of a kind of state whose institutions allow it to guarantee rights. Regarding limits to the concept of democracy, he suggests that the main problem lies in a lack of rigor in characterizing the regimes that actually exist. Norbert Lechner asks how it may be possible to go beyond a procedural vision of democracy without ending up with a general theory of society. Reducing democracy to the democratic regime is unsatisfactory, he argues, but the definition should not be expanded to include social life in its entirety. He admits that he has no answer to the dilemma but believes the search, in itself, to be valid.

The second group of comments combines conceptual treatment of the theme with concern for comparative aspects, especially those related to evaluation of the quality of democracy as proposed by the citizen audit. María Hermínia Tavares de Almeida highlights the issue of states' capacities to guarantee civil and social rights. In this sense, she admits that the financial and fiscal limitations of many Latin American states threaten their potential to develop these capacities. Accordingly, the problem is not so much the absence or limitations of legal norms but rather the effective exercise of rights guaranteed by the state. Catherine Conaghan highlights the merits of presenting a convincing argument to demonstrate the link between material life and the exercise of rights in a democracy. In her understanding, O'Donnell and Vargas Cullell's chapters lay the foundation for a new approach to democracy and democratization. She suggests that the nexus between the political and the economic defines the next frontier for efforts to promote democracy. Osvaldo Iazzetta discusses efforts to go beyond the limits that have made reflection on democracy a prisoner of narrow theoretical frameworks. He points out that the expansion of the concept must be undertaken with care so that it can go beyond the explanatory deficiencies of currently prevailing categories while avoiding an overly broad approach that compromises its comparative potential. Manuel Alcántara Sáez emphasizes the need to consider political culture as a relevant factor; he suggests that the audit not be limited to a focus on citizens' "democratic aspirations" but also should focus on their civic and political aspirations. Likewise, he suggests taking into account the views of elites as well as the international context and the impact of globalization on the quality of democracy.

The third group of comments provides discussion of conceptual issues as well as methodological suggestions related to measuring the quality of democracy and the experience of the citizen audit in Costa Rica. Michael Coppedge highlights the citizen audit's relevance as a self-evaluative task for democracy and as a tool for stimulating participation in the democratic process. At the same time, he points out the problems involved in measuring concepts generated through citizen consultation and suggests that in future projects stronger intellectual guidance be provided in selecting the concepts to be measured by researchers. Sebastián Mazzuca employs a distinction between political philosophy and political science to delimit prescriptive and descriptive levels that may enter into conflict when measuring the quality of democracy. Consequently, identifying the peculiarities and tensions between these levels becomes indispensable to defining the concept of democracy and evaluating its quality. Gerardo Munck focuses on methodological aspects that researchers must consider when formulating concepts for measurement. He concentrates on examining some attributes that are included in and excluded from the concept of democracy and evaluates the citizen audit as a source of information that can be used to measure democracy using dimensions that exceed Dahl's concept of polyarchy.

In Search of a New Paradigm

*Quality of Democracy and Human
Development in Latin America*

GABRIELA IPPOLITO

Introduction

The project organizers' call to debate the theoretical foundation of
the concept of "quality of democracy" and its possible empirical applications
could not have come at a more opportune time. Prompting the call, undoubtedly, is the paradigmatic crisis that current theories of democracy (basically
understood as theories of the political regime) are undergoing, as well as the
limited results of democracy promotion efforts (mostly devised from such
theories) that governmental and multilateral institutions have tried out in
the last two decades.[1]

This paradigmatic crisis (which Kuhn[2] defined as the emergence of growing anomalies or divergences between theoretical assumptions about, in this
case, democratic theories and the observations of the democracies that actually
exist) stems from the rapid expansion over the last two decades of political

regimes that have adopted electoral forms of democracy while at the same time showing great deficiencies in other, no less important, attributes of democracy. According to Freedom House's ratings for 2001, more democracies currently exist than ever before in the history of humanity, 121 in all. These democracies include Ukraine, Venezuela, Sweden, Turkey, Costa Rica, and Russia, to cite a few examples. A glance at the day-to-day reality in these democracies shows wide divergences among them, both in terms of civil, human, and social rights and in the effectiveness of basic aspects of the workings of the political regime, understood narrowly as a set of political freedoms. Although elections appear in some of these regimes as the principle mechanism for gaining political power, these elections are far from clean, free, and (most importantly) institutionalized.[3] Furthermore, in practice political power is exercised through a complex network of informal and essentially undemocratic institutions. In short, the very meaning of citizenship is at issue in many of these countries.

A no less relevant fact is that in the majority of these countries an unprecedented growth in poverty and economic inequality has accompanied the implantation of democracy. As a corollary, we find a high level of citizen dissatisfaction with the functioning of democratic institutions. Today it seems taboo to bring poverty and social inequality into the definition and evaluation of democracy. Yet we must not forget that in the nineteenth century the redistributive thesis of democracy[4]—that is, the supposition that introducing majority rule and universal suffrage would lead to greater social equality—was considered a legitimate and central issue in the debate about political democracy. The electoral path appeared to be the antecedent and to a large extent the *raison d'être* for social citizenship.

In this context of growing anomalies between democratic theory and praxis, and between citizen aspirations and social reality, it is legitimate to question the pertinence of assessing the regimes of such countries as democratic. Social scientists have adopted two strategies in response to these anomalies. On the one hand, they have produced a series of conceptual refinements about democracy, leading to the birth of so-called "democracies with adjectives." Thus we find democracies of various types: oligarchical, delegative, electoral, semidemocratic, etc. While the use of adjectives initially was useful for advancing the classification of "hybrid" political regimes, their proliferation has generated more confusion than precision; consequently, democracy's definitional horizon has been lost. When we speak of "democracy," it is not clear to what we are referring. More recently, and partly in response to this conceptual confusion, other scholars have chosen to reclassify some doubtfully democratic regimes as authoritarian, attributing to them only a few of the characteristics belonging to a democracy.[5] In my opinion this only adds to the confusion and is indicative of the deepening crisis of meaning that, in any scientific field, precedes paradigm shifts.

In this sense, the debate about the quality of democracy comes at an opportune moment. This concept acknowledges that the question of democracy is not only a question of classifying political regimes or choosing from among current definitions, whether minimalist or maximalist. To the contrary, this concept of quality indicates that the *redefinition* of democracy's very content and the dimensions relevant for its study are at issue. To ask what dimensions are relevant for defining a country as democratic—as the authors of the first two chapters of this volume have done—is a matter not only of academic but practical relevance, with the potential to develop more effective democracy promotion policies throughout the world. In this context, the citizen audit undertaken in Costa Rica is an appropriate tool for examining the reality of democracy, with great potential for its subsequent theoretical refinement.

Human Development, Human Rights, and Democracy

O'Donnell's chapter is a major theoretical effort to integrate in a single framework (that of the quality of democracy) themes such as political democracy, development, and human rights, which until now have been approached from different—and in some ways, even contradictory—analytical perspectives. The text constitutes an invitation to abandon the safe waters of normal scientific praxis and head into stormy seas. In short, this work may be the spearhead of a new paradigm—that is, a different way to conceptualize and approach a question or set of questions, in this case democracy. Like any paradigm shift, the point of departure is an issue that available theories of democracy cannot answer. I believe that the question underlying O'Donnell's chapter is the following: How do we account for the coexistence of a democratic political regime based on the idea of citizenship or political equality in a context of high socioeconomic inequality and/or violation of fundamental human rights?

O'Donnell's proposal does not imply the simple expansion of the concept of democracy (or the democratic regime). Rather, he attempts to understand political democracy in a new way and, in so doing, to prompt a shift of focus in the definition of problems and questions that are relevant and likely to be carefully analyzed, as well as of the standards to be utilized for this purpose. His analysis, based on ideas of human agency and fairness, has repercussions for thinking about the constitutive elements of a political regime *qua* regime and about the relationship of the latter to the minimal conditions for the exercise of political citizenship.

The two central ideas in O'Donnell's work are *human agency* and *fairness*. During the Heredia workshop the debate focused more on the concept of agency than fairness (I will return to this later), yet both ideas are fundamentally related in that they place human beings and the respect for their rights at the center of the analysis of democracy. According to this view, political institutions are crucial to the definition of democracy but only to the degree that they contribute to the constitution of individuals as such, that is, as beings endowed with agency. The question we can draw from this is, what institutions are necessary to protect and promote citizenship? This emphasis on human beings is parallel to the concept of human development that, by making individuals and their capabilities the focus of development, fundamentally changed the terms of the debate and prompted major revisions in the theory and policy of development. I believe that O'Donnell's text points in a similar direction.

Like any paradigm shift, this one will go through advances and setbacks, support and criticism. To link political democracy, human rights, and human development theoretically and to seek their empirical relationship in order to evaluate the quality of democracy implies evading—like Ulysses upon his return to Ithaca—the sirens' song. For it is basically antipolitical sirens who favor governability and stability over a democratic politics that understands the struggles to win rights as its central element. If democracy is based on the ideas of equity and fairness and, as a consequence, on the conquest of citizenship rights, this implies the existence of a public sphere of political conflict in search of significantly reversing the existing asymmetries of power. All of this, in turn, requires a democratic state with the ability to enact appropriate public policies.

O'Donnell's proposal includes both a theoretical redefinition and a meticulous empirical analysis of democracy. Even more important is the work's conviction that a discussion of political democracy remains incomplete if the ethical values that underlie its definition are not made explicit. The question would be, why bet on democracy? Part of the answer that O'Donnell puts forward is that democracy is not only an instrumental arrangement to elect those who govern. Behind the diverse definitions of democracy lie different normative valuations about human dignity and rights. I would call this the *moral logic* of democratic institutions, upon which their political legitimacy finally rests. This line of argument is welcome, particularly at a time when the moral logic of political institutions is regarded as a given, thereby reducing democracy's functioning and improvement to a technical question of institutional engineering.

Democracy, Agency, and the State

O'Donnell defines *agency* as a fundamental element of citizenship and therefore of democracy. Posing the topic from this perspective, the minimal conditions required for the exercise of political citizenship—that is, the thresholds that make agency possible—become a constitutive part of democracy. Expressed in another way, these minimal conditions are no longer external but become intrinsic to democracy. From this it follows that if democracy is based on citizenship, and citizenship is based on the idea of agency, then any violation of the conditions necessary for the existence of agency are violations of citizenship and must be considered part of the *problématique* of democracy. What O'Donnell suggests should not be confused with empirical studies of the relationship between democracy and development, which focus on whether democracies generate more or less economic growth than other political regimes, or if greater economic development raises the probability of achieving or sustaining a democratic regime. The innovative idea is that the violation of the conditions necessary for agency to exist and its impact on the effectiveness of citizenship *define* the degree or quality of democraticness of the political regime. For example, with respect to political equality, even if each person's vote is counted equally, their equality is violated in cases of extreme poverty, in which citizens lack sufficient autonomy to formulate their preferences and may be pressured to vote for candidates who extort them in a clientelistic fashion. In this case, as Fishkin[6] asserts, citizen autonomy and the equal "power" of the vote are violated; as a corollary, one of the basic principles of formal political equality—the possibility that any citizen might cast the decisive vote in an electoral process—is denied.

The second fundamental idea in O'Donnell's text is that of fairness. This idea points to the relationship between democracy and the state. Under a democratic regime, the state is obliged to treat all citizens with the respect they deserve given their condition as agents. This implies providing the basic minimal capabilities required for the exercise of citizenship. This is the problem of the achievement of *substantive justice,* which, following O'Donnell's argument, can only be decided through the democratic process.

Once these minimal necessary capabilities for the exercise of citizenship are decided upon, the question of *procedural justice* emerges; that is, the way policies aimed at facilitating agency, and therefore the exercise of citizenship, are decided and implemented. These procedures usually have a significant effect on the constitution of agency/citizenship beyond the specific content of such policies. In particular, the way social policies are implemented is a crucial sphere for the constitution of citizen identity and, therefore, of agency. In this context, evaluating the quality of democracy is important not only in terms of the state's efforts to generate capabilities but also to register *how* the state gives what it gives. Key questions emerge from this, such as those related to the ways of exercise and discretionality of public power. For example, the law may establish health care as a right, but if implementation of that right is targeted to the point of stigmatizing the beneficiaries, the question arises as to whether this right is facilitating or hampering the constitution of citizenship. Likewise, if social policies to promote equity force the presumed beneficiaries to change their lifestyles or exaggerate their social deprivations in order to obtain benefits, it is worth asking whether this violates the agency of these citizens. Institutions of social welfare are a fundamental element of the relationship between democracy and the state; therefore, it is crucial that they be analyzed in order to understand how state institutions treat citizens; this, in turn, is central to the evaluation of the quality of democracy.

About the Citizen Audit of Democracy

It would be hard to exaggerate the relevance of the citizen audit carried out in Costa Rica. Without a doubt, it is an intellectual and empirical endeavor of major importance. For those of us who make fieldwork a central part of our academic life, the audit provides an excellent example. As such, I suggest that the authors put aside their modesty and stress their contribution not only to academic social science but also as a historical record. The contribution in this regard is the creation of an archive of citizens' democratic opinions and aspirations in a specific time and space. In addition, the audit is not only relevant for subsequent social research but also an excellent tool for identifying and advancing efforts to overcome anomalies in democratic theory, to which I refer above. Regarding the audit's applicability outside of Costa Rica, I share the workshop participants' optimism about the possibilities for doing so at the national, regional, or municipal levels. Therefore, I do not believe that the "size of the country" or "social heterogeneity" variables are definitive obstacles to the audit's viability in other national, regional, and municipal contexts.

The workshop emphasized the audit as a type of accountability and, more specifically, as an instrument of "societal accountability," following the work of Smulovitz and Peruzzotti.[7] My comments on this topic focus on the audit's deliberative dimension. I refer not only to the fact of participation of citizens in the preparatory work of the audit but also to the impact that the audit may have on those who participated in its formulation as well as on those with whom the audit is discussed. In this sense the audit would serve as both an instrument of accountability for public affairs and a mechanism for generating "deliberated opinions" among citizens. In general, citizens possess fragmented information and lack opportunities to interact systematically with one another and exchange opinions on public affairs. Thus the audit gives citizens a chance to deliberate democratically and to generate informed opinions. Consequently, the audit also has important practical potential: its results have prescriptive force because they are the voice of people who meet the special condition of having deliberated with other citizens on matters that affect the entire community. Opinions and standards produced through such deliberation may generate what Fishkin calls "effective hearing."[8]

Despite the existence of an international context that is by and large favorable to democracy, a series of challenges exists today that threaten both the stability and the quality of democracy. Among them are general disenchantment with democratic institutions and growing social inequality attributable to poor economic management, corruption, the lack of rule of law, etc. In this context, I believe that an audit—the result of deliberative action by citizens—has the potential role to serve as an early warning system about threats to democracy. Although the early warning concept comes from the field of security and international conflict studies, a new agenda is developing that considers such issues in terms of *human security,* a broad concept based on the security of individuals that includes as a necessary condition the existence of a high-quality democratic system.

Themes that Should be Incorporated in an Audit

The audit correctly suggests that a fundamental dimension for evaluating the quality of a democracy is the way citizens are treated. In this respect, the context in which social policies are implemented is crucial. This is the area of the state bureaucracy that deals with the most vulnerable citizens; it is there that the exercise of power in relation to the respect for people's rights becomes most crucial and evident. One type of situation consists of encounters with the bureaucracy where, for example, work permits or passports are issued. These tend to be sporadic encounters, where the dignity of a person is not at issue beyond the moment in which the paperwork is completed. In contrast, during exchanges with the state that involve social policies (usually repeated and extended over time), what is at stake is the dignity, the status, and, in many as yet unexplored ways, the very identities of the presumed beneficiaries. It is here we see the best and worst faces of citizen treatment and where we learn whether or not individuals are *really* citizens. Moreover, in these exchanges the level of benefits that a particular state agency grants is as important as the *way* it does it.

The second theme that I believe should be given priority in an audit of the quality of democracy is the treatment of persons who inhabit the territory but are not part of the *demos*. If political democracy is based on the idea of agency and fairness, then respect for the rights of residents who are not citizens must be part of the audit. This is a very important area for exploring the relationship between human rights and citizenship. From it we can derive analytical tools to distinguish, for example, the varying quality of democracy in countries such as Norway and Germany, where the treatment of immigrants is different despite the fact that the two countries are very similar in terms of political rights and social services. To this we should add an analysis of the rights of immigrants at the local level and assess how the exercise or denial of such rights affects the overall quality of democracy in a given country.

NOTES

1. For an evaluation of democracy promotion models, see Thomas Carothers, *Aiding Democracy Abroad: The Learning Curve* (Washington, D.C.: Carnegie Endowment for International Peace, 1999).

2. Thomas Kuhn, *The Structure of Scientific Revolutions* (Chicago: University of Chicago Press, 1962).

3. As Guillermo O'Donnell asserts in "Teoría Democrática y Política Comparada," *Desarrollo Económico* 39, no. 56 (2000): 519–70.

4. Ian Shapiro, "Why the Poor Don't Soak the Rich," *Daedalus* (2002): 118–28.

5. Larry Diamond, "Thinking about Hybrid Regimes," *Journal of Democracy* 13, no. 2 (April 2002): 21–35.

6. James S. Fishkin, *Democracy and Deliberation: New Directions for Democratic Reform* (New Haven, Conn.: Yale University Press, 1991).

7. Catalina Smulovitz and Enrique Peruzzotti, "Social Accountability in Latin America," *Journal of Democracy* 11, no. 4 (2000): 147–58.

8. Fishkin, *Democracy and Deliberation*.

Notes on Human Development, Human Rights, and Auditing the Quality of Democracy

LAURENCE WHITEHEAD

Three Preliminaries

First, three very general comments. O'Donnell's chapter provides a framework for integrating topics and areas of analysis that have grown up as independent fields of specialization. To master the relevant literatures and then rethink them in a more holistic manner requires a very wide range of expertises combined with a firm sense of intellectual discipline. One has to go back to first principles in order to construct a robust framework. But at the same time the project is eminently practical, so one must also have a firm grasp of the relevant social realities: how administrations, legal systems, social policies, and so forth actually function in a variety of very distinct and often troubled settings and how to identify indicators or measurements of these realities that make sense for the purpose of comparisons and can help identify priorities for ameliorative action. This is a hugely ambitious undertaking, and all comments—and especially criticisms—must start by acknowledging the difficulty and originality of the task.

It is also the right general approach, and indeed it is long overdue. Political scientists have segregated a limited range of institutional variables within the framework of "democratic consolidation" and tried to analyze them abstractly and in isolation from their consequences for the citizenry. The *reductio ad absurdum* of this approach is a formally consolidated democracy in Argentina that no one knows how to govern because the people as a whole are utterly disgusted with the achievements of their rulers. Similarly, some human rights advocates have isolated a selection of vital, but in the end partial, legal and civic rights that have been abstracted from their historical and social settings and exalted into absolute desiderata, regardless of other considerations or consequences. Carried to an extreme this can result in criminal trials where the scales of justice are so rigged in favor of the accused that the police give up trying to make arrests and the victims of crime resort to public lynchings.

Even the "human development" community, which has done so much to widen our appreciation of the social dimensions of development not captured by the crude growth rate data, can sometimes be faulted for isolating certain "politically correct" parameters of development performance that may not entirely reflect the aspirations, or even the best interests, of the poor they claim to champion. For example, defense spending tends to be seen as pure waste and a diversion of resources from the satisfaction of human needs. Often, of course, this may well be the case, but there is also an opposite possibility, as illustrated by various "failed states" and the current preoccupation with international terrorism. The preservation of order may sometimes require a large and sustained collective effort, without which hopes of cumulative human development will be frustrated. More generally, effective democratic governance is not an optional add-on to the pursuit of uncontroversial poverty alleviation goals; it is constitutive of human development properly understood. If so, then we need both theoretical tools and empirical instruments for integrating the concerns of the human development community with the priorities of the human rights advocates and the analysts of comparative democratization. This justifies a shift in theoretical emphasis from the incentive structures associated with democratic procedures to the quality of outputs associated with democratic responsiveness to citizen demands. But the shift cannot be purely theoretical. If we are to speak with any conviction about the satisfaction of citizen demands, we need accurate and independent methods of assessing and prioritizing those demands. We need a democratic audit, understood not as a technocratic instrument but rather as an intelligible and practical tool for channelling feedback between the governors and the governed.

On the Language of Rights

What do we mean by classifying any social claim as a "right"? Is it just an officially endorsed collective aspiration, or is it a personally enforceable entitlement that trumps all contrary considerations? At one extreme we have the hazy rhetoric of so many populist orators and at the other the libertarian absolutism of the late lamented Robert Nozick. On the one hand, we have the vacuous amendment to the Mexican constitution promoted by President López Portillo, which guaranteed all citizens the right to a job; on the other hand, we have the "right-to-lifers" who view the sanctity of the fetus as so absolute that the courts may compel a woman to carry an unwanted child to term, even at the risk of her own health. Between these two theoretical extremes most claims about rights are neither entirely vacuous nor unconditionally enforceable. In any case, different rights have different degrees of enforceability. Property rights may be (in some historical contexts) pretty well universal and authoritative. Indigenous rights are almost invariably patchy and contested. Consequently, we need to distinguish between different types of rights, different contexts in which they may be invoked, and different degrees of enforceability. If rights are trumps, some of them are low trumps, and players often pretend to hold an ace of hearts when really their chances of prevailing are far from certain.

O'Donnell's theoretical standpoint on rights is at the heart of the analysis. For him democracy, human rights, and human development all share a foundational conception of the human as *agent*. This condition of agency originates not only in moral claims but also in *universalistic rights*. It is *theoretically undecidable,* however, what minimum sufficient set of rights or capabilities could generate clear and firm generalized intersubjective agreement. What we must do, therefore, is not seek to artificially stipulate any particular set of universal rights but instead *analyze the reasons and consequences* of their undecidability. I hope this is a fair summary of a complex and sophisticated argument. It leads to a critical conclusion with which I am wholly in agreement. If we cannot arrive at a timeless and universal consensus on a minimum set of universal rights, and if merely stipulating the negative (absence of rights) is insufficient to determine the positive requirements for agency, then the crucial issue becomes how can and should we decide which rights are enacted and implemented. The answer provided by O'Donnell is that this only can and should be decided by democracy itself. The consequence of this move is to allow rights to be socially constructed and (within limits) variable. It is also to make democracy not an optional add-on but arguably the master value behind human development and human rights. But we are in deep waters here. Rather than trying to derive democracy from human rights, or human rights from democracy, the logic of O'Donnell's "elective affinity" approach might be to conceive of both as social constructions derived from a common heritage and capable of being made mutually supportive over time.

It would take a long time and much careful work to bridge the gap between the last two paragraphs. I will try to use the standpoint of the first paragraph to probe the limits and implications of O'Donnell's argument as summarized in the second, but these are only tentative notes for a discussion. My first thought is that if rights are socially constructed and contextually located, if they are often just in some sense turbo-charged aspirations, then we can escape the sharp dichotomy between rights and nonrights. Instead of searching for some universal minimum set, we can think in terms of a core of solidly established aspirations that have come to be regarded as rights (that have been socially constructed, for example, over centuries of campaigning for the abolition of slavery;[1] that have been generalized from some social contexts until the remaining exceptions are just shameful dark corners; and that may now carry the credible threat of enforcement by—if necessary—international legal action). Then, growing out from these powerful, but still contingent, core aspirations-become-rights, we can think of correlates that are either not yet so universal (different cultures still have different assumptions about, say, gender equality or the death penalty); or not clearly so integral (is the right to a pension an essential component of agency?); or not so reliably enforceable (the right to work is a glorious aspiration, but we live in a globalized market economy). Thus we would have a relatively solid core of rights, surrounded by a penumbra of associated aspirations of varying degrees of stability, coherence, and enforceability. When democratic processes gave rise to an expansionary use of the language of rights, more of these aspirations would be codified and enforced. But since democracy is also a perpetual error-correction mechanism, if the system became overloaded with too many unmanageable and incompatible claims to rights, the community could always decide to renegotiate the boundaries, to revert to fewer but sounder enforceable rights. The precise line would be theoretically undecidable because it would be "essentially contestable"—permanently subject to democratic deliberation and review.

I am also against posing the questions of the universal nature of rights in terms of a dichotomy. In practice schizophrenics do not have all the same universal rights as Supreme Court justices. As O'Donnell's chapter clearly shows (particularly the quotation from Jeremy Waldron in section 11), the structure of rights potentially available to any bearer of rights is inherently complex. While *some* of these may be clear-cut and directly enforceable, many are tacit conventions and expressions of sociability rather than portable possessions.

Moreover, in new democracies social heterogeneity and policy instability are palpable realities that filter the citizen's subjective experience of her entitlement to rights. The Yanoami do not have precisely the same aspirations (let alone prospects for codifying those wishes into enforceable entitlements) as the executive council of São Paulo's industrial federation (FIESP). There is a socially constructed continuum, and there is constant bargaining and negotiation over the scope and coverage of rights. In what O'Donnell calls the Northwest, it may be that such coverage is relatively stable and clear-cut (although persons of Middle Eastern appearance or origin may not feel so sure of that in the wake of September 11). But certainly in the new democracies that interest us here, and in the democracies where "quality" is most subject to questioning, the scope and coverage of rights is characteristically unstable and volatile. A certain minority may feel reasonably secure in all of their rights. A possibly equal sized minority may be absolutely clear that such rights are not extended to themselves, but in between lies a wide array of citizens who cannot be sure. On good days they can claim some rights, especially if they agitate. If they stay passive, or if their system is subjected to some shock, rights that seemed to be assured can abruptly evaporate. Their pension fund can be seized and allocated to pay off foreign creditors. Their access to information can be abruptly curtailed by censorship or manipulation. The leaders who seemed accountable to them can with short notice turn into inaccessible autocrats or irresponsible incompetents. Experience teaches that as a rule rights are not stable and cannot be taken for granted; rather, they are *volatile*. But this in no way undervalues the importance of generating such rights. On the contrary, those citizens who feel most insecure in their entitlement to rights have the most to gain from collective reiteration of such aspirations.

Another aspect of O'Donnell's perspective on rights also deserves comment. In a laudable attempt to pinpoint foundational principles, he keeps returning to the requirements of *individual agency*. But if rights are socially constructed and enforceable aspirations, and if they come in clusters that do not necessarily follow the sequence postulated by T. H. Marshall, then perhaps some of the requirements of individual agency may not always and necessarily be so foundational. To put the point provocatively, if individual agency is truly the universal core of O'Donnell's conception of rights, then does he not have to follow the libertarians and place private property entitlements in a privileged position? Alternatively, if he resists the pure logic of possessive individualism and prefers to think in terms of more socially responsive variants of agency (which could include heavy taxation, obligatory community service, and other forms of collectivism), then something other than strictly individual rights may become foundational. Do the church, or the state, or the university, or the courts have the status of agency, as well as the individuals composing these corporate entities? If so, the rights of private property can be subordinated, but in addition, then, the cluster of agency rights that may have to be respected is that much wider and more indeterminate—more subject to social construction. Individualists fear the assertion of such collective rights as oppressive. But both O'Donnell and I seem to be at one in arguing that democracy offers (in principle) a way in which such collective aspirations can be codified and enforced without necessarily destroying the foundations of personal freedom.

On Human Development and Democracy

Since the 1990s the conviction has grown that democracy and development are more intimately interconnected and more positively associated than previously thought. Data from many countries has been used to test for such an association (with somewhat mixed results), and various democracy-related terms—"participation," "civil society," "empowerment"—have assumed increasing prominence among the goals pursued by international development agencies. As more developing countries have adopted at least the outward appearance of democratic political practices, the traditional lobby opposed to linking democracy with development has weakened. The majority of developing countries can now hope to benefit if developmental assistance carries democratic conditionality, and donors are increasingly inclined to associate democracy with social development and therefore attach such conditions to their assistance.

If this shift in beliefs and practices is to prove more than just a passing fashion, it will have to be accompanied by a reconceptualization of both democracy and development. Fortunately, such a debate may be getting underway in the relevant scholarly communities. Social development provides the key point of intersection between the separate academic discourses of democratization and economic development. To the extent that these discourses converge, social policies and citizenship entitlements will move from the margins to the center of attention. But it is one thing to shift the focus of attention and quite another to integrate the new objects of study into a coherent and operational analytical framework. Given the intellectual difficulties involved, it is all too tempting for development agencies to maintain an established framework with some "add-on" references to social development, environmental sustainability, gender balance, or political empowerment that sound encouraging but that do not disturb core assumptions or modes of analysis. Similarly, advocates of democratic conditionality find it tempting to treat social welfare as an optional extra.

The established policy framework confronts mounting difficulties, however, both practical and political. On the practical side, with the spread of democracy comes growing demands for decentralization and the devolution of public policies to local levels of government. Similarly, with the spread of market-based systems of competition and allocation comes a shift of economic power away from the government agencies. Moreover, where social development has been allowed to falter, perhaps through omissions arising from too narrow a conception of "good performance," the evidence has increased that such omissions easily produce negative feedback that can eventually destabilize procedural democracy and/or disrupt "sound" growth strategies. Practical considerations of this kind, reinforced by the political preferences of a growing number of both donor and recipient governments, have driven defenders of the old framework to make concessions. Those who favor the incorporation of "softer" styles of explanation and evaluation, however, have yet to develop generally accepted alternative approaches.

It should be possible to move beyond this state of affairs and to reconceptualize both democracy and development in a manner that would provide a superior and integrated policy rationale. The UNDP's *Human Development Report*, UNRISD's *Visible Hands: Taking Responsibility for Social Development*,[2] and a range of academic initiatives indicate that the search for a substitute framework is well underway. It is increasingly recognized, for example, that freedom of expression and association somewhat offset the risks of man-made famines and other preventable "natural" disasters. Citizens with voting rights can exercise some leverage over public policy priorities and may prefer clean drinking water to pharaonic dams and other such projects. If social development elicits local ownership and citizen participation, it may constrain wasteful arms expenditure and tilt international relations toward cooperation rather than conflict. The traditional separation between politics and economics, both narrowly conceived, obstructed investigation of such potential linkages (forgetting what Gunnar Myrdal had once taught us about "cumulative and circular" causation in development studies).

Yet at least four big analytical questions remain unanswered. First, how are developmental priorities to be established, and reconciled, once the traditional criterion of growth maximization has been relaxed? Second, how is good performance to be evaluated if a variety of somewhat competing and partially subjective long-term goals becomes central to integrated "social development"? Third, since in any realistic definition long-term democratic and social developments provoke resistance and conflict, and are therefore prone to periodic interruption and even reversal, how is such turbulence to be interpreted and (possibly) managed? Finally, since even the most optimistic of assumptions about the pace of progress holds that most new democracies will continue for generations to include large numbers of poor citizens whose urgent social policy needs can at best be addressed only gradually, how can democratization and social development be stabilized in the intervening decades? Merely listing these questions is sufficient to demonstrate the scale of the task required before a new integrated analytical framework can fully substitute for the old dichotomy. Here are a few tentative responses.

First, on the establishment of developmental priorities, in principle the answer must lie with the newly enfranchised citizens of these developmental democracies. As democratization proceeds, ownership of the development process is bound to pass from the specialized agencies and ministries toward the local authorities and societies directly and permanently affected. (Admittedly, this assertion rests on a view of democratization as a long-term, cumulative process of social learning.)

Second, on the evaluation of social development performance, international comparative indicators will remain indispensable and will have to be further refined. But an integrated view of development will require all evaluations increasingly to take account of the expectations and perceptions of the citizens in question. That, too, follows from the idea that democratic development requires local ownership.

Third, the realities of conflict and nonlinearity in long-term processes of social development pose a severe analytical challenge that cannot be resolved purely by invoking democratic authority. Local ownership must be qualified by respect for the opinions and experiences of others. Social development in a liberalized international system must be cosmopolitan and constrained within an agreed framework of basic rights and values. For this reason, an integrated approach will require cooperation and coresponsibility across international boundaries. A social catastrophe in, say, Afghanistan or Albania can jeopardize both democracy and development far afield. Recently, there has been some progress in generating norms of conduct for managing such conflicts, but the challenges remain acute.

Finally, at the domestic level, the management techniques needed to contain frustration while gradually diminishing the backlog of legitimate and unmet citizen demands can easily jar with both the standard operating procedures of the development agencies and with the impersonal logic of the market economy. Once democracy is understood as more than the alternation in government of rival parties, politics regains its status as an autonomous sphere of social action with its own messy logic and awkward outcomes. UNRISD is right to refer to the "visible hands" that will then "take responsibility for social development," but more analysis is needed to distinguish the legitimate exercise of democratic authority from the old vices of mismanagement behind a veil of good intentions. Once development is understood as a process of social construction and not just of growth maximization, then local creativity and experimentation can be celebrated. But here, too, lurk the dangers of distortion and manipulation. A strong analytical framework, grounded on solid international consensus and backed by widely accepted lessons of experience, will be required if such experiments are to be more than cosmetic "add-ons" to development and are not to prove costly "subtractions from" conventional growth.

The Method of the Citizen Audit

O'Donnell's chapter contains rich theoretical analysis, but it also gives rise to four excursi on assessing the quality of democracy. The aim is to identify procedures and indicators that are empirically testable and that permit comparison and feedback. He joins Sen in stressing that in order to assess the "real interests" of individuals, both internal and external perspectives are needed. The method of the audit permits the assembly and testing of a widening range of indicators—objective rankings and national performance as in the Human Development Index; subjective perceptions via public opinion surveys like *Latinobarómetro;* cross-tabulated evaluations of such key hidden variables as the incidence of corruption (as in the Transparency International and World Bank enquiries); and in-depth case studies such as the seven municipal governments evaluated in Costa Rica's State of the Nation Project. There is a rapid proliferation of measurements and assessments of this kind. One of the key tasks of our workshop on the quality of democracy presumably was to evaluate the different types of evidence becoming available and to help us put it in order, so that instead of being swamped by floods of partial and inconsistent data we are able to assemble a coherent and collectively intelligible picture of overall democratic performance. For this we need reliable comparisons over time, between countries, and also within single countries at a given moment in time.

Costa Rica seems to be in the vanguard in Latin America as far as democracy audits are concerned. (Although I have also seen UNDP-backed studies of El Salvador and Bolivia that contain much of great value and that, in particular, illustrate my thesis about the "instability" or "volatility" of the rights extended to so many of the citizens of new democracies.) What seems to me critical is that the method of the audit should be sufficiently comprehensive and impartial to provide a basis for collective deliberation, but it should also be sufficiently crisp and relevant to attract popular interest and involvement. Somehow the partial indicators and complex comparisons would have to be structured in such a manner that ordinary citizens, and not just a coterie of experts, could assimilate their implications. The diagnosis has to be sufficiently precise and well founded to generate proposals for improvement and reform that can be made operational by a public administration and a legal system that cannot just respond to moral exhortations. But an audit of democracy is not just an instrument for generating specific measures of reform. It is also a means of collective self-reflection, a component of the very process of democratic deliberation itself. At the risk of sounding pretentious, it struck me that in Weberian terms one might think of a democratic audit as penetrating the *verstehen* of the society, or in Hegelian terms as contributing to its self-realization.

We are at a very early state in experimenting with this method of both assessing and improving the quality of democracy. An audit of democracy can be promoted as a strategic instrument for the social construction of a more responsive and accountable system of self-government. It could fill a crucial gap between elite circulation via competitive elections (the Schumpeterian conception of democracy) and more ambitious conceptions of democratization as a progression toward a more rule-based, participatory, and consensual form of social coexistence. But we should not overlook the possibility that some variants of the audit process could also be subject to distortion or appropriation in the service of other, less noble, causes such as buying time or deflecting blame. In the Heredia meeting, Thomas Carothers made a key point when he warned that too long a list of secondary desiderata could distract attention from the essential problems of centralization of power and lack of participation. There are important conceptual and practical difficulties before the democratic potential of the audit process can be fully realized, but the attempt is of the utmost interest, not only for Costa Rica or Latin America but for the future of democracy itself. That future remains "essentially contested," and an audit of democracy could be a vital weapon in such contexts.

Afterthoughts

One way to view democracy is as a civic religion. It can stabilize otherwise destructive sequences of collective action, it can reinforce national identity, and it can provide individuals with a means of "value discovery" as well as a way of processing and summing up personal preferences. This is certainly not the only way to view democracy, but it is perhaps the implicit view of those who gathered in the Hotel La Condesa in Heredia on the eve of the Costa Rican *fiesta patria* that is election day. If Costa Ricans have adopted democracy as their civic religion, they are particularly likely to embrace methods, such as the State of the Nation citizen audit, that reinforce that self-understanding and that both celebrate and deepen that commitment.

On a more subjective note I could not avoid reflecting as our discussions unfolded that there was a distinct parallel (O'Donnell might prefer "elective affinity") between our proceedings and those of the priesthood of an official religion. Pursuing this slightly far-fetched analogy, the Human Development Report could be compared to an encyclical and the annual audits of democracy to Anglican discussions about the spiritual health of the nation. On the same basis, attempts to generalize this model for other countries bear some resemblance to old debates between Christian missionaries about how far to bend in accepting local religious beliefs in order to generalize the faith.

This is intended as a light-hearted analogy, not a criticism of our deliberations. There is a good case for applying reason and research effort to the task of deepening democracy. This is both a scientific and a normative undertaking. Social scientists who attempt to combine the two may be addressing a deep-felt social need, but they are also filling a space previously occupied by the clerisy. Oxford and Cambridge rose to academic eminence by collaborating to produce the King James Bible, a huge task of research that also addressed a spiritual need and crystallized a civic religion. In a secular age universities no longer preach, but they can still orient their research toward the elucidation of collective values and the production of well-thought-out and carefully validated audits of democracy offer an appropriate way to unite normative and empirical investigating.

NOTES

1. On the paradox of Western historical development, that ideas of precise legal agency and personal responsibility developed first and furthest in association with the slave-owning democracies of Greece—and the United States. See Orlando Patterson, *Freedom in the Making of Western Culture* (New York: Basic Books, 1991).

2. United Nations Research Institute for Social Development, London: Earthscan Publications, 2001.

Latin America

Virtuous or Perverse Cycle

TERRY LYNN KARL

The Costa Rican audit, and especially the chapter by Guillermo O'Donnell, represent an ambitious and daring effort to conceptualize and assess the quality of democracy in Latin America. Not only does O'Donnell's text attempt to connect strands of moral, legal, and political thinking about human development, human rights, and democracy, thereby reinforcing the seminal work of Amartya Sen and past reports of the United Nations Development Program, but it does so by placing human agency at the center of attention. In O'Donnell's universalistic vision, it is the "citizen agent"[1] who makes political democracy work. Agency can only be exercised if the individual has basic conditions or capabilities; these, in turn, are guaranteed by positive rights to an adequate standard of living and protections through the rule of law. Definitions here are certainly not minimalist: democracies are not simply "electoralist"; human rights are not just civil liberties; and development is not restricted to a rise in the gross national product. This insistence on the individual citizen as the primary "agent," on the one hand, and the linkage between development, rights, and democracy in a moral and virtuous cycle, on the other, is the central attraction of O'Donnell's argument. It is a strong statement about the possibilities of democracy, even procedurally based democracy, and one that I share in many ways. But it is also the source of some problematic issues regarding individualism and some latent tensions between human development, human rights, and democracy, as we shall see below. Arguments regarding the possible "virtuous cycle" of democracy, human development, and human rights also need to take into account some of the very real tensions between these three normative visions and goals, and measures of the "quality of democracy" should also try to identify these tensions as they arise.

Excessive Faith in the Rule of Law

Political citizenship, O'Donnell claims, is first and foremost a legally defined and formal status. It results from juridical rules based on fairness, which have been elaborated progressively in a long and complex historical trajectory. The rule of law (meaning in its narrowest sense that laws should be publicly promulgated, predictable, reasonably clear, and prospective and that political, administrative, and judicial decisions, issued by independent and impartial authorities, should be applied to all in accordance with these laws)[2] is seen as a universal moral imperative. Even though this vision of rule of law is contested among legal scholars, given Latin America's weak judicial structures, O'Donnell's emphasis on the importance of the rule of law for a quality democracy is basically correct, in my view. Where I would disagree is in the strong faith running throughout O'Donnell's argument that the rule of law is likely to be democratic and nonideological, thus enabling the individual—the carrier of rights—to have a legally grounded claim to be treated equally in the exercise of agency. In the debate over what the rule of law actually is, O'Donnell locates himself firmly in the "substantive" camp that assesses outcomes like "justice" or "fairness" rather than formal rules or functional performance.[3] Given the strong positive connotations that stem from this definition, the rule of law is treated as an intrinsic normative good.

But the assumption that the rule of law is a substantive public good, even when defined as a democratic rule of law, is problematic. Not only is it possible to imagine a society with unjust laws that manages to achieve significant substantive justice according to some normative criteria (say, Cuba or Singapore), but it is also relatively easy to conceive of a country with normatively strong laws and legal institutions that are relatively marginal to how society actually operates (for example, Colombia). Moreover, it is even possible to imagine a society with "too much" rule of law, in other words, law whose excessive detail, pervasiveness, and rigidity acts as an obstacle to the formation or functioning of the mechanisms of informal conflict resolution that are so important for the quality of democracy.[4] Is it the law that must be moral, the legal institutions that must be extensive and effective, or the substantive outcomes that really matter?

The rule of law has a built-in contradiction. Even a newly constructed or reformed rule of law, one that may be qualitatively different from the laws promulgated by the dominant interests of the *ancien régime,* is necessarily bureaucratic; it relies on its own institutions to regulate the conduct of other bureaucracies in their relations with individuals. But this regulation is carried out by a skilled, specially trained, and elite legal profession. This tends to make the law financially inaccessible, alienating, and removed from the way ordinary people understand their own behavior and their social interactions with individuals and institutions. Furthermore, even though equal protection under the law is a fundamental right, programs that might make this a reality are underfinanced, overburdened, and understaffed. In short, access to justice is highly inequitable everywhere, but even more so in new, economically precarious democracies.

The authoritarian legacies and especially high levels of socioeconomic inequality that characterize most of Latin America complicate the picture because they raise the clear danger that the rule of law, and current efforts to reform the law, will be an instrument for the continued dominance of those who benefit from unfair policies. The top of Latin America's social pyramid is still where the law is primarily utilized. Given the conservatism of the legal profession in general, the enormous social distance between judges and the underprivileged, and the lack of information about making use of the law, the poor are unlikely to make use of the courts. This is not surprising since poorer citizens, even in stable and older democracies, are also reluctant to use the law, although it may be a valuable tool on their behalf. Where inequalities are especially great, judges hearing these unlikely cases are even more unlikely to be sensitized to the viewpoints of the poor. Take Brazil, for example, where surveys demonstrate that 68 percent of Brazilians assume that blacks receive worse treatment than whites, where some valuable legislation prohibiting racial discrimination exists, but where legal instruments are widely recognized to be of limited use for remedying racism due in part to the disinclination of citizens to use them—for very good reasons.[5] Instead, there is arguably a culture of "beating the system" among many of the poor, expressed by admiration for those who can break the law and get away with it. Under these circumstances, relying on the rule of law as the central mechanism to enhance democratization and human development may not work.

Tensions in the Virtuous Cycle: All Good Things Can Come Together Sometimes—But Not Easily

Given these problems, it is not self-evident that the rule of law, as it is currently defined (and not how O'Donnell seeks to define it in his chapter) is necessarily compatible with political democracy and/or human development, or even that it will necessarily enhance the agency of the average Latin American citizen. Latin America, or at least most of it, follows a different sequence than most advanced industrialized countries with regard to the construction of the rule of law and democratization. O'Donnell's claim (and hope) is that the continent's new political democracies, however incomplete or flawed, can provide the basis for the construction of a democratic rule of law. In this respect, they may form a virtuous cycle, which, in turn, makes progress in human development possible. But it is at least as possible that Latin America's elitist political democracies, most of which were not principally the conquest of broad mass movements of the poor and underprivileged,[6] will circumscribe the potential of the rule of law through reforms that continue to bias legality toward the wealthy and powerful. In this respect, the rule of law, even as it is currently being reformed, may be in very real tension with important aspects of democracy and human development as envisioned in the workshop.

In contemporary Latin America, as O'Donnell rightly notes, the rule of law and democracy are being constructed together. What is less clear, however, is that this is a *political* process—one in which the success or failure of one part of the equation greatly enhances or constrains the other. When the cycle is positive, democratization and rule of law are mutually supporting and contribute to the broadening and inclusiveness of each. For example, the recognition in this new wave of democratization that Latin American societies are multicultural and that minorities must be protected has meant new constitutions enshrining collective land rights, customary law and the role of traditional authorities, various forms of local administrative autonomy, new recognition for legal pluralism, and even the possibility of controlling their own resources for the benefit of their communities.[7] In a vision that unites democracy, rights, and development, this is how things should work. But these changes are not necessarily the result of new democratic polities or practices, or even the workings of a virtuous cycle. To the contrary, in a number of cases, they are the result of the struggles of indigenous peoples in alliance with other national and transnational actors; these battles are marked by violence and repression and not just the peaceful exercise of the electoral franchise of freedom of association. Nor is this exercise of agency primarily the act of individuals. Instead, and this is the key point, it is collectivities that matter. Furthermore, these rights may have become more firmly entrenched in legality during some form of authoritarian rule (Nicaragua, Mexico, Paraguay, Peru) or in extremely troubled polities (Colombia, Ecuador) than in marginally more stable but less inclusive democratic polities (Guatemala).

In sum, a positive and self-reinforcing cycle, however hopeful and morally satisfying, cannot be taken for granted. This is especially true when the construction of the rule of law must be devoted to reshaping, redefining, and enhancing the interests of the broad majority of the population in highly unequal societies—and not just the status of corporations through the reform of commercial law or the protection of propertied interests through criminal law. Judicial reform, whatever its merits, is not being promoted by the poor in Latin America. Despite rhetoric claiming that such reform could be the elixir of the underprivileged, it remains to be seen just how much they will benefit, especially from legal mechanisms that transfer power to the market, which is usually not the best place to fight for their rights. Paradoxically, the minimization of the state, when combined with a strengthened judiciary that is socially distant from the poor and not accountable to them in any way, may result in inadequate protection of civil rights as well as enormous obstacles to accomplishing the redistributive policies that are so obviously required to reduce exceptional levels of inequality. Even in new political democracies that are committed to reform, the judiciary itself is embedded in ultraconservative pasts and characterized by internal organizational incentives toward corruption.[8] It can be a powerful barrier to justice and, hence, to progress in the quality of democracy and development in Latin America. This means that quality of democracy indicators need to pay great attention to both access to the law and the content of both criminal and property law.

Citizenship: Is It Individual, Organizational, or Collective?

Decisive in determining whether cycles are virtuous or perverse is organized political action by the poor and the near poor through representative institutions that are capable of forging alliances with often precarious "middle" classes. Without such organizations and alliances, public policies in democracies, functioning at their best, may be able to target successfully the weakest members of society but in doing so may drive a wedge between them and the better organized strata located above them.[9] This potentially threatens progress in human development, the rule of law, and democratic stability. This is why building a "quality" democracy is so eminently political. The degree of inclusiveness of democracy and the extent of the protection of rights is determined more by bottom-up social movements, political parties, and individuals acting through permanent or semipermanent organizations than by any action of an individual citizen. Regardless of the mix of types of representative institutions, the existence of a full panoply of these organizations and associations and their ability to make relatively stable and durable alliances is essential for building a democracy of quality.

Representation is the Achilles' heel of the "virtuous cycle" argument between democracy, rule of law, and human development in Latin America. This is especially true in those cases where democratization is not a "conquest from below," pushed by fear of mass revolution in the model of some European countries, but rather a complicated process designed largely by elites and generally welcomed by them. The paradox of this wave of democracy in Latin America, and of the liberal individualism that places human agency at the center of analysis, is that these democracies are inevitably skewed toward those who have more resources. Since those with time and money can better organize, "the interest group chorus sings with a decidedly upper class accent," as one social scientist famously remarked.[10] Meanwhile, associations of the poor, organized around survival necessities like soup kitchens, mothers' clubs, or group credit schemes, do not provide appropriate mechanisms to link up with middle-class organizations and may lock the poor into a poverty trap that permits neither the mobility nor representation available to other groups.[11]

Thus, what contributes to producing a virtuous cycle between democracy, development, and the rule of law may be something barely mentioned in our discussions: the extent to which new democracies have systems of representation that *actively encourage* the political organization of the poor, the proliferation of associations and parties among precarious middle sectors, and the formation of alliances between the two. Democracy can reduce poverty and inequality if some type of redistributive alliance exists, and this, in turn, depends on forms of representation that actively promote this alliance. In Latin America very different collectivities, with different interests, passions, and needs, may need to be pushed to cooperate with each other through the effective interaction of both political and legal incentives in systems of representation. By this I mean that quality of democracy indicators should examine the extent to which incentives actually exist to encourage the organization of the poor in alliance with other groups, how low or high barriers to organization and association are, and how much the rules of democracy divide or unite the poor and their potential allies.

Agency without Citizenship:
The International Dimension

The inadequacy of representation is especially important due to the huge social divisions in Latin America and the region's deep insertion into a globalized world so strongly defined by its neighbor to the north. This international context, once a central preoccupation of scholars, has been given short shrift in conceptualizations of the linkages between democracy, human development, and the rule of law. Yet current patterns of globalization change the entire equation. One example makes the point. More and more—given the powerful demonstration effect of relative inequalities when standards of living (and consumption) are set in the North—a small minority of Latin Americans "belongs" more to this North, another small minority tries to achieve that same status by hanging on to what may be precarious gains, and a far larger group is in a very different world.[12] Building organizations and alliances between the two latter groups is no easy task because their worldviews are so different, and these differences may be increasing. Thus, poor Latin American countries seem to understand democracy differently from wealthier ones, and poor people within these countries have conceptions that are increasingly distinct from richer citizens within the same borders. This has important implications for both virtuous and perverse cycles.

In wealthier countries and among wealthier people, there is more likely to be a belief that democracy, the market, the rule of law, and development are mutually reinforcing. Here democracy is largely defined in terms of political liberty; and it is seen as desirable in itself. This is probably because there have been clear benefits from new democracies and judicial and economic reforms where they have worked. But at the same time, in countries where large parts of the population still are not ensured a minimal standard of living or where significant sectors are frustrated due to relative inequalities, democracy tends to be defined in socioeconomic terms (as gains in the standard of living or "progress"), and a positive cycle is possible only to the extent that particular governments "deliver." When the attitudes and beliefs of ethnic minorities (or majorities in the case of some countries) are factored in, visions of democracy become even more complicated. For example, democracy can mean "coming together," "agreement," "a spirit of solidarity," or "doing what we need to survive," which is a far cry from notions of electoral competition, alternation in power, or elections as conceived of by a political class or international organizations promoting democracy. These different realities and worldviews, all of which are supported by some (very different) transnational networks, international organizations, and multinational corporations, complicate representation and alliance formation among some groups and facilitate it among others.

In sum, while developing the arguments about the interaction of democracy, the rule of law, and human rights and showing how these can work in a mutually self-reinforcing way to build better societies, we also need to look very closely at the ways that they are in tension. In these tensions (and certainly in some very real cases in Latin America) lies a reality that is different from that which I believe this group seeks—the prospects for new forms of domination in which democracies are either "delegative" or simply inadequate to the task, rights are routinely violated in poor areas, and human development indicators simply do not improve as they should. Indeed, what may be happening in much of Latin America is the coexistence of two cycles linking democracy, human development, and the rule of law—one virtuous (as O'Donnell hopes) and one perverse (as I fear). It is the interaction of these cycles and the mechanisms for strengthening the former that we need to capture.

NOTES

Special thanks to Phillippe Schmitter and Steven Friedman for their comments on the present text.

1. Note that I use this term to refer to what economists might call "the principal"; thus, it does not have the same connotation as "agent" in the principal/agent sense. However, to avoid confusion, agency will be used here.

2. On definitions of the rule of law, see Joseph Raz, *Ethics in the Public Domain: Essays in the Morality of Law and Politics* (Oxford: Clarendon Press, 1994); and Paul Craig, "Formal and Substantive Conceptions of the Rule of Law: An Analytical Framework," *Public Law* (1997): 467–88.

3. For a recapitulation of this debate, see Rainer Grote, "Rule of Law, Rechtsstaat and Etat de Droit," in *Constitutionalism, Universalism and Democracy: A Comparative Analysis,* ed. Christian Starck (Baden: Nomos Verlagsgesellschaft, 1999). Contrast this substantive approach with Hayek's emphasis on the performance of the legal system, most generally its ability to constrain the discretion of government officials. In this view, a polity that permits relatively wide latitude to government officials has a minimal rule of law; the assumption, of course, is that these officials are necessarily arbitrary. See Friedrich Hayek, *The Constitution of Liberty* (Chicago: University of Chicago Press, 1960). More formal definitions concentrate upon the presence (or absence) of specific criteria, for example, a formally independent judiciary, provisions for judicial review, etc.

4. Indeed, it is the failure of overreliance on the rule of law that helps to explain the proliferation of mediators and other conflict resolution mechanisms in longstanding democracies. Within communities that do not use the law (for example, most poor localities of Latin America) or have traditions and customary law of their own, these mechanisms are often very well developed. In countries like Bolivia, where indigenous people form the majority of the population, the broad recognition of customary law occurred in order to reconcile the formal legal system to the reality that justice is largely administered in informal, oral, and local settings. See Donna Lee Van Cott, "A Political Analysis of Legal Pluralism in Bolivia and Colombia," *Journal of Latin American Studies* 32 (2000): 207–34.

5. See, for example, "Color and the Rule of Law in Brazil" by Peter Fry and Joan Dassin's comment in Juan E. Méndez, Guillermo O'Donnell, and Paulo Sergio Pinheiro, *The (Un)Rule of Law and the Underprivileged in Latin America* (Notre Dame, Ind.: University of Notre Dame Press, 1999). In his essay in this volume, O'Donnell develops some of the arguments present in the paper upon which I am commenting, especially the notion of sequence between rule of law and democratization, and he recognizes a number of the points made here. Nonetheless, this paper seems to envision a type of rule of law ("substantive definition") that would be built through democratic means and thus might be able to escape some of the problems I have highlighted.

6. This is clear to me regardless of how their role may have been underestimated by some democratic theorists or overestimated by some social movement theorists in the past. While the demise of authoritarian rule and transitions to new democracies in Latin America are certainly important historical conquests, in most cases they are not the result of the powerful pressure of organized mass movements, the fear of revolution, or war.

7. The constitutional recognition of cultural differences of the region's indigenous peoples, who comprise approximately 10 percent of the population, represents one of the most dramatic legal changes in Latin America over the past decade

8. On the internal incentives for corruption, see Edgardo Buscaglia, "Judicial Corruption in Developing Countries: Causes and Consequences" (Hoover Essay in Public Policy, available online at www.hoover.stanford.edu/publications/epp/95/95b.html).

9. On this point, I am grateful to an email exchange with Steven Friedman of the Centre for Policy Studies, Johannesburg, South Africa.

10. This widely recognized quote is from E. E. Schattschneider (cite unknown).

11. For the socioeconomic aspects of this argument, see Carl Graham and Stefano Pettinato, *Happiness and Hardship: Opportunity and Insecurity in New Market Economies* (Washington, D.C.: Brookings Institution Press, 2002), 32–34.

12. This is eloquently developed in Nancy Birdsall, Carol Graham, and Stefano Pettinato, "Stuck in the Tunnel: Have New Markets Muddled the Middle?" (Working Paper 14, Brookings Institution, 2000), and Graham and Pettinato, *Happiness and Hardship*.

Fundamental Rights as a Limitation to the Democratic Principle of Majority Will

JUAN E. MÉNDEZ

Fundamental Rights and Democracy

The Heredia workshop proved that there is a close connection between people's effective enjoyment of their rights and the quality of the day-to-day functioning of institutions under a democratic rule of law. This relationship has become explicit in recent years among those who work to promote and protect human rights (the so-called human rights movement), after emerging from a long period in which—due to the ideological polarization and constraints caused by the Cold War—democracy as a form of government was excluded from the postulates of this movement.

For the human rights movement, this connection arises from an empirical test: if local protective institutions, especially the judiciary, do not work, then suprastatal protective mechanisms will at best offer palliative solutions and will never effectively replace those local institutions. This practical test has come to acquire normative acceptance.[1] In the Velásquez Rodríguez case, the Inter-American Court of Human Rights affirmed that each state's duty to guarantee the exercise of human rights obliges it to organize all the institutions through which it exercises its authority in a way that makes rights established by international treaties effective.

In any case, the confrontation between the experiences of the human rights movement and the vision of political scientists (which is how I would sum up my own experience in the workshop) suggests that there is an inverse path that may lead to convergence. At the same time, a number of questions arise. The individual and collective rights that we defend in the human rights movement are located outside the decision-making sphere of the majorities, even when they act with impeccable adherence to democratic rules of the game in adopting public policies. Said another way, we argue that individuals and some collective actors have rights that even the majority cannot affect. Thus, if the doctrine of human rights is not profoundly "antimajoritarian," it has little meaning.

The preceding is not problematic if we think about human rights in simple terms: for example, it is clear that democratic majorities cannot order the torture of a prisoner or prohibit the cultural practices of an ethnic minority. Yet some democratic leaders allege the legitimacy of amnesty laws that absolve torturers ex post facto and even keep them in the ranks of the armed forces. The majority's right to development is also offered as a justification for appropriating land and natural resources that are the sole, fragile means of survival for indigenous peoples. Using these and other examples it is still possible to reconcile human rights doctrine with a well-understood notion of the general interest. The problem is that the catalog of rights that lies beyond majority decisions is constantly expanding because the forces and sectors that promote them often prefer to claim them as "rights," not only in the rhetorical sense but as demands that the courts must recognize. Richard Rorty (referring to the United States) warned some years ago against the kind of litigiousness that leads us to bring any legitimate interest to the legal arena as "rights talk," thus removing such interests from the political arena.

The example of torture demonstrates that the problem cannot be solved with the old distinction between civil and political rights on the one hand, and so-called economic, social, and cultural rights (ESCR) on the other. The human rights movement has made an effort to move beyond this dichotomy (inherited from the Cold War) in order to prevent ESCR from being relegated to a perpetual "second generation" status in relation to civil and political rights. Moreover, there is increasing pressure for recognition of a so-called third generation of rights: the rights to development, to a healthy and sustainable environment, and to peace. Regarding the latter, their possible problematic influence on democratic theory is still quite remote since they have no normative acceptance as obligations that states solemnly contract before the international community.

As for ESCR, however, the human rights movement is currently pushing to go beyond civil and political rights and make ESCR fully "justiciable." This means ESCR are no longer considered as merely programmatic norms of our constitutions and that, consequently, we should find a way for their bearers to claim them in court and to obtain redress when they are not observed. It seems to me that the result may place human rights principles and theories of popular sovereignty on a collision course. It might be argued that the insistence of wrapping any discussion of public policies in the language of rights runs the risk of limiting democratic debate and, worse still, eliminating any hope of achieving a consensus on the *common* good. Rousseau's general will has no reason to be equated with majority will; but it is preferable to arrive at a determination of what is good for all through reasoned and informed debate rather than through imposition (even if the latter dresses itself in constitutional or human rights clothing).

For now there is no imminent danger that human rights doctrine will become antidemocratic. Despite the movement's growing influence on international relations, we all recognize that the state is the principal guarantor of rights and the entity responsible for finding effective forms of protection. The "margin of appreciation" doctrine developed by the European Court of Human Rights does not only reflect this intuition; it also recognizes that national authorities (executive, legislative, and judicial) are in the best possible position to find out what formulas adjust best to local idiosyncrasies and cultures, so that universal principles can become a reality. As a consequence, the current panorama of supranational protection systems (in Latin America, the Inter-American Court and the Commission on Human Rights) presents a useful ambiguity. On the one hand, it imposes limits on state authority, with some pretension of justiciability under penalty of international isolation or economic sanctions. On the other hand, it gives rise to a healthy emulation among our countries by disseminating positive experiences in some that may be adapted in others, without recommendations in such cases having a binding character.

Within each national community, however, the discussion about democracy and rights will have to be resolved in the short or medium term. Agreement will have to be reached on the catalog of those personal and collective rights that remain beyond the realm of decisions made by majorities. Furthermore, our political classes must be encouraged to adopt an attitude of self-control in the exercise of power, against tendencies toward sultanism or delegative democracy. This will be especially difficult at a time when abuses of majoritarianism coexist with a feeling in our societies that the levers of power controlling important decisions are completely out of the reach of ordinary citizens.

Democratic Theory's Contribution to Human Rights

My second set of comments refers to the contributions of democratic theory to improving understanding of the challenges facing the human rights movement. (I believe that the social experiences of democratic transitions, with their insistence that the recent past of massive human rights violations not be hidden, have also contributed to theoretical development in this area.) On the new horizon of international human rights protection, several themes figure prominently: accountability (which some Latin Americanists prefer to call the "struggle against impunity"); the above-mentioned justiciability of economic, social, and cultural rights; and the struggle against the social, economic, and political exclusion of vulnerable sectors in each of our societies.

In the struggle against impunity for past violations, it has been very useful to be able to demonstrate that self- and pseudo-amnesty laws not only ignore the state's international obligations (something that is only now being recognized as an emerging principle in international law). The struggle against impunity that our societies have waged—with support from the international human rights movement—has gained legitimacy by demonstrating that accountability is an essential ingredient of democracy. In this sense, accountability has become a powerful weapon in the struggle not only against impunity for violations committed by dictatorships in the recent past but also against "endemic violations" (José Zalaquett) that have persisted and become more visible in our current democracies (rural violence, police brutality, street children, inhumane prisons). It also gives citizens arms for battling corruption, which is perhaps the Achilles' heel of the democracies we live in.

Furthermore, international human rights protection is developing norms for due legal process that relate closely to the rule of law and, consequently, to the quality of democracy. Accordingly, protective institutions no longer look as closely at a single rights violation by a state agent (as was true some years ago) as at the state's *institutional response* to the fact. The emphasis today is on analyzing whether the state has effectively organized its institutions in a way that remedies human rights violations. As a result, the topic of international protection has become more complex because the respective institutions feel obligated to analyze both substantive and procedural national law to determine if these are compatible with the norms of international treaties, and even to examine the day-to-day functioning of the administration of justice. Due process is not only applied in the situation of a person accused of a crime; it also translates to the right to a hearing in any controversy that affects internationally recognized rights. For this reason (and following methods of analysis developed principally in constitutional and administrative law), the new doctrine of due process in international law determines variable levels of severity according to what rights or interests are at play. In other words, the process that is "due" is different depending on whether, for example, the case deals with the guilt or innocence of a person accused of a serious crime (with a consequent loss of liberty or—in some countries—of life) versus the application of a disciplinary sanction to a high school student. The important point is that a minimum of due process, a minimum right to be heard, is always applicable (Articles 8 and 25 of the American Convention on Human Rights).

As might be expected, this trend has consequences for the organization of administrative and judicial structures in each state and even for the way that the provision of public services is organized. Moreover, it is possible to think about ways the concept might be broadened to determine how public policies should be adopted. Of course, international law does not require (for now) any special process for the creation and adoption of laws and decrees beyond the general principles of transparency and auditing of institutions of representative democracy. But the quality of democracy is expressed, at least partly, in the degree to which the voices of all interested parties are incorporated at the moment when a consensus is being created to adopt public policies. In this sense, it is possible to conceive of a criterion for the quality of democracy based on the degree to which the sectors of the population affected by public policies are heard during the policy formation process.

In the struggle against social exclusion and its political and economic correlates, the human rights movement has begun to pay preferential attention to the perspective of vulnerable sectors and to the need to defend cultural diversity in our societies. The rights of indigenous people and more recently of African-American communities necessarily require a differential treatment to make up for the decades of neglect and subordination that their special interests have experienced. Even though the principle of nondiscrimination has been among the rights included in our discipline from the beginning, only recently has it begun to receive special attention.

The doctrine of due process and the more generalized application of regulations against discrimination on the basis of race, national origin, gender, disability, sexual preference, and age may allow the formulation of a practical and effective strategy to promote economic, social, and cultural rights. Although both principles are integral to lists of civil and political rights as well as of ESCR, their stubborn and creative implementation promises to overcome the conception that wrongly asserts the existence of various "generations" of rights. At the same time, through nondiscrimination and due process, civil society begins to have an instrument it can use to fight against social exclusion.

On the Concept of Democracy

Finally, I return to the discussion of the problem of defining democracy, especially in light of the fact that Latin America is now experiencing a period in which virtually all its countries have governments with unquestionably legitimate origins in popular suffrage. At the same time, it is difficult to explain why these democracies seem defenseless against growing poverty and even seem to favor the regressive distribution of income; they also seem especially incapable of containing the scourge of corruption. On this point, I allow myself to echo the feelings of those participants in the workshop who proposed that the problem is not one of definition of democracy, nor that democracy has inherent structural weaknesses that impede it from solving these and other problems. I am convinced that the problems of Latin America's democracies should be resolved by deepening democracy itself, although sometimes the political systems tend to undermine this process through delegation and sultanism. Emergencies always seem to crop up that allow leaders to try to solve problems through less-than-democratic methods, using their electoral legitimacy to impose de facto authoritarianism.

The problem may not reside in the definition of democracy we use but rather in the less than rigorous way we characterize the regimes that actually exist. When I served as director of the Inter-American Institute of Human Rights, we used the concept (not originally ours) of "insufficient democracy" to characterize our vision of the problems of democracy and human rights in Latin America and the Caribbean. In doing so, we meant to emphasize the period's full superiority to the years that preceded it, during which many of these countries had military dictatorships or weak civilian governments with domestically powerful armed forces. Another goal was to point out the party systems' deficiencies in channeling public opinion and political decision-making, the weakness of governing institutions and the systematic attacks on their independence and impartiality, the hostility of many leaders to the notion of an independent and spontaneous civil society, and their weak commitment to the notion of limits on the exercise of power. In conclusion, what seems particularly significant is the general weakness of Latin America's institutions of horizontal accountability (although this does not mean that vertical accountability works well, either).

NOTE

1. See, for example, Thomas Franck, "The Emerging Right to Democratic Governance," *American Journal of International Law* 86, no. 1 (1992): 519–23.

On the Imaginary of the Citizenry

NORBERT LECHNER

The Perspective

My comments share the workshop's basic theme: the relationship between democracy and human development. What relationship exists between the quality of democracy and human development in a country? We can focus the discussion on two questions. First, how can we go beyond a procedural vision of democracy without ending up with a general theory about society? Second, how can we expand and strengthen citizenship, building on the conquests already attained?

The background for my observations comes from the case of Chile and my participation in the preparation of its *Informe sobre Desarrollo Humano* 2002. From this perspective, I propose some reflections for the debate and in particular for the discussion that O'Donnell's text has opened. I do not attempt to offer suggestions for the Costa Rican case nor generalizable hypotheses.

The Notion of Agency

I share O'Donnell's central focus on "agency" as a fundamental aspect of democracy (citizenship) and of human development (the ability to be the subject of the former). I see in his chapter, however, an identification of agency with the idea of "subject of rights," which, while useful for operationalization, seems insufficient for explaining social reality.

The first attribute of agency is probably the "freedom to choose." Such freedom to choose and to decide is, without a doubt, a basic attribute of democracy. But it is also a basic attribute of the market, as Milton Friedman pointed out. Hence the frequent association or identification of democracy and the market. Nonetheless, the citizen's freedom (choice of ends) is different from the consumer's freedom (choice between available goods). The so-called principle of the freedom to choose is not enough.

Yet O'Donnell is right in highlighting this trait because it is the "democratic argument" face-to-face with the current "naturalization of the social." We are witnessing the tendency to view the social order as a kind of natural order removed from human will. Apparently, no alternative exists to adapting oneself to the "market society." This naturalization has a dual consequence: on the one hand, it denies the freedom to choose and to intervene in relation to the organization of the social; on the other hand, it establishes what we are supposed to understand as "rational." A political action or theoretical reflection that goes against this "natural order" would be irrational and excluded from citizen debate.

Naturalization is a type of ideological discourse in the style of the "invisible hand" of the market. But it also refers to a real process: society's growing differentiation into diverse "functional systems" that are relatively closed and self-referential. We should analyze freedom of choice in this context. O'Donnell qualifies freedom to choose according to the "range of possible options." From which options are we able to choose? He puts forth the question of "the possible." Yet we know that the menu of possible options to which citizens' choices are subject is restricted. A large number of choices and decisions are made beforehand in a nonpolitical sphere. These options are "filtered" by the so-called de facto powers (business interests, the church, the military). At the same time, a structural filter is created by the relative autonomy of the "functional logics" of diverse systems. Politics (the political system) seems to have lost its hierarchical centrality in relation to such systemic "logics." What weight, then, does the political have in relation to diverse functional systems, including the economic and legal ones?

The tendency toward naturalization obliges us to pay greater attention to the role of the imaginary in defining the possible. O'Donnell alludes to this in regard to the "objective illusions" of the poor, whose imaginary universe may make it difficult to comprehend the real range of alternatives. Both low levels of literacy and the naturalization of the economic "model" restrict the image of available possibilities. Therefore, the notion of agency must include the perspective from which we approach reality. To be a subject one must place things in perspective: an active process of selection, codification, and assessment. I mean that the imaginary conditions the "mental maps" through which we perceive the "possible" as the area opened between the impossible and the necessary.

Yet not only the possible action but the very idea of being the subject of action are anchored in the imaginary. Both popular sovereignty and the principle of equality are part of a "social imaginary." Agency only exists if there is a collective imaginary in which people can recognize themselves as subjects. We must therefore ask, what force does the idea of citizenship have in the social imaginary of the popular sectors? People's spatial and temporal horizons offer one approximation. Our survey in the above-mentioned *Informe* revealed a clear fact. For those interviewed from the lower strata, the most important things in their lives take place in the neighborhood and in the present—that is, in the here and now.

O'Donnell points out the "exercise of rights" as a third attribute. Actually, the capacity for fulfillment is as important as freedom to choose. Zygmunt Bauman is right when he notes that today greater freedom of choice seems to coincide with greater collective impotence.[1] There seems to be both more market and less citizenship. Widespread feelings of impotence in regard to citizenship (at least in the Chilean case) may have more to do with a lack of capacity for collective action than with freedom to choose. People may feel they are able to choose, but in the end "nothing can be done"—nothing changes.

Impotence may reflect the individual's perception that society has abandoned him and will not help him get ahead. The lack of social resources suggests an additional point: I believe that the approach discussed here should more clearly indicate that it wishes to avoid both a liberal view (and methodological individualism) and the simple opposition of individual and society. Instead, it should emphasize the interconnectedness of individual and society. In contrast to the first *World Development Reports* (which were centered on the individual person's perspective), one might affirm that there is no individual capacity to choose and act without social capabilities. Essentially, society's capabilities determine the resources that the individual has at his disposal.

The Question of the State

Democracy implies a democratic state. According to O'Donnell, this is foremost a legal system, a rule of law. Forgive me for returning to some vaporous aspects: for example, what is the "spirit of the laws?" The legal system operates in the framework of a certain "community of meaning," that is, certain shared values and presuppositions. This is because any "application" of the law (the subsuming of a case under a norm) implies "giving meaning" to an act. Moreover, O'Donnell himself indicates that justice and fairness are basic principles, which are not objective facts but subjective values whose realization depends upon people's subjective perceptions. When the 2002 *World Development Report* defines *governance* as fair rules and fair institutions, what does *fair* mean?[2] Fair for whom? This could be a universal principle or the awareness of what is fair at a specific historical-social moment in time. In German legislation and adjudication, for example, "human dignity" (the first article and basic principle of the constitution), as well as "defense of public trust" and "good faith," are principles that inspire formal laws. Actually, their interpretation and validity depend, essentially, on political struggle. This struggle unfolds in the cultural sphere, around the criteria of what is fair and unfair and what is licit and illicit.

The second characteristic that O'Donnell emphasizes is that no one is above the law. Truly, Latin America's democracies no longer allow the type of impunity that was common in the years of dictatorship. Yet it is no less true that de facto powers enjoy enormous influence. They are not above the law, but they make the laws or at least have the right to veto them. As a result, there are nonpolitical actors (not subject to democratic elections and legitimization) that decide upon the regulation or, in some cases, deregulation of various matters.

A little-explored theme in Latin American countries is the social accountability[3] of these de facto powers. With respect to the media, it is worth asking, who is guarding the guardian? In Chile's case, the press tends to exercise "market accountability;" that is, it monitors governmental activity in terms of its contribution to the smooth functioning of the market (as spelled out by the Washington Consensus in its updated version).

In his oral presentation in Heredia, O'Donnell pointed out the following three characteristics as defining a democratic state: the rule of law, the state's relationship with citizens recognized as such, and its aim to provide a focus of collective identity (the credibility that it normally tries to pursue the common good). I would like to emphasize this last aspect: the state's symbolic dimension. The state symbolizes the nation as a collective identity that permits each member to feel that he belongs to and participates in a community of citizens. I would say that, in the tradition of Marxism or of Castoriadis, the state is a physically metaphysical synthesis of the social. Beyond its "apparatus," the state embodies that imaginary realm through which a society recognizes itself as a collective order. I say this to highlight what the Anglo-Saxon world and particularly economists tend to forget: the state is more than public administration, public services, and a treasury. It is a specific configuration in (national) space and time (history). And this re-presentation of the social totality—an aspect that current state reforms have completely ignored—seems crucial for both the articulation of social diversity and the country's systemic insertion in global processes.

This leads me to highlight a point that I have come to consider as crucial. The current redrawing of the state, along with the expansion of the market, has provoked a weakening of the image of "We." Without a strong image of ourselves there is no agency, no active citizenship, no human development. In positive terms, the idea of "We" must be strengthened in the collective imagination in order to have agency, and this has a great deal to do with people's experiences of society and collective action.

The Democraticness of the Social Context

The quality of democracy depends in good measure upon how democratic social life may be. In his day, Lipset spoke of the social requisites for democracy (and Hirschmann questioned that focus); much earlier, Marx referred to the formal character of human rights and democracy in relation to society's divisions. What I mean is that the relationship between the social and the political continues to be a problem. As our workshop ended, I was tempted to conclude that there is no way to delineate a specific set of social conditions for democracy. This, in effect, is an "undecidable limit." Yet how can we self-limit ourselves from embracing too many factors in assessing the quality of democracy?

I refer to two factors mentioned by O'Donnell. One is access to information. Without a doubt, there are no free elections without information about possible options, but the range of the possible has to do with available mental maps. In the past, the ideologies of political parties offered these maps. They can be understood as interpretive codes that allow citizens to structure the "social magma" into an intelligible panorama, and in so doing to visualize the available alternatives. Today, the interpretive guides that were familiar seem obsolete, and we have not replaced them with new ones. Granted, we have always interpreted social reality, but lately the power relationships that influence interpretive thinking have become more opaque. A prime example is television's "visual construction of the real." Who codifies the image of reality that we make for ourselves? How do we de-codify it?

O'Donnell likewise alludes to a "minimal set of capabilities and rights" while acknowledging that such a set is undecidable. Even so, let us look at some of the social capabilities that influence citizen action and at the obstacles that the social context presents. Citizenship implies *organizational capacity.* Nevertheless, organizing collective action is difficult due to the high degree of social distrust that permeates our societies. Citizenship includes *cognitive capabilities* that allow us to discern the possible. But, as I noted, the "naturalization" of the social process creates the appearance that there are no alternatives to what exists. Citizenship demands, of course, *moral capabilities* in the sense of a normative framework. Currently, however, an individualistic ethic prevails that does not generate social ties. Citizenship implies a *capacity to symbolize social relations,* but how long can symbols endure, given the oversupply and saturation that audiovisual media and consumer society produce? It also requires the *capacity to establish an emotional and affective relationship with democracy,* yet we see daily proof of the weakness of this bond.

I want to summarize two points. On the one hand, citizen action depends on an (undefined) set of social capabilities that are shaped by a specific social context. On the other hand, the current context hampers the creation and strengthening of such capabilities. Carried to its conclusion, the current discussion would reopen the old debate about democracy and capitalism. The capitalist market economy shapes the practical experiences and collective imaginaries that nurture citizens when the time comes to give opinions and make decisions on matters of general interest. If this is the case, what is the specific content of the problem today?

Democracy and Human Development

I have summarized some of the comments that grew out of my reading of O'Donnell's chapter. Yet I am aware that they are not very constructive; that is, they do not include a proposal for reformulation. I lament this all the more because I share the text's underlying perspective. Limiting democracy to the democratic regime fails to take into account the reality of our societies. Yet, we cannot broaden democracy to include social life in its entirety. I have no solution to the dilemma, but I continue to believe we are on the right path.

I propose to continue exploring the quality of democracy by using society's human development as the reference point. I understand human development to mean the process that allows people to become effective subjects and beneficiaries of development. The nucleus of human development would thus be what O'Donnell proposes: the search for "agency." As an underlying argument, we could argue that the strengthening of citizenship occurs to the degree that it broadens opportunities and counteracts restrictions on people's ability to be subjects of social development.

Note that this conception of human development is very general and lacks a solid operationalization. Nevertheless, it is a useful approach, in my understanding, because it allows us to consider the development of society as a whole, joining a normative perspective and an analytical focus. It offers a normative criterion ("being a subject") that—like the method employed in the Costa Rican audit—permits analysis of social reality from the perspective of its degree of "nearness" to an "aspiration." That said, I still doubt whether human development can be "measured."

It is possible to put forth the following as a general thesis: the higher the capacities to be an individual and collective subject the better the conditions for citizen action. Citizenship has, in effect, a dual face. Citizens evaluate the effectiveness of politics based on their concrete experiences as private persons. This assertion directs our attention to a sphere on which O'Donnell casts little light: that of "the public." This sphere can be considered the "converter" that translates the elements of human development and democracy between each other. Focusing on the "quality of the public" perhaps allows us to relate the social and the democratic. In other words, a problem of human development such as social distrust influences the quality of democracy because it has a negative impact on the public sphere. Conversely, a strengthening of the social rule of law, for example, favors public dialogue with the anonymous Other and in so doing generates favorable conditions for human development.

I ask myself if perhaps we should look to the public sphere as one of the reasons for the deficient quality of (Chilean) democracy. By public sphere I mean the place where citizens pose "matters of general interest." What effect does the transformation of public space as a result of the prominence of television and consumerism have on people's daily lives? The gradual displacement of "the public" by segmented "publics" restricts the practice and representation of social coexistence among individuals. It can be affirmed that human development would be hampered by citizens' difficulties in experiencing society in this kind of public sphere. The resulting weakness of such collective experience makes it even harder to visualize a social dynamic. Tendencies toward self-referential (naturalized) systems and a "negative individualism" keep people not only from experiencing the social but even from forming an idea of their own country. It is striking that 6 out of 10 people interviewed in a 2001 United Nations Development Program survey did not identify with *lo chileno*—that which is Chilean. A national identity undoubtedly exists, but it no longer provides the social roots and the affective sense of belonging that it used to.

If the invocation of "we Chileans" seems vacuous, perhaps we can refer to ourselves collectively as "we the citizens." Nevertheless, democracy seems to have brought a cultural deficit along with it. In the Chilean transition, the self-referential nature of the political system, the silencing of collective memory, and the inability of politics to generate future prospects are factors that threaten the possibility that the collective democratic imagination might represent a "We" as collective subject. In spite of the country's notable socioeconomic advances, fewer than half of Chileans prefer a democratic regime above any other. One-third say that they are indifferent to the type of regime. Such tendencies suggest that politics has given up on trying to create a "common world" that articulates social diversity. The accords produced by the political system, important as they are to institutional stability, seem to have a limited reach. It seems that political discourse has not given words or images to people's experience. It is probably not in the political sphere that Chileans will find the meaning of living together. And if democracy does not help citizens to find meaning in their common experience, it should not be surprising if citizens find democracy itself to be meaningless.

NOTES

1. *En busca de la política* (Buenos Aires: Fondo de Cultura Económica, 2001).

2. See the United Nations Development Program (UNDP), *Informe sobre Desarrollo Humano 2002: Profundizar la democracia en un mundo fragmentado* (Madrid, Barcelona, Mexico City: Ediciones Mundi Prensa, 2002).

3. See Catalina Smulovitz and Enrique Peruzzotti, "Societal Accountability in Latin America," *Journal of Democracy* 11, no. 4 (2000): 147–58.

State, Democracy, and Social Rights

MARÍA HERMÍNIA TAVARES DE ALMEIDA

The opportunity to read Guillermo O'Donnell's work and the reports from the citizen audit, and to participate in the workshop on the "Quality of Democracy and Human Development," was an extremely gratifying intellectual and human experience. O'Donnell's work reiterates a common trait of his previous writings: the intellectual courage to go beyond the limits of established knowledge, to suggest new approaches and new ways of thinking and, above all, new doubts and questions. The citizen audit constitutes an important effort to advance in the direction of applied knowledge; moreover, it is an intellectually daring, analytically rigorous, and empirically well-founded effort. The comments that follow should not be taken as criticisms of the work presented but as ideas prompted by their reading and discussion. My observations are casual and hardly begin to exhaust the themes to which they refer.

The quality of democratic systems is one of the biggest challenges facing both normative and positive democratic theory. It is a difficult, if not impossible, challenge to escape since democracy is at once an ideal, a normative horizon, and a concrete, historical experience of political organization. "What democracy *is* cannot be separated from what democracy *should be*. Democracy exists only to the degree in which its ideals and values make it exist," Sartori reminds us.[1] Consequently, the tension between the ideal and the experience in the democratic systems that really exist is constitutive of democratic life. The tension is present in citizens' and political actors' perceptions and in those of the academic analysts. The quality of democracy is not, therefore, an inquiry externally imposed by political scientists or philosophers. It is a question that springs from the very functioning of democratic systems. In Dahlian terms, it is a question that emerges from the comparison between democratic ideals and values with the reality of polyarchies.

Often the question of the quality of democracy is not explicit, and it enters self-proclaimed positive analyses as a kind of normative smuggling. A glance at the extensive academic production on new democracies reveals innumerable examples of surreptitious normativism. The disadvantage of not treating the theme of quality explicitly is that the criteria and parameters used for making judgments are not defined. The best that we can do is to accept the theme and treat it in a systematic fashion.

Nevertheless, taking the theme of the quality of democracy seriously is not a simple task. It implies expanding the focus on institutional design and its consequences for the behavior of political actors—dominant today in political science—to include the *results* of the democratic process in relation to some definition of political equality. The discussion that O'Donnell proposes on the *core* of rights that can guarantee the condition of citizen-agent reveals the complexity of this task.

Perhaps a first step in the discussion might be to establish what legitimately can be included, and what must be excluded, from discussions about the quality of democracy. Preliminarily, we should recognize not only the institutional diversity of existing democratic systems but also the fact that different institutional arrangements can produce conditions that are favorable to agency. Thus, to advance the discussion about the quality of democracy we must abandon the frequent idea that there is an unmistakably superior institutional design, as long as we are talking about systems in which the requisite minimum of free electoral competition is guaranteed. Nor does there seem to be an institutional design that simultaneously maximizes all the ideals and values associated with democracy. In other words, from the point of view of the quality of democracy, there is no way to decide, for example, between the Westminster model of fusion of powers and the model of separation of powers with checks and balances. Moreover, one must begin by acknowledging that there are limits on what democracy can deliver in terms of guarantees of rights and satisfaction of citizen demands and aspirations. These limits are not fixed once and for all. They change over time; they can be pushed and expanded. But they operate permanently, and they cannot be ignored.

Without pretension of exhausting such a complex theme, I would like to call attention to one external limit to democracy: a country's level of development and its consequences for the capacity to finance government activity and for the complexity of state structures. Levels of national wealth impose very concrete limits on what democratic governments can do to ensure conditions of agency and/or attend to citizen demands and aspirations. The capacity to finance public spending limits the action that democratic governments can take to guarantee civil and political rights, regardless of how determined and committed they may be to doing so. All of the above assumes state capacities that require significant resources. Let us take Costa Rica and Ireland as examples. The two countries are similar in terms of population—3.7 million and 3.8 million inhabitants, respectively—but they are significantly different in terms of national wealth. The distance between the two in national income levels is great. In 2002 per capita income, measured in purchasing parity power, was $7,880 in Costa Rica and $22,460 in Ireland, according to the Population Reference Bureau. Even supposing that the two countries' governments were equally democratic and committed to guaranteeing citizen rights, undoubtedly less can be done in Costa Rica than in Ireland.

Democracy does not only have external limits such as those mentioned above. Internal limits, related to historical trajectories, may also restrict what democratic systems can produce at a given time in relation to conditions for the exercise of citizenship and agency. Here I think of path dependence phenomena that are extremely important to understanding the situation of social rights in Latin America.

The notion of social rights as components of citizenship, as outlined by T. H. Marshall and his many followers, refers to a specific modality of social protection. It brings with it the principle of universality of a defined nucleus of benefits and guarantees—the idea that, to quote Marshall, "Social Policy consists of services provided by society as a whole, to society as a whole."[2] Linking the quality of democracy to a *core* of rights that allows for the existence of the citizen-agent implies considering the need for universalistic systems of protection.

Nevertheless, the legacy of most Latin American countries in this matter is a different model of social protection. Whether called conservative, corporatist, or meritocratic, it is not based on the principle of universality. Its central feature is the differentiation of rights and guarantees according to social groups or categories. It is a model that creates, reproduces, and at times deepens inequalities, producing different classes of "citizens." Moreover, the model creates and reinforces strong interests committed to maintaining it.

In Latin America democracies based on citizen-agents would demand radical changes in existing systems of social protection. We know a great deal about the political conditions that allowed universalistic systems to emerge. Yet we know almost nothing about how institutionalized corporatist systems can be transformed into more universalistic ones. Moreover, the dominant trend toward emergency policies focusing on the poorest of the poor, while obviously necessary, do not lead to the conception of universalistic protection systems.

To conclude, I would like to make an observation about the theme of civil rights. I share O'Donnell's conviction that civil rights constitute an extremely problematic issue for Latin American democracies. A deficit exists in relation to civil guarantees, and in Latin America it has a clear class bias: their effectiveness is associated with individuals' social position. Nevertheless, the problem is not an absence or limitation of legal norms defining such rights. It is instead a deficit in *enforcement,* of effective exercise of rights guaranteed by the law. As such, the main challenge is to understand why institutions do not function in practice. Part of the problem probably relates to the financial and fiscal limits on the development of state capacities. In Latin America and in some other new democracies, states are poor and have a low tax-collecting capacity. Certainly there are also problems of poor institutional design, which create perverse incentive structures. The theme of police and judicial system reforms is central to the discussion of the quality of democracy.

Even so, there is a dimension of political culture that should not be overlooked. In order to integrate it consistently into the discussion, we must promote a revolution in theories of political culture. Neo-institutionalist critiques of conventional culturalist theories are absolutely correct. Such theories were excessively ideological and ethnocentric and did not offer useful analytical tools for understanding democratic transitions and expansion beyond North America and western Europe. Nevertheless, even when we accept the principle of citizen-agent rationality, we cannot dispense with inquiries on citizens' cognitive maps, beliefs, and attitudes, through which their preferences are defined and their strategies for action designed. Consequently, in the specific terrain of the effectiveness of civil rights, it is worthwhile to conceptualize the role played by political culture. We should also try to learn more about prevailing beliefs about social hierarchy, racial and gender differences, relationships with authority, and other representations that tend to offer justification for discriminatory and arbitrary behavior.

NOTES

1. Giovanni Sartori, *Democratic Theory* (New York: Praeger, 1967), 4.
2. T. H. Marshall, "Citizenship and Social Class," in *Class, Citizenship, and Social Development* (Garden City, N.Y.: Doubleday, 1965), 8.

Deepening Civil and Social Rights

CATHERINE M. CONAGHAN

O ne of the most important contributions made by Guillermo O'Donnell in his chapter is his compelling argument regarding the relationship between material life and the exercise of rights in a democracy. As O'Donnell underscores, the political and civil rights that we expect as part of the package of a functioning democratic system cannot be exercised by people in any meaningful way when they are severely deprived and cannot live a minimally "decent life."[1]

This observation alone may not appear to be especially surprising. But, as Thomas Carothers has emphasized in his recent work, it is something that "democracy promotion" advocates and the international community may have lost sight of in their frenzied work over the last decade.[2] Using the minimalist procedural definition of democracy, international promotion of democracy has tended to focus on projects like election monitoring, judicial reform, etc.—all of which, of course, are important in their own right. Nonetheless, this privileging of the procedural dimensions of democracy has turned democratic promotion into its own sphere—a sphere often removed from international debates on economic policies, development, and poverty.

O'Donnell's analysis clearly shows that no meaningful discussion of how to advance democratization in Latin America (or elsewhere in the developing world) can ignore the catastrophic effects that material impoverishment has on the exercise of democratic citizenship. The real challenge posed by O'Donnell's analysis is not so much academic as practical and political. How can this concern for establishing the minimal material conditions of democratic citizenship become part of a new paradigm of democratization shared by the international community? What role can academics and organizations like UNDP play in promoting more coordinated approaches to economic and democratic political development?

The nexus between the political and the economic is the next frontier in democratic promotion. As Carothers noted during the workshop, economists must become a part of international discussion of democracy. Policies promoting democratic and economic development cannot and should not be segregated. One of the fundamental causes of popular malaise and discontent with democracy in the region is rooted in the divorce between economic policy making and democratic mechanisms. With good reason, people become skeptical about the authenticity of democracy when essential decisions affecting their quality of life are simply imposed by governments responding to the strictures of international financial institutions. A good example of the rage (and political crisis) such conduct evokes has been evident over the last several years in popular mobilizations against privatization in Bolivia, Ecuador, and Peru. Disgruntled citizens have taken to the streets and confronted their respective governments in order to halt privatization. While many economists might deride and dismiss these events as yet another example of "irrational" politics, the situation certainly underscores that economic policy cannot be separated from democratic procedures without great cost.

In the short term, O'Donnell suggests that a more full-bodied commitment to the development of *civil rights* would be an important advance in the establishment of social rights. The reasoning is that improved access to civil rights would invigorate social movements and other organizations pressing for improvements in the quality of life. O'Donnell's idea is compelling, but as a practical matter, it would be useful to see more specifics regarding exactly *which* civil rights need to be given priority and what kinds of policies/actions need to be taken in this regard. As Iazzetta notes in his comments, the implementation of rights costs money.

Given the current economic constraints faced by most Latin American countries, governments have tough choices to make concerning spending priorities and could use more concrete guidelines as to how to go about strengthening (at least selected) civil rights. My preceding remark presupposes that governments are, in fact, interested in civil rights (which perhaps is too generous an assumption). Governments that are currently confronting contentious social movements (as in Ecuador and Bolivia) probably would be loath to reinforce civil rights as they find themselves struggling to impose the neoliberal and coca eradication policies. This raises yet another practical question regarding O'Donnell's suggestion on the expansion of civil rights. Exactly how and where will this impetus for expanding rights come from (especially in the context of post–September 11 where "contentious politics" may be susceptible to new scrutiny and suspicion, at least in the eyes of U.S. policymakers)?

In light of how the new, post–September 11 anxieties may be (negatively) affecting international sensibilities and fueling a conservative backlash, O'Donnell's reminder that "democracies are made from below" is especially timely and important. It is an observation that bears repeating over and over again in international forums. As important as elite pacts have been in processes of political transition (as noted by Karl in her comments), subordinate classes and marginal groups have always "pushed the envelope," advancing democratization well beyond the right to vote.[3] Any evaluation of the quality of democracy in the region needs to take into account the contributions that "contentious" movements are making in the region—and regard their existence not simply as indicators of a "poor quality" (unresponsive) democracy but as the *sine qua non* of democratic advancement.

The UNDP/State of the Nation research team has designed and authored one of the most comprehensive and methodologically rigorous research projects ever attempted in the field of democratic studies. The team has established a template for research that will be useful for years to come. The ambitious and extensive nature of the research project (encompassing surveys, focus groups, ethnographic studies, etc.) makes it a rich source of data; it is unlikely, however, that such a wide-ranging, national-level audit could be undertaken in many of the other countries in the region. No doubt the relatively small size of Costa Rica made a national-level audit feasible. Moreover, the social homogeneity in Costa Rica probably reduced the problems involved in reaching consensus on the standards to be used. In the discussions at the workshop, Karl rightly raised the question of how audits could be effected in countries where ethnic and linguistic divisions and social inequalities complicate the environment far more than in Costa Rica. I agree with O'Donnell and Coppedge that any subsequent stage of this project should focus on the question of how to tailor a more manageable package of research issues and methods (a "*núcleo duro*" in the words of O'Donnell) so that audits could be undertaken elsewhere. Also, as noted by Daniel Zovatto during the workshop, developing a package for subnational or municipal audits may be an especially promising avenue for promoting the use of citizen audits in the region.

From a methodological perspective, the most audacious and original aspect of the approach used by the research team was to use the "democratic aspirations" articulated by citizens themselves as the benchmark for evaluating the quality of democracy (instead of using a static set of criteria defined by experts). This synergy between researchers and the public is one of the most innovative features of the project—and certainly takes the study out of the realm of being a strictly academic exercise. By using citizens' expectations as a point of departure, the project is an interactive experiment that invites the public into a deliberation on democracy. Clearly, this national "self-definition" of democracy creates prospective problems regarding the comparability of cross-national results of audits in the future. However, the advantages that can accrue from using the audit as a vehicle of national "consciousness raising" about the state of democracy probably outweigh the losses in methodological purity and comparability. The approach also has the potential of illuminating, with great specificity and subtlety, the variations among different national interpretations of what makes for quality democracy.[4]

The audit produced fascinating findings. I will just briefly highlight a few. In the discussion of the problems in Costa Rican democracy, I was struck by those that continue to lurk beneath the surface (clientelism, discriminatory views), even in a system that is so obviously advanced in other realms. Moreover, I think some of the compelling areas for future research are to be found in the areas where the panels could not agree on the standards to be applied or were problematic to research. The issues located in these areas—media conduct, corruption, the internal governance of organizations—go to the heart of how the public sphere operates in Latin America and pose some of the greatest challenges to democratization in the future. The fact that the expert panels could not agree on how to evaluate some of the issues indicates how complicated empirical study of these areas is and how "contested" these areas are when it comes to interpretation. Future research will have to grapple with them again in some form. These are some of the real frontiers (or perhaps "no man's lands," to continue with the geographical metaphors of the audit) for future democratic development in the region.

NOTES

1. As I was writing this text, I contemplated an appalling report on the degrading conditions confronting millions of slum-dwellers in Bombay, India, that appeared in the *New York Times* on February 10, 2002. Because of a lack of running water and the absence of public toilets, people are forced into a humiliating daily search to find places

to relieve themselves. Given expectations of modesty, women are especially affected by this public health crisis. That snapshot of daily life in India underscores how underdeveloped our concepts of democracy remain when they do not incorporate a consideration of the socioeconomic dimension. According to Freedom House, India is an "electoral democracy" and ranks as a "free" country in terms of political and civil liberties.

2. Thomas Carothers, "The End of the Transition Paradigm," *Journal of Democracy* 13, no. 1 (2002): 5–21.

3. On this argument see Dietrich Rueschemeyer, Evelyne Huber Stephens, and John D. Stephens, *Capitalist Development and Democracy* (Chicago: University of Chicago Press, 1992).

4. For a study that uses survey research to illuminate different national conceptions of democracy, see Roderic Ai Camp, ed., *Citizen Views of Democracy in Latin America* (Pittsburgh: University of Pittsburgh Press, 2001).

Unfinished Business for Latin America's Democracies

OSVALDO M. IAZZETTA

Democracy and Quality

O'Donnell's text establishes new parameters for reflecting on democracy that go beyond the narrow limits that have imprisoned the issue within prevailing theoretical frameworks. The effort expands that vision by grounding itself in an interpretation that connects political theory to other disciplines, while offering a new foundation on which to build a theory of the state and explore the close links that connect it to democracy.

Likewise, the work rightly integrates categories and dimensions whose connections have been explored little until now. This is manifested mainly in (a) the philosophical basis that it offers for elective affinities among *human development, human rights, and democracy,* highlighting the common traditions from which these currents originate; and (b) the development of a new framework that extends concern with *democratization* beyond the limits of the *political regime,* projecting it to include the *state* and the *social context* surrounding it. This broader approach is taken with caution. While it assumes the explanatory insufficiencies of currently prevailing categories, the approach avoids becoming so overreaching that it compromises its own potential to be empirically useful.

Actually, one of the text's main merits is to encourage redefinition of the concept of political democracy, introducing aspects that are silenced in the current "minimalist" literature. Nevertheless, this elevation of the requirements that allow a regime to be classified as democratic does not affect the concept's usefulness for distinguishing and classifying regimes through comparative analysis. Its particular achievement, therefore, is to grasp nuances—especially evident in new democracies—that other approaches have not illuminated sufficiently. In the following pages, I examine key aspects of O'Donnell's chapter that merit disaggregated analysis.

Broadening of the Concept of Democracy and Its Limits

As noted, O'Donnell's text gives expression to the search for a conceptualization of democracy that goes beyond the limits of the concept of the political regime. Undoubtedly, this category defines minimum components that allow us to distinguish a democratic regime from an undemocratic one. While such a minimalist concept provides appropriate parameters for establishing this difference, it tells us little about the *degree of democraticness* of such democracies. Nor does it permit us to recognize variations and nuances that coexist within the broad spectrum of democratic regimes in Latin America.

O'Donnell's text begins with a dual assertion: democracies have had an unsatisfactory performance in Latin America, and available concepts are insufficient for explaining why. This is the void to be filled, not only to identify democracy's principal failings but to outline tasks for addressing them in the future. The broadening of the concept of democracy results mainly by associating the political regime and the state, accepting that while a democratic regime is a system of rights in which all people become citizens, its mere existence is not enough to make rights effective; it is the state's task to guarantee them. O'Donnell vindicates this legal dimension by noting that without an *effective state,* there can be no democracy. By highlighting the state's legal dimension as a crucial component of democracy, he also avoids a double conceptual reductionism and allows us to broaden our cognitive maps. On the one hand, he conceives democracy beyond the limits of the political regime, but by highlighting the state's legal dimension, he goes beyond the conceptual impoverishment that results from restricting the state to its bureaucratic face.

This healthy expansion of the concept of democracy is undertaken carefully to preserve the concept's operationalism for comparative purposes.

O'Donnell moves on ground between two extremes in tension with one another. On one side lies a "minimalist" concept that reduces democracy to the political regime, and on the other hand is a wider ranging concept, in which the frontiers between the political regime and the socioeconomic sphere disappear, subordinating the evaluation of democracy to its socioeconomic performance and to the social equality or inequality that it eventually helps to promote.

The conceptual boundaries that O'Donnell draws have analytical foundations; if we include "everything" in the concept of democracy, the category becomes unapproachably vast. Furthermore, his view avoids the practical problems that such broadness can cause when it encourages disproportionate social expectations of what democracy can effectively provide and fulfill. The alternative that O'Donnell chooses avoids both the "smallness" of the concept of the political regime, and the excess of the second approach, which entrusts democracy with responsibilities that exceed its potential for effective action and creates fertile ground for frustration when its performance is unsatisfactory.

Faced with the implications that stem from this latter approach, I share O'Donnell's caution and accept the idea that the conceptual ground he proposes should not be confused with what seems to be the prevailing opinion in Latin America. Despite this clarification, it is apparent that in some Latin American countries there is a widespread feeling that democracy has done little to ameliorate situations of extreme social inequality or current processes of worsening inequality. Nevertheless, this says less about democracy and more about the incapacity of its actors and leaders, who have failed to take advantage of the possibilities that democracy provides to reverse such asymmetries peacefully.[1]

Experiences like Argentina's, where the affirmation of democracy has coexisted with the rapid increase of social inequality, illustrate in a paradigmatic fashion the tension between a political regime that is capable of guaranteeing the universality of political citizenship and a socioeconomic system that threatens the chances for uniformly extending the social rights that complement such citizenship. This tension cannot be understood without considering that when democracy returned to Argentina in 1983 and awakened an unprecedented civic faith in pluralism and diversity, the foundations had been laid for a destructive socioeconomic process in the previous authoritarian period. This paradox and asynchrony have become increasingly apparent, feeding widespread feelings that democracy has failed to remedy social asymmetries.

Such concerns go beyond the agenda set by the Costa Rican workshop and the present volume. For the moment, to have reached a relative consensus on the inadequacies of the concept of political regime—and to recognize its links with the notion of the state as an acceptable way to overcoming them—represents a far from negligible milestone. Thanks to this conceptual advance, we are better positioned not only to determine *what* regimes are democratic but also to evaluate *how* democratic they are. Yet while this step is important, we need to complement it with additional efforts that allow us to recognize factors that can explain *why* our democracies may lose *legitimacy* and see their support gradually erode.

Clearly, the evaluation of democracy must not be reduced to its perform-ance and effectiveness; that is, the concept must be separated from the issues of unemployment, inflation, or economic growth so that it is not overbur-dened with demands that exceed its purview. Yet, although it seems excessive to overwhelm democracy with such demands, the persistence of negative indi-cators is likely to have an impact on democracy's legitimacy. While democracy is valuable in itself, the persistence of such conditions threatens to open the floodgates to those enemies of democracy who offer themselves as the best interpreters of what society needs to get through difficult times.[2]

Reassessing the Idea of the State

The reassessment of the idea of the state is intimately linked to the notion of *agency*. That is, the moral conception of the individual as an autonomous being and carrier of subjective rights refers inevitably to the state as the guar-antor of those rights. This foundation constitutes the nucleus around which O'Donnell organizes his chapter. It not only explains the convergence between human development, human rights, and democracy but brings back the state as a central factor in thinking about democracy. This reassessment is timely, since many of the faults of Latin America's democracies stem from the limited effectiveness of the state in uniformly guaranteeing such rights.

Furthermore, this broader focus pushes us to explore democraticness beyond the political regime and to ask additional questions about the quality of the bond linking the state to its citizens. O'Donnell is correct in noting that Latin America's democracies' main deficits are registered outside the limits of the political regime, in the state's abuses or disregard for nominally established rights. We find there a long list of "problematic frontiers" resulting from the state's treatment of its own citizens.

I agree with this broader approach. Nevertheless, I would point out a ten-sion between the *explicit* limits and accomplishments assigned to the state—mostly identified with its legal dimension—and the *implicit* contents and tasks that the text attributes to the state for sustaining such rights. The state's effectiveness depends on the availability and effectiveness of a broad network of institutions that require appropriate financing. An effective state is not free of charge; it requires resources and budgets. Thus the implementation of rights, as O'Donnell's text suggests, costs money that usually comes from tax revenues.

By limiting the idea of the state to its juridical and legal dimension—understood as the legal order that organizes institutions—such a reassessment overlooks the fact that much of the state's effectiveness stems from its infrastructural capacity. This is particularly the case for "anemic" and "stunted" states whose capacities have been undermined by economic adjustment policies, which encouraged the reduction of infrastructural capacity with the argument that "less state" implied "more democracy." To trust in the effectiveness of the state without discussing this material dimension—associated with the availability of resources—may provide us with inadequate maps for identifying the state's current failings and the tasks that lie ahead for perfecting our democracies.[3]

The Convergence between Human Development, Democracy, and Human Rights and the Expansive Role of Political Rights

One of the main contributions of O'Donnell's text is to solidify the connections between these three currents, identifying both their *elective affinities* and varying possibilities for effectiveness. Likewise, this convergence expresses a more inclusive conception that benefits the approach as a whole, suggesting that the effectiveness of political rights is intimately linked to civil and social rights.

I agree with the recognition of this convergence. Nevertheless, we cannot ignore that the demand of achievement of human development capabilities exceeds the frameworks of the political regime and state—if we hold to the broader conception of democracy that O'Donnell's text suggests—and extends to the socioeconomic sphere. In other words, the elective affinities between democracy and human development (especially because of the latter's social importance) reopen a certain tension related to the limits of the concept of democracy, even after having drawn a convincing demarcation between the political regime and the socioeconomic system. The difficulties of reconciling this circumstance with the rest of O'Donnell's arguments does not mean, however, that we must reject the convergence that he notes between these three currents in a normative sense.

At the same time, this topic contains one of the text's most suggestive propositions by highlighting the *expansive* role that political rights may acquire in contexts where social and civil rights suffer significant deterioration. Despite their notorious insufficiencies and deficits, Latin America's democracies have guaranteed a *relative universality of political rights,* which are the only rights that the popular sectors can enjoy in a more or less complete fashion. The element is a new one in Latin America, and the utilization of these political rights can pave the way for struggles for more civil and social rights. This is the available "threshold" of rights to which O'Donnell refers, and it reveals the "comparative advantage" of political rights, which have a greater chance of becoming universal since they can be demanded of the state or to other individuals through the legal system. Recognizing this singularity is crucial for understanding how such rights may serve as a lever or springboard, providing opportunities for launching other struggles that allow the conquest of new rights.

Certainly this has not occurred in the North Atlantic countries' experience: there the expansion and rootedness of the vision of the individual as a carrier of subjective rights *preceded* the "democratic wager." The sequence was different in Latin America, as demonstrated by the current existence of democracies that guarantee political rights while proving themselves incapable of guaranteeing the universalization of civil and social rights. This specificity has theoretical implications, since in the democratic theory inspired by the experience of the North Atlantic countries, such a distinguishing trait becomes an unaccountable anomaly. Accepting the specificity *threshold* sustained by political rights—given that they are guaranteed in a relatively universal way—might allow us to assign to these rights the same expansive and supporting role that civil rights previously had in the North Atlantic countries.

After highlighting this potentiality of political rights, O'Donnell poses a crucial question. Where should the struggle begin, when there is such widespread privation of so many interconnected rights and capabilities? The answer is far from simple, not only because it is not a matter of linear processes but also because, given the extensiveness and severity of existing privations, any choice implies the postponement of other important rights and needs. While such struggles cannot be settled in the academic realm, it is imperative to incorporate them into our agenda for discussion.

Definition of the Quality of Democracy

In evaluating the quality of democracy, O'Donnell mentions the difficulties caused by the absence of a *complete* theory of democracy that would allow the clear identification of a minimum of rights that guarantee democracy's existence and satisfactorily identify questions concerning the "how" and "where" of democracy. Because of this absence, measuring these concepts and operationalizing them demands an inductive strategy that allows us to partially fill the theoretical gap. I agree with this strategy since it defines an appropriate way to advance gradually toward creation of a complete theory.

Consistent with the initial theoretical formulation, democracy's evaluation is not limited to the notion of the "democratic regime" but extends to the state and society, seeking to recognize "different degrees of democraticness" and of "relative democraticness" through the following three-dimensional approach: (a) democraticness of the political regime; (b) democraticness of the state (effectiveness of the state, state-citizen treatment); and (c) democraticness of the social context, which includes a minimum of human rights and human development capabilities and a diverse social context.

Within this approach there are nuances that prompt us to place new emphasis on certain matters. On the one hand, the state becomes a crucial indicator in the study of democracy and its quality. On the other hand, the approach assesses the vitality and autonomy of civil society to demand accountability (social accountability) as well as social conditions that favor agents' autonomy and their acquisition of capabilities.

Social issues, while not absent in reports concerning the audit preceding Vargas Cullell's chapter in this volume, never took on the centrality that they acquire in this chapter. Perhaps the fact that social issues do not constitute such a pressing problem for Costa Rica, with its relatively homogenous society, led to the assumption of a minimal floor of autonomy and social equity for all agents. Nevertheless, and to the degree that attempts are made to extend the experience to other countries, this minimal social "floor" is not guaranteed uniformly. This social aspect must be considered if we wish to extend the approach to diverse situations.

Toward a New Regional Typology Based on Levels of Quality of Democracy

In principle, I consider the criteria that O'Donnell uses to classify countries to be correct, with one observation to be made below. It is undeniable that an exercise of this nature requires both skill and knowledge of the diversity of situations throughout the region. Even so, its parameters could be adjusted and enriched with contributions from research that is now underway. The effort constitutes a lucid and imaginative synthesis that will generate inevitable—and necessary—controversy related to the consideration of certain national peculiarities within the proposed groupings.

It seems correct to join the political regime (political democracy) and the state when putting national cases together in a group. In any case, it seems difficult to find a minimal and operative concept without sacrificing aspects that seem relevant for enriching the classification. (Here I think of "authoritarian enclaves" in Chile or executive/legislative relations, not covered by the concepts of regime or state according to the criteria used in the classification.) Certain elements that determine institutional quality (such as the independence of powers and patterns of public policy making) that would allow inclusion of additional nuances in the national cases are not considered in the classification. Yet these additions would increase the complexity of the comparative exercise at an empirical level.

I note that the countries of the region are classified on the basis of three criteria, according to the degree to which each is present in a country. These criteria take into account the variations that these countries exhibit in the following areas: political democracy and effectiveness of the state and its legal system; levels of support and compliance with the democratic regime and evaluation of its performance by public opinion; sequences of development of civil, political, and social rights. With respect to the first item, it seems convenient to consider the caveats that several participants in the Heredia workshop expressed in relation to Chile, as O'Donnell admits by referring to "authoritarian enclaves." Regarding Uruguay, placed in the first group along with Costa Rica, no qualms are necessary if the elements of the political regime are defined based on the existence of rights derived from the concept of polyarchy. Nevertheless, recent research has called attention to some negative aspects of *institutional quality* in Uruguay associated with decision-making patterns for the implementation of economic reforms. The research does not invalidate Uruguay's location in this group, but it adds nuances that should not be overlooked.[4]

The final observation, related to the "claims of singularity" that surely will be made as soon as this typology comes under scrutiny, relates precisely to a nuance demonstrated by Argentina's experience in the sequence of citizen rights. It is correct to accept that as a result of populism, Argentina moved prematurely forward to a stage of social rights—today in decline—that launched a process of acquisition of other rights. While we accept this in general terms, we must also note that historical research has made an important contribution to reconstructing the process of acquisition of political rights in Argentina. Such studies demonstrate that the right to vote was recognized early on— especially in Buenos Aires province—even though its formal existence did not guarantee, for several reasons, the effective exercise of this right. The turning point came in 1912, when the *right* to vote was given mandatory status, henceforth making it a *duty*.[5] Obviously this does not refute the typology here proposed, but it reminds us of the contribution that historical and empirical studies can make to our understanding of the peculiarities of each national case within such a classification.

Extension of the Audit and Evaluation of the Quality of Democracy

This section focuses on more operative issues, particularly those related to comparability and the possibility of undertaking evaluations of the quality of democracy in other countries.

First, I would like to note that despite the protestations of its coordinators, the innovative audit carried out in Costa Rica is not devoid of theoretical underpinnings. The task they have undertaken, despite its inductive character and the denial of theoretical ambitions, could not have achieved its goals without the guidance of some basic conceptual notions. The very distinction between a "minimal threshold" (identified with the notion of polyarchy) and a "superior threshold" of democracy (alluding to the traits that define its quality) presupposes a theoretical grounding without which the whole task would have lacked orientation—which happily is not the case.

On the other hand, the fact that the audit does not begin with an explicitly defined theory results from its nature as an exercise inspired by practical goals rather than by the demands of academic research, as well as the existing theoretical and conceptual gaps in this matter. In this sense, the chapter by O'Donnell provides a new conceptual map that, while not definitive, may be sufficient to guide future audits and gradually move them beyond the inductive character that predominates at this time.

Comparability and Extension of the Audit to Other Countries

During the Heredia workshop, participants raised two issues that I want to highlight here. First, they recognized that the fact that an audit of the quality of democracy could be undertaken at all was proof of its worthiness. Second, they rejected the notion that audits or evaluations of this kind are only meaningful for well-performing democracies. Granted, those who least need an experience like the audit are the most likely to accept it. Yet this does not mean the effort should not encompass countries with recognizably low thresholds or parameters of democratic quality.

The audit report as well as the chapter by Vargas Cullell are cautious in recommending this experience for other countries. The authors remark that "there is no manual for conducting a citizen audit." Accordingly, it is not a matter of exporting the audit indiscriminately, without noting the advantages and peculiarities that make Costa Rica a distinctive case. The greater regional heterogeneity, population, and size of other countries in Latin America make them more complex cases. While such characteristics may make the audit less viable on a national scale, this does not impede its undertaking at the provincial (departmental or state) or municipal levels.

Two distinct orders of problems exist. The first relates to the viability of the comparative exercise, such as political conditions, dimensions, and diversity of the country under comparison. The second alludes to the difficulties inherent in any comparative exercise, which require that minimal common denominators be found to translate empirically the essential elements in the concept of the quality of democracy. The main challenge, in this case, is to find a common minimum that condenses the idea of democratic quality without omitting contextual elements that, if overlooked, would affect the validity of the comparative endeavor. Another issue is how to create a common nucleus without sacrificing the unique traits of each national case, which might be individually relevant but lack correlation to other national cases. In this sense, the proposal that O'Donnell suggested—combining "three layers" of data[6]— seems appropriate since it allows common and unique traits to be made compatible.

I make a few observations related to the definition of the empirical anchors that allow us to operationalize indicators of democratic quality. Two questions are worth emphasizing. First, how far can we expand the list of indicators for comparison? Second, how should this list of comparable indicators be drawn up?

Definition of the list—the first issue—will depend upon whether comparisons are being made on a national scale or at the subnational level. Whatever level is chosen, a common nucleus must be maintained that encompasses the three main aspects of democraticness suggested by O'Donnell: the levels of the political regime, the state, and the social context. I believe that to this common nucleus should be added two variants: on the one hand, "the three layers" proposed by O'Donnell (for comparisons on a national scale) and on the other, adjustments derived from changes in scale if the evaluation is done at the subnational level.

Since not every country in the region may be evaluated at the national level initially, bringing the exercise down to the subnational level would require revising some indicators that are appropriate at the former but not at the latter level. At the same time, it seems important not to discard initiatives that are viable at a local scale—and which would be complex to implement on a national scale—that may be illustrative of the quality of democracy, such as participatory budgeting experiences or decentralization processes. The challenge lies in detecting certain levels or aspects of democraticness that exceed the mere evaluation of governmental administration.

To the degree that other countries adopt the Costa Rican experience on a national scale, they will need to consider some contextual variables—not contemplated in Costa Rica—to avoid distortions in the comparative character of the exercise. I am thinking especially about traits such as parliamentarism vs. presidentialism, party and electoral systems, and mechanisms of political party financing, among others.

Drawing up the List of Problems and Quality Standards

In terms of the themes for comparison, these may tend toward a mix that integrates the best of the Costa Rican experience (aspirations and expectations defined "from below") with other experiences inspired by the International Institute for Democracy and Electoral Assistance (IDEA International), in which the issues to be assessed are defined a priori. One of the audit's merits is to favor citizen participation, since as Vargas Cullell indicates, the effort is a self-evaluation of shared democratic life viewed from within the citizenry. Consequently, data collection is guided by looking at the democratic problems and aspirations that are important to citizens, thus articulating a vision of democracy "from below." The great civic potential of this initiative comes from its stimulation of citizens' debates about the quality of their own democracy.

Given the audit's approach, the methodology chosen to define the principal problems of democratic life (135 such "problems" were identified) entrusted their identification to citizens who were consulted through diverse techniques. This process of "detection" combines inductive and deductive techniques, but it deliberately avoids a priori definition of the problems. Two factors explain this approach: first, the audit is a collective construction of agreements for evaluating the political life of a country (or part of it); second, no theoretically defined view of the quality of democracy exists that might serve to determine such a selection. The audit's methodology does not consist of the simple, passive act of registering problems indicated by ordinary citizens, however; instead, these opinions are processed in a pluralist and independent "civic forum" (the Consultative Council) that discusses and approves the standards of democratic quality. This characteristic is worth emphasizing since, as the audit notes, it is not an academic exercise imposed by third parties to grade a country but a self-examination and a tool society can use to critique and improve itself.

Without disparaging this methodology, some workshop participants expressed concern that a "self-evaluation" of democracy with indicators designed by citizens "from below" might lead to a kind of "naturalization" of the prevailing opinions at a given point in time. They based their concern on the idea that using such opinions to set agendas might lead to the silencing of issues that should not be omitted from an evaluative exercise of this nature. In the context of this discussion during the workshop, a reference was made to the evaluative methodology that IDEA International employed in Peru, in which project coordinators formulated problems and quality standards a priori, using parameters taken from comparative academic research.[7] This approach represents a different modality and conception of the task. It deserves consideration, since it also moves us toward the goal of finding ways of perfecting and deepening democracy.

During the present phase of building experiences, and of exploring techniques and conceptual refinements about the quality of democracy, all efforts are welcome. Nevertheless, to enrich and perfect these evaluative tools we may have to choose a mix that includes, on the one hand, problems mainly indicated by citizens, and on the other hand, problems that prevailing opinion has forced into a "spiral of silence." Thus, without meaning to question experiences that are now in progress, I would encourage a kind of methodological "squinting" that would keep one eye on society's aspirations and unease as indicated by citizens themselves and another eye conceptually guided on those problems that have not emerged in the prevailing wisdom but should be present. In so doing, we would move beyond prejudice, sectarianism, and other impulses that exist alongside the "nuclei of good sense" always inherent in prevailing social wisdom.

On a final note, I want to praise the spirit that has guided this effort and the valuable experience now in progress. I share O'Donnell's view that democracy's deficits can be cured with "more democracy" and that the citizen audit and other current attempts to evaluate democratic quality are very useful tools for contributing to this task. Likewise, I understand that the best contribution we can make toward perfecting democracy is our refusal to be complacent about its defects, conducting what O'Donnell in other works has called—with his usual ability to condense democratic agendas and tasks—"a democratic critique of democracy." For this reason I share the exhortation of the audit and the chapter by Vargas Cullell to pay close attention to democracy's day-to-day dimension and the revalidation of its legitimacy on a daily basis. Citizens' bond and commitment to democracy is renewed and played out every day in the little things.

NOTES

1. We should remember Juan Linz's suggestion that "the distinction between denying legitimacy to the political system and denying it to the socioeconomic system is basically analytical. In reality, the two are difficult to tell apart. Certainly a profound hatred for the socioeconomic order leads, almost inevitably, to denial of the legitimacy of the political system." See *La quiebra de las democracies* (Buenos Aires: Alianza, 1991), 27–28.

2. As Juan Linz argues (in *La quiebra de las democracies*), support for and legitimacy of the political regime do not exist independently of the actions and attitudes of specific people, and members of a society grant or withdraw legitimacy to it on a day-to-day basis in response to its performance. In short, a democracy does not have guaranteed support independent of its policies and results for different social groups.

3. It is worth noting that O'Donnell has developed a more inclusive conceptualization of the state in the article "On the State, Democratization and Some Conceptual Problems: A Latin American View with Glances at Some Postcommunist Countries," *World Development* 21, no. 8 (1993): 1355–69. In this paper he offers a three-dimensional characterization of the state that includes its legality, a set of bureaucracies, and a form of collective identity. In this same text, he warns about the deleterious consequences unleashed by the indiscriminate dismantling of the state, an aspect of the "neoliberal" policies implemented in the 1990s.

4. A study of Saguinetti's second presidency (1995–99) suggests that Uruguay has also shifted toward a very executive-centered pattern of decision making, in which the president's historic supremacy relative to Congress has turned, more recently, into absolute supremacy. See Carlos Moreira, "Una mirada a la democracia uruguaya. Reforma del estado y delegación legislativa (1995–1999)" (paper presented to the Quinto Congreso Nacional de Ciencia Política SAAP, Río Cuarto, November 14–17, 2001).

5. Among these I would highlight the work of Hilda Sábato, *La política en las calles: Entre el voto y la movilización. Buenos Aires, 1862–1880* (Buenos Aires: Sudamericana, 1998), and Leandro Gutiérrez and Luis A. Romero, *Sectores populares, cultura y política: Buenos Aires en la Entreguerra* (Buenos Aires: Sudamericana, 1995).

6. O'Donnell recommends thinking about a methodological strategy of three layers or levels of data. One would be a hard comparative nucleus shared by all cases. Another would gather specificities of each case. A third layer, "between" the other two, would consist of data that the respective national teams should attempt to make comparable, but not to the point of ignoring or disregarding specificities that may be considered important.

7. See Rolando Ames, Enrique Bernales, Sinesio López, and Rafael Roncagliolo, *Situación de la Democracia en el Perú (2000–2001)* (Lima: Idea Internacional, Pontífica Universidad Católica del Perú, 2001).

Quality of Democracy or Quality of Politics?

MANUEL ALCÁNTARA SÁEZ

The chapters by O'Donnell and Vargas Cullell set an excellent standard of quality. Written with the highest rigor, they are very stimulating intellectually. To reflect on the themes proposed with Latin America as a background is extremely timely, since the region represents one of the most dramatic scenarios combining democratic institutional development, inequality, and generally poor economic performance. Costa Rica itself is an excellent laboratory for an audit given its fifty years of political stability, its reasonable size in demographic terms, and the population's concentration in the central valley.

I would like to make a general comment about the title of the workshop—"Quality of Democracy and Human Development in Latin America"—that relates both to O'Donnell's text and to the citizen audit and refers to the substantive use of the term "democracy." Although this matter was discussed at different times during the Heredia workshop—and while I fully share O'Donnell's idea that a continuum exists for democracy with a merely institutional framework at one extreme and at the other a description of democracy as "everything that one might like"—I understand that the object we are reflecting upon is "politics in democratic contexts." In this way, I believe that we can distance the immediate discussion—and this is more obvious in the case of the audit—from the emotional and valuative content that the concept of democracy brings with it. In the workshop, Vargas Cullell indicated that we cannot begin with theory but rather with the mental map that people have of democracy, yet I think this is an exceedingly ambitious criterion that runs the risk of leading us down a dead end. First, the very term "democracy" has been the focus of reflection in political theory for a long while; and second, it relates to processes of cognitive construction among individuals, an aspect that touches upon the phases of psychosocial learning of abstract concepts. By focusing the discussion on "politics" or the political system (I prefer the latter term to political regime, for reasons I am about to defend), we increase our capacity to identify variables that affect the political process. We also unburden our analysis of the emotional controversies involved in discussions that focus on democracy. On the other hand, why did the audit evaluate democratic aspirations rather than civic or political ones? As we know, Robert Dahl was concerned with this matter when he wrote his famous *Polyarchy* in 1971.[1] Since then, practically all of us have come to agree on polyarchy's constitutive elements, but we have not accepted the term to the point where all of us include it in our discourse as teachers or researchers. I therefore defend my right to refer to a title that argues for an "audit of politics," understanding politics as a polity in the Anglo-Saxon view. I would define *politics* as the political system that accommodates four different types of elements, which interact in a systemic way: formal and informal institutions; societal actors; historical memory embodied in each country's unique political culture; and a fourth dimension of a spatial nature, in which each political system relates to other(s) of a different rank. I believe that this view facilitates the search for indicators that can become explanatory variables and is fully consistent with the work undertaken by the Costa Rican audit.

O'Donnell's text lucidly outlines a series of issues that are of vital importance to political theory. In my opinion, a central element of his work is rooted in the moral and fully universal conception of the human being as an autonomous, responsible, and reasonable agent. He or she is an elector and can be elected. This situation constituted the central nucleus of legal systems in the originating countries before democracy, but it is a situation that finds itself clearly limited to a small number of cases today. In Latin America, looking at the case of Colombia in a period as recent as the last fifteen years, the assassination of three thousand party militants campaigning for local elections has made it impossible to create a left-wing political party. Likewise, the extreme poverty that characterizes most Latin American societies makes it consistent and very rational for individuals to sell their votes for t-shirts, sandwiches, or shoes—a common practice—and in so doing to limit their autonomy as agents. These circumstances relate to the second point in O'Donnell's vision, which describes an effective state as a legal system that provides a normative fabric to society, even though—as the foregoing discussion indicates—the weakness of this type of state is one of Latin America's most serious characteristics. Some countries have traditionally had a weak state (Colombia, for example, and those with sultanistic experiences like Nicaragua or the Dominican Republic), and others have seen it weaken over the last decade as a consequence of the processes of privatization and shrinking of state institutions (Argentina). From this follows the claim of existence of a "friendly state"—a state because without it there are no fundamental rights, and a friendly one because this is the face it should show to those who most need it.

O'Donnell expresses his conviction that "the presumption of agency is another institutionalized fact." That is, certain procedures have become routine, linked with formal aspects through a process of emergence of political rights with others of a valuative nature, which grow informally from the efforts of individuals. This brings us to the cultural conditions of the democratic political system, drawing both on the classical approach to civic culture as well as the more modern concept of social capital. According to either view, the existence of certain values (tolerance, trust, etc.) in a given community—and the community's ability to create networks based on the development of these values—is a key element to the establishment and progress of the democratic creed. Certainly, as O'Donnell points out, the dimension of citizenship implied in the possibility of being elected has been neglected in many theories. Yet it is worth remembering that, independently of institutional and economic factors, other factors of a cultural nature can explain the absence of standards for agency in human beings who, in their cultural codes, fail to "step forward" as political participants by making themselves candidates. This reflection does not appear to be present in O'Donnell's text, although it did emerge during the discussion among the Heredia workshop participants. Nor was it an element that was incorporated in the audit, owing to its methodological orientation, as mentioned above. Nevertheless, the classic studies deserve vindication because they have made a major contribution to our understanding of this theme.

The picture that O'Donnell offers of Latin America is correct. It is evident that the new element that supposes the expansion of political rights contrasts with the persistence of old patterns, especially in regard to the deficit of basic civil and social rights among the popular sectors—aspects that are nothing more than a reflection of the profound inequalities that prevail in the region.

Nonetheless, the classification formulated for the region's democracies is imprecise in terms of its taxonomic criteria and reflects the Latin American reality in a very impressionistic way. I suggest that it be reformulated to indicate more precise and consistent criteria than the ones used.

Neither of the two main texts in this volume seems to take into account the role of leaders. Neither discusses their performance, or the effects of the exercise of patrimonialist power in Latin America. The region is a place where individuals who rise to power—in a framework of relationships characterized by extreme inequality—tend to forget that their right to exercise that power comes from those who are below them, who confer rights that demand complete consideration and respect. Given this fact, it would be extremely interesting to conduct an evaluation from the viewpoint of the elites, who should have been given a space of their own in the audit. Even in seemingly more egalitarian societies like Costa Rica's, the elites' role takes on major importance and should be the object of specific study. In fact, it would be meaningful to compare the results of a "popular audit" with an "elitist audit." The divergence between the two would reflect a distorted country, while any overlap would show an integrated one. If an audit is a collective construction for evaluating political life in a country or part of it, why not undertake an audit in the dual direction suggested above? Moreover, in many countries strong leadership by elites is significant when it comes to understanding where the country is going; thus, the matter is not so much to know what citizens expect but what its elites do. This view might give rise to a paradox that reflects the tension between the strong defense of democracy (politics under the democratic creed) and what citizens expect from their country. Citizens and elites can be vectors of opposing feelings, with elites conducting politics in conflict with citizens.

Finally, in a scenario like the current one—in which no book or paper fails to mention the term "globalization"—it seems shocking that neither of these essays nor practically any of the workshop sessions dealt with the internationalization of politics. Nor did they offer a framework for analysis that might assess the impact of the quality of democracy on actions or omissions of an international nature. The policies of individual agents like the United States and multilateral actors like the International Monetary Fund, to cite two relevant examples for Latin America, have a notable impact on national politics throughout the region, yet they are absolutely impervious to citizen demands. Other actors project their influence through "demonstration effects" by showing "facts that must not be committed" (Yugoslavia) or presuppose that the rule of law must be implemented through the creation of international authorities. Something similar is occurring with the forces that have been articulated by the latest explosion of globalization. Specifically, there are two forces of a very different nature that have a major impact in Latin America and throughout the world. One of these is the Internet, which serves as an ever-present instrument for unrestricted information and communication. The other is the impact of powerful financial markets that function in real time on a universal scale and that move huge quantities of money with few domestic controls through a region that has historically lacked capital—and in which the economy often dramatically drags politics along with it.

NOTE

1. *Polyarchy: Participation and Opposition* (New Haven, Conn.: Yale University Press, 1971).

Quality of Democracy and Its Measurement

MICHAEL COPPEDGE

About the Citizen Audit

I am impressed with the achievement of this audit as an audit: that is, as an intervention. It is difficult to imagine any other group, in any other country, carrying out such a task with the same success. It would be impossible for an audit that is so determined to prompt frank reflection about citizen perceptions and values to be imposed from outside; the project must be conceived and executed by citizens themselves. Moreover, if any nation were interested in carrying out a similar evaluation or "settling of accounts," only one as democratic—and as sincerely interested in deepening its democracy—as Costa Rica would be willing to examine itself with such honesty. The project leaders and all of its participants deserve sincere congratulations.

I believe that the audit has accomplished its goals. The authors have discovered, in rich detail and with convincing documentation, how Costa Ricans of all social classes view the quality of democracy. The authors have collected an impressive quantity of useful data to evaluate how well Costa Rica's institutions and practices respond to popular aspirations. They have stimu-lated participation in the democratic process and institutionalized a prominent place for quality of democracy on the national political agenda. They have also proposed or helped to propose a large number of reforms, and they have already influenced the training of the next generation of public officials. Again, this is high praise.

Nevertheless, I understand that the State of the Nation Project is specifi-cally interested in my comments on the project's more academic aspects, including the rigor of the research and its potential to shape political science research agendas. I believe that the audit will make two valuable contribu-tions to political science. First, the audit will help persuade more political sci-entists of the need to broaden the concept of democracy. Political science dominated by the United States has fallen into a routine of conceiving of democracy in minimalist institutional-proceduralist terms, equating democ-racy with polyarchy instead of treating polyarchy as a minimal acceptable degree of democracy. While the number of so-called democracies in the world has increased, there are obvious differences in quality among them, and mini-malist concepts offer an insufficient guide to help us distinguish among them. Because scholars must make these distinctions, many of us have begun to refer to the quality of democracy, albeit often in imprecise ways. The audit should be considered the most ambitious effort to define the content of the quality of democracy (as applied to Costa Rica). Given its ambitiousness and rigor, the effort lends dignity to the emerging debate over what "quality of democracy" means.

Second, the audit takes a bold position with regard to what the concept should mean. It adds two conditions to the polyarchical minimum: the state's respect for the rights and dignity of all citizens, and the *convivencia*[1] among citi-zens at an individual level. It also proposes to bring socioeconomic conditions back into the definition of democracy through the claim that a certain minimal level of human development is an essential requirement for democracy. In the workshop some participants resisted this attempt to recover the state and human development in the definition of democracy. Although I will argue below that there may be an analytically more useful way to incorporate some aspects of these factors, I am pleased that these items are on the agenda again and that they are being debated.

I would like to suggest a few areas in which the State of the Nation Project could be improved, if it were to be repeated in Costa Rica or if its methodology were exported to other countries. In so doing I do not mean to diminish the many achievements of the citizen audit in any way, since every social science method has both defects and areas that can be improved.

The Costa Rican audit was very participative and open. Citizens made a great number of contributions, and the authors took great care to respect those citizen contributions as much as possible, as well as the desires of the representative interest groups that participated in the advisory committees. I agree completely that it was valuable to follow these procedures in the first undertaking of the audit. In fact, they are the source of some of its most interesting conclusions. Nevertheless, these benefits have a price, which the authors recognize: the price of finding themselves burdened with some vaguely defined concepts as a result of having to compromise between opposing interests or as a reflection of the fact that some citizens shared vague beliefs. If there is a second Costa Rican audit, I recommend less consultation and stronger intellectual guidance from the project directors in defining the criteria that will be used to evaluate the quality of democracy and the indicators capable of accurately measuring progress in meeting these objectives.

I recommend this for two reasons. First, to reach its full potential, this project must be both politically and intellectually respectable, and to be intellectually respectable it must treat conceptualization, operationalization, and measurement as the essentially academic tasks that they are. It is commendable that ordinary citizens should suggest their interests through surveys and focus groups and that researchers should understand these interests in the same way that citizens do. But this does not mean that untrained citizens should define the concepts that researchers seek to measure. Instead, researchers should exercise their professional responsibility by converting those interests, as appropriately understood, into analytically useful socioscientific concepts and by deciding which of these concepts can be naturally articulated in a coherent theoretical framework. With a few exceptions, the concepts were unusually concrete and useful; yet in some aspects the aspirations and standards of the audit reflect qualities that probably should not be considered as defining characteristics of the quality of democracy but rather causes and effects of it. I will say more about this later. Second, the benefits of extensive consultation have already been achieved and will extend to the next audit; additional consultation in a second audit would bring with it diminishing returns. To spend as much time and energy in consultation on the second audit as in the first would constitute an inefficient use of resources. Extensive consultation would be more necessary, however, if the audit were undertaken in another country.

I hope that this study will be repeated, both in Costa Rica and in other countries. But as the authors have observed, an exact replica of the entire audit process in Costa Rica at another time could lead to the appearance of different aspirations and standards, and its replication in another country would certainly require the addition of whatever standards might be especially relevant there. If each study considers only those standards that seem relevant at that time and in that country, then no two studies would be alike or comparable. The lack of comparability limits the study's interest to those concerned with the problems considered relevant in Costa Rica; those concerned with different issues might discard the study as irrelevant. Striving for comparability is a good way to increase the audience for the study's findings.

The only way to make all such studies comparable is to standardize the criteria for evaluating the quality of democracy so that these same criteria can be used at all times and in all countries. The easy route to doing so is the traditional one: to put on blinders and designate as irrelevant any of the idiosyncratic traits of different times and countries. The harder and better road to achieving comparability is to measure all of the standards that are considered relevant in each country. This may be a practical impossibility since we cannot know exactly what those standards are until the audit takes place, but it is the objective toward which we must move. Using a more exhaustive set of criteria would produce either a more favorable evaluation if the audit has omitted standards that Costa Rica takes for granted, or a less favorable one if the audit has omitted standards that are very controversial. But if the State of the Nation Project values comparability, it must adopt a more exhaustive set of standards even if these are not on Costa Rica's agenda and even if they are controversial.

Overall, the citizen audit used much more comprehensive standards than any other study of democracy I know of. I believe that to obtain comparable measures of the quality of democracy, however, a somewhat longer list is needed. Specifically, I would suggest adding the following standards:

> If national elections are held with sufficient frequency to reflect major changes in public opinion, and if there are constitutional mechanisms that enable citizens to remove elected officials between elections.

> If electoral laws respect the principle of one person one vote, awarding legislative seats to political parties in proportion to the votes they receive.

> If the executive is elected by a procedure that ensures the selection of a person who is acceptable to the majority of voters or their representatives.

> If state institutions implement laws in a way that is faithful to the intentions of the elected officials that created them, and if these officials systematically control the execution of laws to ensure that their intentions are faithfully respected.

> If political parties and candidates devote themselves to a wide range of issues that are meaningful and important to citizens, and if they take

positions on these issues that appeal to voters. If the party system, as a whole, offers voters clear and meaningful alternatives.

If representatives, once elected, continue to advocate for policies that they claimed to defend during their campaigns. If citizens trust their representatives to do so.

I also believe that there should be a condition for an audit's relevance that precedes even the "minimal threshold of democratic guarantees," namely, that a state exists that exercises effective control over its territory.

This first audit was, very appropriately, highly disaggregated. That is, it observed and reported information about at least 210 indicators, which were reduced to no less than 33 democratic aspirations and 10 thematic areas. This was an excellent way to ensure the collection of a great variety of (highly exhaustive) information that, as I warned the group three years ago, was the highest priority and the safest way to begin. For many readers, however, the results will be burdensome and difficult to assimilate; therefore it would also be desirable to condense the information a bit more, if possible reducing it to a smaller number of dimensions. Reducing the data to a manageable quantity of dimensions would also help to connect this empirical research to the abstractions involved in academic theory.

The task of reducing the quantity of data essentially consists of discovering which indicators tend to inform one another. If a high value of one indicator usually corresponds to a high value in another, it often makes sense to say, roughly, that both indicators are measuring the same underlying dimension. If, on the other hand, knowing the value of one indicator tells us little or nothing about the probable value of another, then the two are mutually independent and probably correspond to different dimensions. Scholars typically use factorial analysis to identify these dimensions empirically and then recur to more than one "art" to interpret their meaning. Aníbal Pérez Liñán has already undertaken this type of analysis based on a study of citizens done as part of the audit, and he identified around a dozen dimensions. Nevertheless, most of these dimensions correspond to the question of *convivencia* (civic culture) and the problem of abuses committed by the state. I agree that these are the problems that head Costa Ricans' list of concerns. But once again, a comparative perspective helps us to discover that many other considerations are relevant to the quality of democracy, even if ordinary citizens are not concerned with them. The indicators for these additional considerations must also be part of the analysis of dimensions. We must not worry that the number of dimensions resulting from such an analysis will be even less manageable, because the number of dimensions is highly dependent upon the variables introduced in the data set. If in addition to the civic/citizen variables we introduce variations in institutional design, the effectiveness of the state, and other considerations, it is very possible that fewer dimensions will emerge.

The obstacle to doing this type of analysis, however, is the synchronic, photographic nature of this first audit. Dimensions cannot be analyzed unless variation exists, and variation is difficult to find when a single observation is made about a number of indicators in the present time. This is another good reason to shift toward reproducing the audit experience in other countries and other time periods: doing so would provide the type of variations we need to know about so we can commit ourselves to reducing the data. In the meantime, it might be possible to find some variations within Costa Rica: among municipalities and districts, for example. I echo the suggestions to replicate this type of audit at the local level, in a couple dozen municipalities.

Another way to begin simplifying the findings is to propose a causal process that produced what the audit observed. Even if all the indicators were presented as requirements for a high-quality democracy, some could be seen as results that imply that a democratic process took place, others as direct evidence of the process itself, and still others as prerequisites for the process and as factors that influence the manner in which it functions. For example, freedom of association and expression are a prerequisite for the formation of a competitive party system; access to information, public financing, regulations for party financing, etc. all influence how competitive the party system eventually will be; and the number and size of parties and their distinctive programmatic characteristics reflect how competitive the process was.

If the causal process were better understood, findings could be presented in a more meaningful way. It would be possible to explain better why the quality of democracy is what it is. There is relatively little research on the causal questions embedded in the concept of quality of democracy, but it is beginning to appear. The State of the Nation Project already has some especially relevant data that could begin to answer questions about, for example, the impact of race, ethnicity, gender, and age on mistreatment by the state. Nevertheless, the answers will only have real meaning when they are integrated with a coherent theory on the quality of democracy. This brings me to O'Donnell's text.

About O'Donnell's Text

Despite the fact that this imaginative and erudite essay penetrates political theory more deeply than I am able to, I believe I can appreciate some of its important contributions. First, the text applies a vast body of erudition to the goal of broadening our understanding of democracy. It does so by basing a theory of democracy, human rights, and human development on a set of rights that are required in order to assume that (adult) human beings are morally responsible agents. It argues that if we recognize that other people are agents (and if we believe in reciprocity), we must guarantee them certain rights, and from these rights we inevitably derive the principles of democracy, human rights, and human development. Of particular relevance for the citizen audit, it shows that the same defining assumption of liberal democracy also demands respect for civil rights, which can include the relevant standards for *convivencia* and dignified treatment by the state. All of these arguments are sustained from a comparative, long-term historical perspective, which leads to the fascinating denunciation that the quality of democracy suffers when civil rights were not respected before liberal democracy was in place. Along with this argument, O'Donnell demonstrates that democracy is not only a quality of the regime but also of the state. He also asserts that some minimal levels of human development (including a long list of objectives of a progressive social agenda) are necessary to achieve a high-quality democracy.

Although I consider it to be a stimulating, penetrating, and undoubtedly impressive work of erudition, and although I agree with the majority of its main points, I tend to think about some of these questions in a different framework. My framework is somewhat less coherent than O'Donnell's and certainly inferior, but perhaps it can be useful for the citizen audit.

The affirmation of a categorical and absolute right is too inflexible and demanding for my mind, which is mathematically organized. If we guarantee someone a right, we are saying that that right must be verified in practice and that anyone who places himself between a person and his or her rights is committing a grave injustice. Moreover, rights are conceived as universal and supported by a certain type of natural law. I, on the other hand, prefer to think of most of the norms that O'Donnell calls rights as goods or objectives desired by the majority of people, but not necessarily by all of them, and certainly not required by any natural law. We can provide people with the majority of these goods—with the best of them, in my opinion; but others may disagree in both principle and practice, and so the failure of attempts to provide these goods completely and immediately does not necessarily justify moral censure. These decisions are, as O'Donnell notes, political; but in my opinion they are also a question of degree.

Given that "rights" are a question of degree, we do not need to accept the impossibility of attaining consensus on a list of rights that would be essential to a high-quality democracy. Such a categorical instrument would only be necessary if we were looking for a one-to-one correspondence between a certain "floor" for each "right" and some categorical threshold that separates "high-quality" from "minimal" democracy. I believe that we do not need to—nor should we—go looking for such categorical answers. Instead, we should seek the path of finding out what constitutes "more" and "better" democracy and what implies "less" or "worse" democracy. To do so, we need not formulate any absolute right or list of absolute rights; we only need to know how much of each good corresponds to what degree of democracy.

Empirical research, rather than definitions or applications of normative theory, provides the best chance for answering these and any other types of questions. This is especially true if we conceive the relationships between the components of democracy as causal relationships. Thus, for example, we can examine what degree of freedom of association permits the formation of a certain number of political groups. We can assess the impact of an additional year of education on the ability to elect a party that better represents one's own interests; or how many calories a day are enough to make someone want to go and vote. Basically, these seem to be the kind of causal relationships that are better understood through empirical research than by using theoretical definitions.

In the end my liberal, North American, Dahlian training is too powerful: I prefer to keep social and economic conditions analytically separate in measurements of the quality of democracy. Nonetheless, I propose to do so in a more sophisticated way than usual. We tend to evaluate the quality of democracy in a way that attributes to the regime (and the state) all the beneficial forms of social and economic equality that exist "naturally" or historically in a country. That is, we do not differentiate between political equality that results from socioeconomic advantages and equality that is the result of a political regime. I believe that it would be better analytically to understand "democracy" as the state's capacity to close the gap between current social equality and the idea of political equality to which we aspire. This goes hand in hand with my preference of conceiving of the state as an actor and the regime as that which the state does (formally and informally, but in general, the important things that the state does repeatedly and predictably).

As an analogy, we might look at the preferred paths for evaluating the quality of education offered by a school. In the United States, for example, schools located in wealthy neighborhoods tend to graduate students with a good education, and those located in poor neighborhoods tend to graduate students with little education. Yet this does not mean that all rich schools are doing a better job educating people because they have the advantage of teaching students from families who value education and began educating their children even before they enrolled them in school. Such children probably would have received a good education at any school. Rich schools, therefore, do not deserve all the credit for the education that rich children have. To evaluate educational quality, then, one must maintain the students' socioeconomic context constant. I would argue that a similar approach is warranted when we evaluate the quality of a democratic regime. This may not be practical yet, but I would still prefer to keep socioeconomic impacts on the results of democracy separate from the definition of democracy. I prefer to consider human development—even at a basic level—to be a cause that contributes to high-quality democracy and not a defining element of it.

Because it is based on rights, O'Donnell's theory on the quality of democracy inclines strongly toward liberal democracy. But as he himself has recognized, there are also other, equally valid versions of democracy, especially the concept of democracy as popular sovereignty. In addition to guaranteeing basic civil rights, political rights, and state respect for dignity and *convivencia,* I believe that a democratic state is obliged to carry out popular will—or some reasonable facsimile thereof—when this reveals itself. A state that systematically ignores the political preferences of its citizens would not be democratic even if it respected all civil and political rights, supported elections, and encouraged people to be pleasant to one another. Therefore, this essential goal of democracy must be given equal importance in any theory on the quality of democracy.

As O'Donnell has pointed out, having different goals for democracy can lead to theoretical dead ends. I believe that fact poses a problem for a coherent theory, especially if the theory is forged in absolute terms instead of in a question of degrees. But it presents no obstacle to measurement. Moreover, if in principle people must cede some of their sovereignty in order to enjoy their rights (or vice versa), this does not mean we should not consider a country to be more or less democratic, in one or more dimensions. In other words, measurement does not demand that these theoretical difficulties be resolved since they are only theoretical in nature.

Introducing popular sovereignty also involves the theoretical problem of the impossibility theorem: that is, there is no universally fair procedure to aggregate individual preferences into social preferences. Nor does this create a problem for measurement. Even if no procedure is absolutely fair for all possible decisions, we can still measure how fair a particular procedure was for making a particular decision (or an average for a set of decisions). In fact, measurements of this type were what allowed Arrow to prove the impossibility theorem. As such, the practical problem of measuring the quality of democracy is really not a problem at all.

NOTE

1. For years, Spanish-speaking political scientists have had to deal with terms in English that have no exact equivalent in Spanish, such as "accountability." It is only fair that English speakers should confront *convivencia,* which has no close English equivalent. Nevertheless, I think the term is quite close to Almond and Verba's notion of civic culture. As such, the idea has a long and distinguished pedigree in political science, although more as a cause of democracy (and especially of democratic survival) than as one of the characteristics that *defines* democracy.

Democratic Quality

Costs and Benefits of the Concept

SEBASTIÁN L. MAZZUCA

Close examination of the workings and results of the Citizen Audit of the Quality of Democracy in Costa Rica reveals that there is much to admire about the effort. Indeed, the audit provides the encouraging confirmation that social science tools, used creatively and critically, have civic potential. My comments can thus be summarized with a single recommendation: that the analysis that the audit team carried out in Costa Rica be replicated in other countries and across time. As I will argue, this would allow the audit's academic potential and political usefulness to be exploited fully. Specifically, my aim in the following pages is twofold. First and most importantly, I attempt to justify the need for deepening the audit's scientific component, clarifying how it serves civic and reformist purposes. Second, I suggest research strategies for maximizing the audit's academic potential by extending its program to other contexts and across time.

About the Concept of Democratic Quality

The concept of democratic quality holds great theoretical and political promise; this promise is fulfilled when the concept is in the hands of O'Donnell and the audit team, who are undoubtedly responsible for the most sophisticated and successful effort made to refine it to date. My purpose in this section is to suggest how the theoretical side of this potential might be exploited to the maximum. In particular, I put forth the idea that the concept of democratic quality is an "amphibious" species that has two lives—one prescriptive and the other descriptive (or normative versus scientific). Furthermore, I argue that this amphibious nature—which has been extremely productive until now—may henceforth interfere with empirical analysis, as illustrated by the apparent dead ends and controversies in the workshop over what attributes to include in and exclude from the definition of the quality of democracy. Unfortunately, these controversies have no obvious solution; nevertheless, we can draw a more or less obvious distinction (between philosophy and political science) that helps us begin to confront them.

The division between political science and political philosophy is analogous to the difference between two questions about political life in societies. While the philosopher tends to wonder, "What is the best form of political organization that societies can give themselves?" the scientist asks, "What causes a change from one political organization to another, and what causes stability in each type of organization?" To think about the division of labor between political philosophy and political science, it is useful to imagine two different "contests." In the realm of political philosophy, the contest is waged between conflicting public goals and values, often summed up in antagonistic forms of government or political programs, whose virtues and vices are exactly what philosophical inquiry seeks to explain. The scientific contest, on the other hand, features alternative causal explanations of why certain forms of political organization prevail in some contexts, and others in different contexts. A typical example of the philosophical contest is illustrated by the question, "What type of political organization fits better with our ideals: popular or autocratic sovereignty?" Or, less trivially, "If sovereignty is popular, is it better that it be limited or unlimited? And what do we prefer, unlimited popular sovereignty or limited autocratic sovereignty?"

The scientist *qua* citizen (especially the informed one) may have convincing answers to these questions, but scientists lack the tools to resolve the philosophical contest between antagonistic political values and forms of government. Simply, no scientific method—whether statistical, experimental, or comparative—can answer the philosopher's questions. Such methods are as

useless for resolving philosophical disputes over ultimate values as a ther-
mometer is for taking a person's blood pressure. What statistical, experimental, and comparative methods can do, nonetheless, is tell us—independently
of the scientist's political preferences—what causes the emergence, stability,
and decline of different forms of government. What has more bearing on the
emergence of democracies—economic development, the secularization of culture, or a combination of both? And what factors promote the creation of constitutional limits on governments? Obviously, such questions do not seek to
ask whether democracy is a better or worse form of government than authoritarianism, or if limited power is better or worse than unlimited power. The
questions deal strictly with the various causes of one or the other (although the
scientist, as a philosophically informed citizen, may prefer a limited democratic government to any other combination).

Exploring the normative virtues and defects of different forms of government is a different task from investigating their causes. Just as important is the
fact that the methods used for one task are useless to the other—their cross-
application produces no results. This division of jurisdictions is a purely
logical topic, limited to the Kantian-Weberian assertion that normative
conclusions cannot be deduced from empirical experiments (in the same way
that universal propositions cannot be deduced from particular ones). Yet this
in no way implies that philosophy and science cannot be combined, often in
the same person. In a stylized portrait of this combination, philosophy takes
on the task of justifying what form of government (A, B, C, D . . . K) best fits
certain ultimate normative values. Next, with the conclusions gained from
philosophical inquiry, science tends to indicate in the end that if one wants a
particular form of government (for example, A), *then* it is necessary to take into
account that its causes are: $\times 1$, $\times 2$, $\times 3$ (and not $\times 4$, $\times 5$, or $\times 6$). Heaven forbid
that the politician who wants to produce form of government A pushes the
wrong button and gets B instead! Viewed from this angle, the distinction
between philosophy and political science boils down to a division between
means and ends: philosophy outlines and justifies political *ends,* while science
examines the *means* to achieve them (or the means to achieve those means)
without being able to justify with its tools which ends are valuable per se.

The division (and subsequent combination) of tasks between philosophy
and science is fundamental in the analysis of democratic quality. The workshop repeatedly posed the question of whether a country with major social
inequalities should be classified as democratic or not. Participants' opinions
appeared to be more divided than was really the case. The fundamental
point—that the distinction between science and philosophy allows us to
illuminate—is that those who supported the idea of joining political democracy

and social equality in the same concept did so on philosophical grounds. Those who rejected the approach did so on scientific grounds (while agreeing from a philosophical standpoint that democracy is connected to social equality). The case is a rich one for illustrating how different methods (science and philosophy), which are valid in different disputes (those involving causal hypotheses versus disputes between political values), require different conceptual operations. In this case, science dis-connects what philosophy connects. He who argues, from a philosophical viewpoint, that democracy is the best form of government because it best expresses the value of "equality" in the political realm, might also point out that that same value justifies a more equitable redistribution of economic wealth (someone who associated democracy with other values, such as "autonomy," would use another line of reasoning). By pointing out that political democracy and social equality have a common denominator in some broadly shared moral value, the philosopher draws normative connections between both concepts. Nevertheless, by entering the jurisdiction of science, normative connections are transformed into analytical distinctions (they dis-connect), and political democracy and social equality are transformed into different concepts precisely to allow the statistical, experimental, and comparative study of their mutual causal relationships.

At this point it seems worthwhile to introduce a principle related to concept formation that I believe is fundamental for refining the notion of democratic quality. Concept formation has two different objectives and consequently two different evaluation standards depending on whether it is done as a philosophical or scientific exercise. In political philosophy, the formation of a concept such as democracy usually begins with anchoring or grounding the concept in a particular ethical-political value that is considered fundamental (for example, equality, autonomy, rights, agency). Next follows an inventory or systematization of all the logical and normative implications that grow out of this anchoring of the concept in a fundamental value. When the question is, for example, "What form of social organization best fits with the value of autonomy?" the goal is to produce the most exhaustive possible description of the elements that constitute this ideal social organization and that are consistent with this fundamental value. In political science, concept formation aims to meet another objective: finding causal relationships between political processes and institutions, which requires the demarcation of analytical lines between them. While philosophy joins objects normatively (for example, contemporary liberal philosophy joins rule of law and democracy), science separates them analytically because it presumes that, empirically, the relationships between them can vary greatly and a priori assumptions are inappropriate. In fact, science separates them as a preventive measure in order to facilitate a posteriori analysis based on empirical research. Thus, for example, while there may be a strong normative connection between A and B, science separates them in order to evaluate empirically if (1) A and B always exist together, (2) A and B always exist separately, (3) A and B exist at times together and at times separately, (4) A causes B (or vice versa), (5) A and B are both caused by a third factor, C, (6) A and B each have distinct causes, or (7) the presence of A causes the absence of B. Likewise, the more that normative connections between A and B seem justifiable from a philosophical standpoint, the more pressing is the demand that science separate them in order to study which of all the possibilities best explains their empirical relationships. The greater the importance of connections discovered by philosophy, the more necessary it is for science to break them down analytically to enable their empirical study. What Rawls calls a "just" or "well-ordered" society includes both political rights and redistribution of income between the richest and poorest, but we require science to disaggregate the concept of "just society" into several distinct components in order to study their empirical relationships. If they are grounded in the same concept, it is not possible to study the relationship between political rights and social equality—in other words, it would not be possible to answer such important questions as, "Does one cause the other? Are they independent? Does one prevent the other?"

At the risk of sounding counterintuitive, the preceding discussion can be synthesized in the following motto: the better a concept's normative import, the poorer its scientific performance, and vice versa. The standard for judging a concept's normative import is its consistency with fundamental ethical-political values, while the standard for judging its scientific performance lies in its descriptive and explanatory utility. For example, let us say a philosopher finds the normative value underlying a series of political institutions and processes that previously appeared to be disconnected (as Habermas does, for example, in connecting political rights and the legal framework of the welfare state), and in doing so lends newfound coherence and systematicness to the elements on this list ("grounding"). We can certainly call this a philosophical discovery with the capacity to provide practical orientation to politics and citizens in general. Science, at least in its best-known successes, does the opposite: it divides up elements in order to study their empirical relationships, and puts together "atomistic" concepts. We can conclude, then, that the quality of concepts must be measured with two different standards, depending on the goal of who creates them. According to the philosophical-normative standard, the best concepts are those that bring together the most attributes and organize them under a fundamental ethical-political value. According to the scientific standard, the best concepts are those that make the best distinctions between objects that might potentially exhibit diverse empirical relationships, and which therefore must be investigated.[1]

From this we derive what I believe is the most important recommendation that I can offer in regard to the important task of forming and refining the concept of democratic quality. Until now, the concept's attractiveness has lain in its amphibious nature, which serves both to shed light on crucially important normative questions (none less than the basis for democracy and the clarification of its implications) and to open what may be the most interesting agenda for empirical research over the next ten years. Nonetheless, this attractiveness brings with it—now that the concept is mature—a great danger. The concept of democratic quality is judged with a double standard, and it runs the (greater) risk of interfering with causal analysis and the (lesser) one of generating controversies and disputes about its meaning whose results are disproportionate to the energy invested in them.

The heart of the problem is this: while normative criteria are used to expand the number of attributes for the concept of democracy, it is not legitimate to use scientific criteria to shrink the list. For example, O'Donnell justifies the inclusion of a diverse social context or civil rights within the definition of democracy on normative grounds (all these attributes, according to O'Donnell, are based on the value of "agency" or autonomy, which also underlies the very narrow concept of "polyarchy"). But while the criterion for inclusion that is used to add certain attributes is their consistency with a certain ultimate value, the same criterion is not used when excluding other attributes (for example, social equality), with the argument that doing so would interfere with causal inference. If the concept includes attributes like a diverse social context or civil rights because of their consistency with the value of agency (that is, for normative reasons), then we must also evaluate the attribute of social equality with the same standard. And if the attribute of social equality is excluded because its inclusion would create a concept of democracy that is too broad, then we must also consider whether including attributes like a diverse social context and civil rights does not produce the same result.

In sum, while the amphibious nature of the concept of democratic quality had the great merit of creating a dual agenda for unprecedented political and scientific work, we will reach a point where the double standard implicit in discussions surrounding it entails more costs than benefits. Accordingly, I would recommend that we do away with the concept's amphibious nature (before its does away with the concept, as occurred with other notable but forgotten social science concepts, which Clifford Geertz partially inventoried for other purposes in his work on thick descriptions). I believe the most viable and promising alternative is to create two versions of the concept of demo-cratic quality—one for prescriptive use in political philosophy inquiries and another for descriptive use in scientific research. The goal is not to create two labels but simply to remind those of us involved in the study of democratic quality that there are two criteria for concept evaluation and that we must be explicit, in our discussions and controversies, about which of them we are using in each case. When the discussion is philosophical, the goal is the great-est possible clarification of the normative bases and implications of what is meant by a high-quality democracy. When the discussion is scientific, the gov-erning idea is to create a concept that prepares the ground for fieldwork and broadens the chances for drawing causal hypotheses about phenomena of interest (even if the evidence later refutes them).

In addition to recommending that the type of evaluation standard for con-cepts (scientific or philosophical) be made explicit in each case, I would make two more specific recommendations. In philosophical discussions, I believe it is possible (and in keeping with the spirit of both O'Donnell's work and the audit) to take more radical positions when analyzing the concept of demo-cratic quality. Inversely, I believe a more conservative position is appropriate to scientific discussions.

What guides O'Donnell's efforts to expand and systematize attributes related to the concept of democracy is the basic concept of agency. In my opin-ion, in philosophical terms this work must be carried to its ultimate conse-quence, exhausting all of the normative implications that the concept implies for a society's political organization and avoiding the restriction of the argu-ment by criteria alien to the domain of philosophical reflection. O'Donnell observes—just as even the very narrow concept of polyarchy presupposes—that agency is also a basis for human rights, human development, civil rights, and a certain type of state and social context, and that failings in these dimen-sions "truncate" agency. Yet does not inequality do the same? O'Donnell does not provide an answer to this question, although he does affirm that including social equality in the expanded concept of democracy complicates empirical research, and for that reason it must be excluded. Nevertheless, the reasoning that bases broadening of the concept of democracy in the idea of agency must judge the attributes it excludes with the same logical and normative yardstick used for those it includes. Inequality, then, must not be evaluated for its inter-ference with science but rather for its normative connection to agency, in the same way that the included components are evaluated. I lack the capacity to undertake this normative evaluation, and therefore I am not suggesting that social equality (or even egalitarian policies *à la* Dworkin or Sen) be included in the definition of democracy. Yet I do believe that philosophical reasoning demands that exclusion take place on the basis of an argument related to the concept of agency (that is, the same argument that includes the rule of law or a social context of a "diverse texture.")

Ideally, grouping attributes under a single concept should be the conclusion and not the premise of empirical analysis. When the researcher is unsure about the relationship between phenomena (as is almost always the case), the most convenient thing to do is "invert the burden of proof." Departing from the idea that the two objects are different, the researcher will argue that there is no reason to unify them in a single concept, that their reciprocal relationships can be described through an infinite number of different models (causality, concomitance, exclusion, and also identity), and that the model's specification results from theoretically informed analysis of empirical data. Thus, with regard to scientific practice, if economic aspects are excluded from the definition of democracy in order to study their empirical relationships, why not also separate the rest of the phenomena that define the quality of democracy (civil rights, a diverse social context, a friendly bureaucracy) from institutional aspects related to democratic access to power? Of course we may speak of the concept of democratic quality as multidimensional and defend the position that each dimension varies relatively independently from the others. In the same vein, we may argue that countries are more or less democratic in relation to different dimensions. Nevertheless, multidimensionality is also an a priori presupposition about the structure of democracy that must be assessed. Perhaps (we do not know; it must be investigated) rather than dimensions of a single phenomenon we should speak of separate phenomena, and in so doing preserve the chances that they have complex reciprocal causal relationships (with possible asymmetries in causality, trade-offs, sequences with or without intervening variables, interaction effects, etc.). I am not aware of a convincing technique for aggregating the diverse scores that countries normally register for different dimensions related to the narrow concept of "polyarchy."[2] Given the state of our knowledge, even the minimal procedural concept of polyarchy is too aggregated to be analytically useful. It might even be argued that instead of broadening it, we should narrow it even further, and in this way enable the study of relationships between its minimal components, different subsets of these components, and phenomena outside the polyarchical set.

"Democratization" is a term that deservedly inspires great affinity and energy in the academic and intellectual community. My proposal to divide democracy into distinct components, in either its broad or narrow version, has the major disadvantage of implying that democratization is not one political process but several, each with potentially divergent causal histories.

The advantage, on the other side of the scale, is that it suggests a better causal understanding of the variety of political results that interest scholars of democratization. Is it appropriate to speak of democratization as a way to move away from *both* authoritarian regimes and patrimonialist states? I believe that the discussion of quality of democracy (in contrast to the discussion of transitions, although both can be subsumed under the topic of democratization) is more closely linked to the problem of patrimonialist administrations, as defined by Weber and taken up again in much of the postwar historiography on the birth of modern Europe. In these experiences, the causal processes that brought an end to patrimonialist practices were clearly different from the causal processes that ended authoritarianism. In keeping with the Weberian spirit, rather than *democratization*—which is reserved for discussions related to the end of authoritarian regimes—one should speak of *bureaucratization* when the underlying problems relate to patrimonialism (or re-patrimonialization, when speaking of the expansion of "brown areas" and informal institutions). In suggesting that problems of democratic quality can be seen more usefully as problems of bureaucratization (and not democratization) my purpose, of course, is not to coin another fashionable term. Rather, by shifting from a description to an explanation of problems of political quality, I aim to point out that the causes for improvements in quality may be different from, or contrary to, those of the transition from authoritarianism. I believe that separating processes and slimming down the terms used to refer to them is a better way to prepare the ground for empirical research than subsuming various subjects under the topic of democratization. In fact, the change of diagnosis (bureaucratization instead of democratization) brings with it the suggestion that new lines of causal investigation can be opened since the topic of de-patrimonialization of "public" administrations draws from a series of literatures, causal theories, and data that until now ran parallel to the discussion of democratization.[3]

In addition to divergent causality, a litmus test for measuring the utility of distinctions between processes, at least in political science, can be conducted with a simple question: Are the winners and losers in one process (or institutional scheme) the same as the winners in another? It is relatively clear empirically, and it is possible to model theoretically, that the actors who have an interest in maintaining democratic access to state power often also have an interest in maintaining patrimonialist practices of exercising that same power. Moreover, those who were formerly oppressed by authoritarianism are not the same people who today bear the costs of patrimonialism. Therefore, the actors that promoted democratic reforms may not always coincide with those who might potentially promote bureaucratic reforms.

The Comparative Question in the Citizen Audit

Once political philosophy has clarified which topics deserve investigation, causal analysis needs no justification. Without knowledge of their causes, it is almost impossible to put an end to public evils and produce public goods. As with any public good, the concern with quality of democracy pushes us to study its causes. These final suggestions are based on the following principle: causal analysis becomes much easier with variation. By variation I simply mean the study of both negative and positive cases. Following this principle, for example, I would argue that to understand the causes of economic development we must also examine cases of economic failure. The point is to prevent the error of citing as causes of economic growth antecedent variables that are present both in positive cases of growth and in negative cases (that is, cases of economic backwardness). If we only look at the positive cases, it is not possible to eliminate as a cause those variables that are also present in negative cases.

The extension of the audit to other cases in Latin America is the most obvious way to obtain variations that facilitate causal analysis. It would allow us to obtain variation across cases—the ideal situation—but also, with additional work on Costa Rica, we could obtain variations within a case and over time. Each of these three types of variation involves different research strategies, for which the audit is well prepared.

To extend the audit across cases, two strategies are most important. First, it is legitimate from a methodological standpoint (with adaptations in each case) to study the quality not of national but of provincial and even municipal governments. In addition to generating variations, the virtues of studying subnational contexts have been well documented,[4] both in terms of their greater practical viability (in the cases of Argentina, Brazil, Mexico, and Venezuela) and in theoretical terms.

The second recommendation related to study across cases is that conceptual tools and empirical indicators be developed that can capture negative cases "less negatively." We have adequately outlined what a high-quality democracy would look like, but we have few tools for describing the "other institutions" of cases of low quality. Furthermore, it must be recognized that there can be a wide variety of alternative institutionalities (subtypes within negative cases). The mere possibility that each subtype could have different modes of functioning and different causal histories justifies the development of such tools.

Regarding variations over time, the recipe is obvious: repeating the audit as a study year after year. One point that is not obvious, but which seems pertinent to emphasize, relates to evaluation standards. The strategy of creating quality evaluation standards with direct citizen participation is a brilliant innovation.[5] To maintain it, we must nevertheless bear in mind that this approach will cause standards to change over time; therefore, the audit will end up measuring different things at different points in time. Causal analysis requires that the object of study be stable in order to draw explanatory inferences. Therefore, I would suggest that along with the standards that are deliberatively gathered each year, a hard nucleus of indicators be established that remains stable as the experience is repeated, through which it will be possible to make causal inferences. To obtain variation across time, the same phenomenon must be measured in every case, and their evolution monitored.

Finally, with respect to variation within a case, I would offer a question rather than a suggestion: Has the audit found that, for example, courts do not work the same way in different locations around the country or that the offices that issue identity cards treat citizens one way in the cities and another way in rural areas? If this is the case, the variations should be explored for the valuable causal inferences that they allow: they provide positive and negative micro-cases that may allow research strategies that eliminate antecedent variables as explanatory factors.

NOTES

1. These Russellian affirmations should be qualified, but space does not allow for it here. I merely sustain that they are not an attempt to make a fundamentalist defense for some kind of conceptual hyperatomism. On the contrary, I believe that the "burden of proof" in the scientific realm (but not in the philosophical realm) falls on attempts to "aggregate" attributes in a single concept. Conceptual disaggregation is a preliminary measure, taken at the outset of research, and the joining of more or less aggregated concepts must be the conclusion (not the premise) of empirical research.

2. See Gerardo L. Munck and Jay Verkuilen's excellent piece, "Conceptualizing and Measuring Democracy: Evaluating Alternative Indices," *Comparative Political Studies* 35, no. 1 (2002): 5–34.

3. On the distinction between types of access to power and types of exercise of power, and the use of the terms democracy/authoritarianism to characterize access and the terms bureaucracy/patrimonialism to characterize exercise of power, see Sebastián Mazzuca, "¿Democratización o burocratización? Inestabilidad del acceso al poder y estabilidad del ejercicio del poder en América Latina," *Araucaria* 4, no. 7 (2002): 23–47.

4. See work on the "subnational comparative method" by Richard Snyder, "Scaling Down: Subnational Analysis in Comparative Politics" (photocopy, Department of Political Science, University of Illinois at Urbana-Champaign, 2001).

5. I refer to the fact that the audit establishes most of its indicators through consultation with citizen groups and intends to update them from year to year.

Conceptual and Methodological Notes on the Quality of Democracy and Its Audit

GERARDO L. MUNCK

O'Donnell's chapter seeks to broaden the set of issues that are currently a focus of attention in the analysis and debate about Latin American politics. In this sense, it is an extremely ambitious, conceptually rich, complex, and provocative text. It makes a major contribution to a fundamental debate. These comments do not address the substantive issues raised by O'Donnell. Rather, they focus on some methodological issues related to the formation of concepts that need to be addressed if the ideas discussed by O'Donnell are to be measured and used in the course of causal analysis.

The formation of concepts entails, as a central task, the identification and justification of the conceptual attributes that are going to be included in the definition of the concept and at least a brief discussion of why some attributes that could be considered as plausible candidates for inclusion are actually excluded. This aspect of concept formation is addressed extensively and in great detail in O'Donnell's chapter. Indeed, the core contribution of

O'Donnell's chapter resides in the way in which it discusses what attributes should be included in the concept of democracy and what attributes should be excluded from the concept. However, two other tasks affect the degree of clarity of the conceptual discussion and also deserve attention.

One task is to ensure that the various attributes used to define a concept are identified in a way that distinguishes them from each other and also from attributes used to define other closely related concepts. This issue is particularly relevant in the context of the discussion of such broad concepts as democracy, human development, and human rights. Put succinctly, if we do not know where one attribute ends and others begin and where one concept begins and ends, any analysis on the basis of such concepts is bound to give rise to much confusion. Another task concerns the need to make the logical structure of the concept clear and explicit by distinguishing the attributes used to define the concepts by levels of abstraction. By making this distinction, the point of departure of measurement efforts—the least abstract attributes—will be identified. Moreover, this distinction serves to clarify the level of abstraction at which any effort at aggregation should start and the conceptual attributes such an effort at aggregation can draw upon.[1] These are issues that are barely addressed in O'Donnell's chapter. Indeed, the key aim of the text is to offer some initial and very critical steps in the process of concept formation. But these additional methodological steps play a role in concept formation and should be addressed with some care.

An important clarification, that I believe is worth raising in the context of the chapter by O'Donnell, concerns the distinction between conceptual issues, which are established by definitional fiat and thus are resolved conceptually one way or the other, and empirical questions, which are subject to testing and thus actually might be right or wrong. This distinction seems relevant when O'Donnell discusses the concepts of state and regime. If I read O'Donnell correctly, what he says is that the state—understood as the *Estado de derecho*—is a conceptually necessary condition of a democratic regime and hence part of the concept of democracy. This is certainly one way of thinking about the matter. But it is worth considering whether a different approach might be more fruitful, taking into account the potential benefits of turning this issue into an empirical question, which would mean that the link between the *Estado de derecho* and a democratic regime would be treated as a hypothesis to be tested through empirical analysis.

In my view, this approach is recommendable. A decade ago Juan Linz made the argument that different political regimes might be associated with different levels of respect for human rights—an aspect of the *Estado de derecho*[2]—and an interesting debate has emerged concerning the precise form of this empirical relationship.[3] More recently, Mazzuca has suggested that the dimensions of access to state power and exercise of state power, two dimensions that resemble to a great degree O'Donnell's concepts of political regime and state, vary independently and actually develop as different points in time, sometimes separated by centuries.[4] Thus, we have a body of theory and some empirical analyses that suggest that the relationship between O'Donnell's concepts of political regime and state should not be resolved at a conceptual level. Of course, it may be the case that the *Estado de derecho* is related to a democratic regime and thus has to be present if a democratic regime is to be found. If this were the case, then there would be a stronger basis than mere conceptual argument for tying these two concepts together.

Over the last several decades O'Donnell has made a series of substantial contributions to the study of Latin America and comparative politics. One of O'Donnell's strengths has been his knack for concept formation, especially through the identification of attributes that are particularly relevant for understanding contemporary politics. These comments suggest that it is necessary to build upon and go beyond this first step in the formation of concepts. Indeed, only inasmuch as the issues addressed in these comments are tackled can other key tasks such as the generation of data and the analysis of causal relationships be confronted.

The *Final Report of the Citizen Audit on the Quality of Democracy in Costa Rica* and the chapter by Vargas Cullell in this volume constitute major contributions to the discussion of current politics in Latin America and pioneer a methodology that had not been used in Latin America before and that has great potential. My comments focus on two core aspects of the citizen audit in Costa Rica and entail suggestions to build upon the considerable work that went into the *Final Report*.

The work done in the context of the citizen audit in Costa Rica could contribute to our thinking about the concept of democratic quality in a different way than the work by O'Donnell. Essentially, O'Donnell approaches this issue from a conceptual perspective, drawing upon and attempting to synthesize large bodies of literature mainly in political theory and political philosophy. The citizen audit in Costa Rica draws inspiration from O'Donnell's work, but it also approaches the issue of democratic quality in a fairly different way, in that it brings a large amount of extremely rich data to bear on the question.

I think it is possible to capitalize on this rich data by addressing the question of what democratic quality is in an empirical, as opposed to conceptual, manner. The challenge would be to carry out an analysis of these data with the aim of seeing how many and what dimensions underlie them. It might be possible, in this way, to show that the data measure a concept that is different from the traditional, Dahlian understanding of democracy and also to say something about how such a new dimension might be conceptualized. Some exercises along these lines have been attempted,[5] but they have used relatively thin and poor-quality data, such as the reports generated by Freedom House. Using the richer and better data gathered in the context of the citizen audit in Costa Rica would lead, I believe, to some new insights that would represent an important contribution.

The other important line of work on the basis of the citizen audit in Costa Rica concerns the extraction of an exportable methodology from the experience already accumulated. To my mind, this line of inquiry could yield some very significant fruits. The task of extracting an exportable methodology is quite complex, and is probably best left to the people who organized the audit from start to finish: Jorge Vargas Cullell, Miguel Gutiérrez Saxe, and Evelyn Villarreal. Thus, I hesitate to offer any advice in this regard beyond some fairly generic points.

In seeking to develop such a methodology, I would suggest that three existing models be studied carefully. One is the methodology developed and used by the International Institute for Democracy and Electoral Assistance (IDEA International).[6] I think the IDEA International framework has some very positive features. It offers a clear and overall easy to comprehend but still broad framework. Moreover, because this framework was developed prior to the application of democracy assessments in specific cases, it has the advantage of making the resulting reports comparable. Indeed, this approach has enabled IDEA International to not only publish case studies but also to pull together the eight case studies they have conducted using this methodology and to draw some lessons that go beyond the specifics of each case.[7] Some drawbacks of this methodology should also be noted. In this regard, I would highlight the fact that the conceptual framework was derived and was driven in large part by the prior experience with a democracy audit in the United Kingdom. In addition, though the preparation of national reports draws upon the expertise of local researchers, the methodology calls for less involvement by various national actors and contributes less to fostering a real dialogue than was the case with the citizen audit in Costa Rica.

I would merely point to two other efforts at developing a methodology for democracy assessment (this is not in any way an exhaustive list). One is the effort by the United States Agency for International Development (USAID).[8] My reaction to this framework is that it is overly cumbersome and hard to apply in a systematic way that would generate comparable results. Another effort is that by the Democracy Dialogue project of the United Nations Development Program (UNDP).[9] The strength of this project is that it is aimed at building local capacities, a definite plus. Overall, however, the framework used in this project lacks a clear basis in democratic theory and leaves considerable room for improvement.

The citizen audit of the quality of democracy in Costa Rica is a unique study that makes a contribution to current debates about the concept of democratic quality and pioneers a methodology that has important academic and political payoffs. Its impact can be increased, however, inasmuch as the data it has generated are further analyzed and the methodology it uses is systematized in a way that makes it easily transportable to other settings.

NOTES

1. For more on these issues, see Gerardo L. Munck and Jay Verkuilen, "Conceptualizando y midiendo la democracia: Una evaluación de índices alternativos," *Política y Gobierno* (México) 9, no. 2 (2002): 403–41.

2. Juan J. Linz, "Types of Political Regimes and Respect for Human Rights: Historical and Cross-national Perspectives," in *Human Rights in Perspective: A Global Assessment,* ed. Asbjørn Eide and Bernt Hagtvet (Cambridge, Mass.: Blackwell, 1992), 177–222.

3. See, among others, Christian Davenport, "From Ballots to Bullets: An Empirical Assessment of How National Elections Influence State Uses of Political Repression," *Electoral Studies* 16, no. 4 (1997): 517–40.

4. Sebastián Mazzuca, "¿Democratización o burocratización? Inestabilidad del acceso al poder y estabilidad del ejercicio del poder en América Latina," *Araucaria* 4, no. 7 (2002): 23–47.

5. See David Altman and Aníbal Pérez-Liñán, "Assessing the Quality of Democracy: Freedom, Competitiveness, and Participation in 18 Latin American Countries," *Democratization* 8, no. 2 (Summer 2002): 85–100.

6. See David Beetham, Sarah Bracking, Iain Kearton, and Stuart Weir, eds., *International IDEA Handbook on Democracy Assessment* (The Hague: Kluge Academic Publishers, 2002).

7. See International IDEA, *State of Democracy: Trends from the Eight Pilot Countries: An Overview of Democracy Assessment Reports in Bangladesh, El Salvador, Italy, Kenya, Malawi, New Zealand, Peru, and South Korea* (Stockholm: International IDEA, 2001).

8. The methodology is outlined in two documents: USAID, "Conducting a DG Assessment: A Framework for Strategy Development" (USAID Center for Democracy and Governance, Technical Publication Series PN-ACH-305, 2000; available online at http://www.usaid.gov/democracy/pubsindex.html); and USAID, "Handbook of Democracy and Governance Program Indicators" (Center for Democracy and

Governance, Technical Publication Series PN-ACC-390, 1998, available online at http://www.usaid.gov/democracy/pubsindex.html).

9. See Katrin Käufer and Bettye H. Pruitt, "UNDP RBLAC Regional Project Democracy Dialogue: Promoting Multi-stakeholder Consensus Building as a Tool for Strengthening Democratic Governance" (unpublished paper, 2001).

Manuel Alcántara Sáez is Professor of Political Science and Administration and Director of the Inter-University Institute for Portuguese and Ibero-American Studies at the University of Salamanca, Spain.

Catherine M. Conaghan is Associate Professor of Political Studies at Queen's University, Kingston, Canada.

Michael Coppedge is Associate Professor in the Department of Political Science at the University of Notre Dame.

Osvaldo M. Iazzetta is Professor in the School of Political Science and member of the Research Council at the National University of Rosario, Argentina.

Gabriela Ippolito was coordinator of the Social Policies Project at the Kellogg Institute for International Studies at University of Notre Dame until 1997. In 2001–2002 she was a researcher with the MacArthur Foundation's Program on International Cooperation and Security at Stanford University.

Terry Lynn Karl is Professor of Political Science at Stanford University and the European University Institute, Italy.

Norbert Lechner was coauthor of the United Nation Development Program's Human Development Reports on Chile, and Professor and Director of the Facultad Latinoamericana de Ciencias Sociales (FLACSO), Chile.

Sebastián L. Mazzuca is a doctoral candidate in Economics and Political Science at the University of California, Berkeley.

Juan E. Méndez is Professor of Law and Director of the Center for Civil and Human Rights at the University of Notre Dame.

Gerardo L. Munck is Professor of Political Science and International Relations at the University of Southern California.

Guillermo O'Donnell is Helen Kellogg Professor of Political Science, Fellow of the Kellogg Institute for International Studies at the University of Notre Dame, and Fellow of the American Academy of Arts and Sciences.

María Hermínia Tavares de Almeida is Professor in the Department of Political Science at the University of São Paulo and member of the governing council of the Coordinação de Aperfeiçoamento de Pessoal de Nível Superior (CAPES) from 2000 to 2004 in Brazil.

Jorge Vargas Cullell is Coordinator of the Citizen Audit on the Quality of Democracy in Costa Rica and Assistant Director of the annual report on the State of the Nation, Costa Rica.

Laurence Whitehead is Director of the Centre for Mexican Studies and Official Fellow in Political Science at Nuffield College, Oxford University.